"This book represents a comprehensive and challenging overview of the world of temperament. Dr. Rettew describes how integrating an individual differences perspective into the diagnostic process can lead the clinician toward a better understanding of the child's behavior. *Child Temperament* should be required reading for all researchers in the developmental personality field."

—Barbara De Clercq, Researcher,
Department of Psychology, Ghent University, Belgium

"Dr. Rettew has channeled his career-long pursuit of the concepts surrounding temperament into a fascinating, comprehensive, and most of all clear and sensible working model. *Child Temperament* will be of enormous value to clinicians, scientists, parents, and all who are interested in the development of children. Beautifully written in a style that is amazingly enjoyable to read, with tables and summaries that students and scientists alike will find indispensible, this is a major compilation that should anchor all future exploration of temperament and help illuminate the path forward for future work in this field."

—John N. Constantino, MD,
Blanche F. Ittleson Professor of Psychiatry and Pediatrics at Washington University School of Medicine; Director, William Greenleaf Eliot Division of Child Psychiatry; Psychiatrist-In-Chief, St. Louis Children's Hospital

Child Temperament

A Norton Professional Book

Child Temperament
New Thinking About the Boundary Between Traits and Illness

David Rettew, MD

W. W. Norton & Company
New York • London

For information about permission to reproduce selections from this book, write to
Permissions, W. W. Norton & Company, Inc., 500 Fifth Avenue, New York, NY 10110

For information about special discounts for bulk purchases, please contact
W. W. Norton Special Sales at specialsales@wwnorton.com or 800-233-4830

Manufacturing by Quad Graphics, Fairfield
Book Design by Paradigm Graphics
Production Manager: Leeann Graham

Library of Congress Cataloging-in-Publication Data

Rettew, David.
    Child temperament : new thinking about the boundary between traits and
illness / David Rettew. — First edition.
        pages cm. — (A Norton professional book)
Includes bibliographical references and index.
ISBN 978-0-393-70730-4 (hardcover)
1. Temperament in children. 2. Personality in children. 3. Personality disorders
in children. I. Title.
BF723.T53R48 2013
155.4'18232—dc23
                            2013009455

ISBN: 978-0-393-70730-4

W. W. Norton & Company, Inc., 500 Fifth Avenue, New York, N.Y. 10110
                        www.wwnorton.com
W. W. Norton & Company Ltd., Castle house, 75/76 Wells Street, London W1T 3QT

1 2 3 4 5 6 7 8 9 0

To my wife, Valerie, for her enduring support and inspiration, and to my children, Jackson, Craig, and Henry, who bring the world of temperament spectacularly to life.

Contents

Acknowledgments

Child Temperament represents a summation of many years of work and thought. As such, it is an amalgamation of the ideas, experiences, and writings of a great number of people who have been influential in my life, both professionally and personally. Like a glacier slowly moving toward the sea, this book has picked up and incorporated little pieces of its surroundings along the way.

The smartest thing I have done in my professional life has been to align myself with excellent mentors over the years. I wish I could take credit for making a conscious decision to do this, but the truth, at least at first, was that I found these individuals purely by dumb luck. In fact, one could argue that the pivotal step at the beginning of my career was when I was the only one to type my application for a summer research internship at the University of Pennsylvania. This experience led me to the lab of Martin Seligman, who opened the door for me to the world of mental health research. After graduation, I was fortunate to work at the Child Psychiatry Branch of the National Institute of Mental Health, conducting studies with the amazing team of Judy Rapoport, Susan Swedo, and the late Henrietta Leonard. The branch was doing some of the most fascinating neuroscience research I had ever seen, and my mentors gave me all the support and responsibility I could handle. In medical school at the University of Vermont College of Medicine, I again was fortunate to encounter strong mentors, this time in the laboratory of Thomas Achenbach and Stephanie McConaughy.

From that point on, I finally realized that I could no longer rely on fate to pair me with great teachers. Consequently, I chose my adult and child psychiatry residencies at the Massachusetts General/ McLean Hospital

Program not only for its excellent clinical training but because Jerome Kagan, Nancy Snidman, and Dina Hirshfeld-Becker, whose landmark work in child temperament had piqued my interest in the field, were there. At Mass General I was surrounded not only by these wonderful scholars by many other outstanding teachers of research and clinical psychiatry as well. My training directors, John Herman and Eugene Beresin, set a standard that motivated me to eventually develop my own child psychiatry training program. Also of particular significance to me was John Gunderson, who brought me into the Collaborative Longitudinal Personality Disorders Study and showed me what it meant to be a good mentor, whether by putting me (as a trainee) next to the famous speaker at a dinner gathering or by taking the time to share his wisdom over a round of golf.

From my residency, I moved back to Vermont to take my first faculty position. As difficult as it can be to pull oneself away from the strong orbital pull of Mass General, I did so to work with great people and great mentors. In Vermont, I have been privileged to continue to learn from teachers such as Professor Achenbach and to work closely with our director, Jim Hudziak. Dr. Hudziak is one of the funniest, most charismatic, and most passionate people I know, and it is hard to imagine any successes I would have had without his mentorship. His generosity, vision, and humanity have motivated and inspired me since I arrived. I am also thankful to our entire team at the Vermont Center for Children, Youth, and Families, and in particular to my colleague and friend Robert Althoff and the many valuable and hilarious discussions we have had that have helped guide my path.

It is also important to thank the many children and families with whom I have worked clinically and in research projects over the years who have been brave enough to share their very personal struggles with me. I want to thank my editor, Deborah Malmud, who was the one to suggest that I write this book in the first place and who, along with the team at Norton including Sophie Hagen and Kevin Olsen, has been so helpful in seeing this manuscript to fruition.

Most important, I have to thank my family. My mother, from a very early age, encouraged me to read and write as much as I could. She gave me encouragement and guidance even when my stories were morbid and contrived. My father, who died when I was 18 years old, instilled in me a work ethic and commitment that helped me override my more natural tendencies to be idle. My brother Jim, now my closest friend, always asks about my writing projects (and keeps pushing me to finish that novel I started in 8th grade). My children, whose development and emerging personalities have been amazing to observe, gave me such support and understanding when it came to writing this book; I hope the project helped them understand the value of taking slow steady steps toward a long-term goal.

The biggest thank-you must go to my wife, Valerie. She has been my greatest advocate in pushing me to keep going on this book, even when that meant she was stranded on weekend mornings with a baby while I shut myself in a room to write. Without her steadfast encouragement and support, this book never would have happened.

There are many people who also have made significant contributions but who are not specifically named—for that I apologize. It is time, however, to stop telling my story and start telling the story of child temperament and its history with psychiatry.

PART I

Temperament and Its Links With Psychiatric Illness

Chapter 1

A Brief History

My youngest son was born in June 2012, in the year of the dragon. According to Chinese astrology, this fact alone portends that he will be brave, passionate, and unpredictable. And because he was born in the year of the water dragon, the news gets even better, as he should also show an ability to control these outward tendencies. Despite this auspicious sign, however, it is quite likely that when my son begins kindergarten with others born the very same year, the class will not be filled with similarly behaving children. Likewise, two siblings born to the same parents who do their best to bring up their offspring the same way are not likely to have carbon-copy personalities. Temperament is good at finding ways to mix things up, to introduce variability under conditions that appear to be the same. Even genetics, which many people expect to reign supreme, can seem to lose power in this arena. Two thrill-seeking parents can easily wind up with a shy, risk-averse child. A driven and meticulous adolescent can emerge from a mother and father who are freewheeling and scattered. Adding more complexity, some early traits that arise in young children stay rock solid all the way into adulthood, while others disappear in youth never to return again, and still others fade from view like an underground stream, only to emerge later in life stronger than ever.

The mysteries that surround our developing personalities have fascinated parents, teachers, and scientists for thousands of years. Personality traits have been linked not only to the stars and the year of birth, but also to the basic elements of the earth, the temperature of the blood, the secret and forbidden drives of our libido, and, more recently, to the complex code embedded in our DNA. As diverse as these proposed influences are, a common and enduring thread is the idea that at least some of the factors that make us who we are exist well beyond our control.

The topic of temperament and personality has long been a source of engaging conversation around the dinner table, a focus of academic discussions, and even a subject within political debates. But more and more, a clinical aspect is being added to the mix. For decades in the mid-20th century, the ever-expanding fields of temperament and personality generally existed in parallel with the vast medical literature on disease. The study of behavioral differences among people tended to be housed in university psychology departments, while the medical school downtown focused on psychiatric illness and the emergence of "true pathology." As odd as it may sound to those working outside of the mental health fields, the experts on clinical depression have mostly not been concerned with trying to understand happiness, and studies of human anxiety usually excluded the examination of thrill seekers.

This picture is slowly changing. The critical work of Chess and Thomas and their colleagues in the 1950s and 1960s thrust the concept of temperament into mainstream psychiatry, although many others before them laid the groundwork for this shift. Today, temperament and its role in psychiatric disorders, from major depression to attention-deficit/hyperactivity disorder (ADHD) to autism, are major areas of investigation. This book addresses what is known about this important topic and explains how such knowledge can be used in schools, in homes, and in clinical settings. Before examining the accumulating evidence demonstrating that temperament is inextricably linked to psychopathology, however, it is worth a brief look back at how our thinking about temperament has evolved.

Historical Theories of Temperament

The idea that certain factors lead to differences in how people habitually act and feel is hardly new. For millennia, philosophers and physicians have tried to account for the readily observable fact that different people have different behavioral tendencies. In ancient Chinese culture, the belief emerged that mental functioning is related to a balance in the forces of energy (or *ch'i*) between the more active and action-oriented *yang* and the more cautious and inward *yin*. This essential dichotomy, which splits temperament into an *approach* dimension and a *withdrawal* dimension, has been maintained in many current theoretical structures of temperament. Linked to energy levels that are always in flux, one's temperament under this perspective is hardly locked in as a lifelong trait. Rather, behavior patterns are ever changing and subject to the fluid instability of the world.

Ancient Greco-Roman Physicians

Early Western theories of personality, however, subscribed to a somewhat more constant view of behavioral predisposition that was derived not from the heavens or from constantly changing energy levels, but from within. Galen (ca. 131–200), a Greek physician who traveled widely throughout Roman Asia Minor during the rule of the emperor Marcus Aurelius, became one of the most influential medical scholars of his time, with many of his works enduring as the definitive authority for well over a thousand years. Drawing upon the work of earlier scholars such as Hippocrates and the Greco-Roman physician Vindician, who lived a couple of centuries earlier, Galen developed a unified theory of personality. His theory maintained that one's basic pattern of emotional behavior was due to the relative internal concentration of the four humors: yellow bile, black bile, phlegm, and blood. These four fluids, in turn, were related to a person's relative balance of the four basic substances: fire, earth, water, and air. The word *temperament* is derived from the Latin word *temperare* meaning "to mix," and the balance, or imbalance, of these humors was hypothesized to lead to four main personality types called choleric (ambitious, labile), melancholic (thoughtful, worried), phlegmatic (relaxed, content), and sanguine (social, pleasure seeking). A more detailed description of Galen and his theories can be found in a book that bears the ancient physician's name (Kagan, 1994).

When I describe some of these past theories of temperament to audiences today, it often provokes a bit of a smug smile and perhaps a feeling of gratitude for being able to live in a more enlightened age, when scientists no longer study bile in order to understand personality. Nevertheless, if one simply substitutes serotonin, dopamine, norepinephrine, and GABA (gamma-aminobutyric acid) for phlegm, blood, black bile, and yellow bile, it becomes clear that in some fundamental ways, not much has changed. An important parallel between ancient temperament theories relating to the four humors and modern biological hypotheses of temperament relating to levels of neurotransmitters is that in both frameworks, the same substances play key roles not only in determining personality traits, such as overall mood, but also in disease states, such as clinical depression or melancholia.

While the balance of the humors was thought to be intrinsic to the individual, it was also believed to be responsive to the environment, especially the weather. Personality could thus change with the seasons, and societies living in different climates were predicted to have different predominating traits that characterized that culture. People from dry and cool areas, for example, would be expected to possess a generally melancholic personality in comparison to those living in warm, moist areas. These ideas provided a basis for some ethnic stereotypes that persisted well into the 19th and 20th centuries.

In the earliest theories, we can see temperament and personality described both in terms of dimensions (e.g., larger relative amounts of black bile corresponded with traits such as sad and reserved) and in terms of types into which groups of individuals with a similar constellation of traits can be categorized. This dual classification scheme remains with us today and is discussed in detail in Chapter 2.

Early 20th-Century Ideas

While a casual telling of the history of temperament may leap from Galen all the way to the 1950s and the work of Chess and Thomas, much happened in the interim. Many important scholars and researchers of the early 20th century are not household names, even among scientists. At the same time, more famous theorists such as Carl Jung and Ivan Pavlov, who are popularly known in other contexts, crop up in the literature as unexpected advocates for the notion of innately driven personality predispositions.

In 1896, Bernhard Hellwig wrote *The Four Temperaments in Children*, in which he discussed not only the four main temperament types but also the optimal way in which parents and teachers could work with these different types of children. With little modification, he maintained the historic temperament categories of sanguine, choleric, melancholic, and phlegmatic. The sanguine child (about 20% of the population) was mainly happy with a lot of nervous excitement, but also prone to deceit. Choleric children (10%) were bold but prone to angry outbursts. The melancholic type (5%) described a more sullen and dejected predisposition, and the phlegmatic type (also 5%) was cool and often unmotivated. The rest, it is important to note, did not fit easily into any of these categories. These temperaments were thought to be related to the temperature of the blood and therefore to the climate of a particular country, but other factors could figure into the equation. Some children, Hellwig argued, had a temperament determined by "outward circumstance," thus contributing to the age-old nature-versus-nurture debate. Perhaps most notable, however, was his early attention to the importance of what would later be called a temperament "goodness of fit" between a child and his or her surroundings, and the need to shape a child's environment so that it optimally adapts to the child's traits. Hellwig wrote that parenting and teaching practices need "to suit the different temperaments of various children" (1896, p. 3) well before the emergence of Individualized Education Programs.

In the early 20th century, psychodynamic theories of personality became popular, led of course by Sigmund Freud and later by scholars such as Carl Jung. Although a full summary of their contributions is well beyond the scope of this book, a few aspects have particular relevance. While some of Freud's early writings allowed for the possibility of innate behavioral differences between infants, his core theories de-emphasized temperament as it is understood today and focused on personality as based in universal sexual and aggressive drives and how they are handled in early stages of life. In contrast to the idea that various substances are responsible for different traits, Freud espoused the idea of a more unified type of energy or libido that is present in everyone, with variations among people arising from how the ego and superego defend against these urges.

Freud's daughter Anna further developed the idea of defense mechanisms and personality traits in children. While she remained a strong proponent of psychoanalysis throughout her career, Anna Freud was also able to acknowledge the existence of child temperament without naming it as such. In her well-known work *Normality and Pathology in Childhood*, she describes the existence of "general characteristics of the personality" that are part of a child's "individual constitution." Using psychoanalytic language, she wrote, "experience shows that a child's chances of remaining mentally healthy are closely connected with his reaction to the unpleasure which is released whenever drive derivatives remain unsatisfied. Children are very different in this respect, apparently from the outset" (Freud, 1965, p. 134).

One component of Freudian theory that has important implications for the boundaries between normal and pathological behavior is the idea that the processes that shape normal variation in personality and those that lead to pathological symptoms are one and the same. Indeed, the central focus on a person's attempt to defend against quite inappropriate sexual and aggressive impulses was a primary reason many people began to move away from Freud's concepts.

In the 1920s, Swiss psychiatrist Carl Jung hypothesized that an individualized personality could be described as a point in three-dimensional space along the following three axes: thinking-feeling, intuition-sensation, and, most famously, introversion-extraversion. Although he may be better known for more mystical-sounding constructs such as archetypes and the collective unconscious, some of Jung's writings suggest a willingness to consider a child's predisposition along these three axes—a perspective akin to what is now described as temperament. In his 1923 work *Psychological Types*, Jung seemed to struggle somewhat against the prevailing "psychological" theories of personality development, writing that this view needs to "yield before the equally unarguable fact that two children of the same mother may at a very early age exhibit opposite types, without the smallest accompanying change in the attitude of the mother. . . . This experience compels me to conclude that the decisive factor must be looked for in the disposition of the child" (Jung, 1923, p. 415). Jung's work in this area paved the way for the development of other personality structures and instruments such as the Myers-Briggs Type Indicator and the Keirsey Temperament Sorter, both of which helped push the focus away from the academic study of children and toward the assessment of adults for commercial and vocational purposes.

Around the time of the Great Depression, early versions of many modern concepts of temperament and personality began to take root. American psychologist Gordon Allport is credited as one of the founding fathers of personality psychology and the idea that personality is made up of individual traits that he categorized as cardinal (dominant), central (consistent), and secondary (exhibited under certain situations) (Allport, 1961). Temperament was thought of as a component of personality. Also around that time, researchers began to design observational studies of children. Psychologist Mary Margaret Shirley followed a small group of infants and toddlers and described the changes she observed during the first two years of life. She described temperament traits as a "nucleus of personality" (Shirley, 1933).

Emerging Behaviorism and Medical Models

Also emerging in the early 20th century were researchers who took a more experimental approach to temperament and personality through the use of animal studies and, for human studies, the now-ubiquitous questionnaires. Along with these instruments came early versions of a statistical technique called factor analysis, which investigators used to coalesce the many items of a questionnaire into a relatively small number of higher-order factors or dimensions. Much of this work was done with adults and college students. Using these techniques, researchers such as Webb and Burt from England, Heymans and Wiersma in Germany, and Cattell in the United States converged on the idea of major temperament dimensions such as extraversion or conscientiousness (Rothbart, 2011; Webb, 1915) that are part of the "Big Five" scheme used today (Digman, 1990; McCrae & Costa, 2003). These early studies laid the groundwork for additional scholars such as noted personality researcher Hans Eysenck (1967) to begin systematic investigations into the underlying neurobiology of major traits.

The second half of the 20th century was also witness to a major challenge to then-dominant Freudian theories of child development—behaviorism. Under this view, children do not come into the world preprogrammed to act in particular ways because of humors or the temperature of their blood. Neither is their development shaped by channeling instinctual sexual and aggressive drives. Instead, infants are more like a "blank slate"—to use English philosopher John Locke's term—to be shaped by learning and experience. The two main types of learning that were studied at that time included classical conditioning and operant conditioning. In classical conditioning, exemplified by the work of Russian physiologist Ivan Pavlov, learning occurs through *association*. He demonstrated in dogs that if the *unconditioned stimulus* of food presentation is paired with another *conditioned stimulus* such as a ringing bell or a whistle, then over time, the physiological response of salivation can be triggered by the presence of the conditioned stimulus alone (Pavlov, 1927).

Interestingly, Pavlov was also a major student and proponent of temperament, although that work receives far less attention in Psychology 101 classes than does his salivation work with dogs. Ironically, these same dogs and the way they seemed to differ from one another behaviorally led Pavlov to investigate further the way these traits affected the dogs' ability to be conditioned (Gray, 1980). Toward the end of his career, Pavlov applied his studies of temperament to psychopathological states. He examined how animals develop an "experimental neurosis," during which they became increasingly agitated and disturbed as they were put through more challenging experimental procedures (Plaud, 2003). He also studied how quickly people shut down under extreme stress or pain, a reaction called transmarginal inhibition, which has direct implications for conditions such as post-traumatic stress disorder (PTSD).

Coming back to behaviorism, the other broad type of learning—operant conditioning—occurs when the probability of a behavior occurring increases or decreases based on whether the behavior is *reinforced* or *punished*. A child will continue to act defiantly, for example, if he or she learns that such behavior works to produce the desired effect. Anxious behavior can also be learned, and therefore unlearned. When a child performs an elaborate ritual to ensure that nothing bad happens to her family, and then nothing bad occurs, that ritual has just been reinforced and will therefore be more likely to continue.

The behaviorists, including luminaries such as John Watson and B. F. Skinner, drew a stark contrast both with the Freudians and with those who emphasized the inherited aspect of personality. Their focus was on the observable and measurable behavior itself rather than the inner workings of the unconscious, which was reportedly accessible only in fleeting and indirect glimpses. Proponents from each of the two schools of thought were predictably quite critical of each other, but in many ways managed to keep themselves apart, arguing from afar in separate conferences, seminars, and scientific journals. This divergence was partially due to different educational pathways, with the Freudian or psychodynamic theories taught as part of the training for psychiatrists and behaviorism taking root in academic psychology. The ability of prominent scholars of one theory to remain insulated from evidence being produced by researchers in the same field, sometimes even on the same university campus, seems remarkable. While one group of psychologists was vehemently defending the supremacy of a blank slate model of children whose behavior is shaped through association, punishment, and reward, a lab down the hall was successfully breeding animals on the basis of their inherited behavioral tendencies. This type of disconnect continues today, despite the modern revolution in information accessibility.

Chess and Thomas

It was into this world of the feuding behaviorists and Freudians that the work of Stella Chess, Alexander Thomas, and their colleagues emerged. In what came to be known as the New York Longitudinal Study (NYLS), the husband-and-wife research team, who were both psychodynamically trained child psychiatrists, began to follow a group of 138 white, middle-class infants and 95 economically disadvantaged infants of Puerto Rican descent (Chess, Hertzig, & Thomas, 1962). While such a project in and of itself was not completely novel in the 1950s, Chess and Thomas directly observed the children rather than relying on maternal reports, and they further included other aspects such as IQ testing and a clinical psychiatric assessment. The study began in 1956 and was designed with mainly psychoanalytically oriented goals in mind (Klein, 2011). However, their observations began to hint at mechanisms that did not seem to fit with any of the dominant frameworks of child development at the time. Siblings raised under very similar conditions were often observed to be quite different. Children of loving and skilled parents could be extremely challenging behaviorally, while other children who were raised under quite adverse conditions sometimes proved to be remarkably resilient. These findings propelled Chess and Thomas to suggest that child behavior was at least partially due to more innate and autonomous biological factors.

This constituted a major challenge to both of the dominant schools of thought at the time. The idea that behavioral traits could be somewhat inborn ran counter to both the behaviorists' notion of rewards and punishments and the analytical view that prioritized the role of early traumatic experiences and internal conflict. While Chess and Thomas certainly did not pretend that their theory was completely their own, their willingness to advance these ideas and challenge the status quo caused them to take a significant amount of academic heat.

The idea that children are born with significant behavioral tendencies was not only scientifically incongruent to the prevailing theories of child development but also potentially dangerous politically. Many scholars in the 1960s had lived through World War II and had seen the horrific misuse of power in Nazi Germany, which stemmed from the central premise that certain groups of people were intrinsically different and superior to others. Furthermore, the fabric of moral life from a religious perspective depended on a person being responsible for his own behavior. When it came to young children, that responsibility was held by the parents, such that negative child behavior was seen as a reflection of parental deficiencies. The practice of "mother blaming" for all kinds of childhood conditions was particularly prominent during this era (Caplan & Hall-McCorquodale, 1985). Thus, the idea of innately driven temperament traits stood to undermine fundamental concepts of individual responsibility and was seen as a potential platform for further prejudice and discrimination.

Fortunately for Chess and Thomas, they were able to back their ideas with compelling data that were not easily dismissed, and the study of child temperament was brought back into mainstream discourse, even if not everyone was ready to accept it. As for the political concerns, it became apparent that what the researchers were suggesting was a far cry from the eugenics movement. While it is important to be mindful of the way scientific concepts can be misinterpreted and misused, it does not make sense to ignore data because of the possibility that some people may go to the extreme. As we will soon see, the genetic influences on child temperament in no way translate to inevitability or destiny. Parenting, morality, positive and negative life events, education, and many other environmental factors can shape temperament traits and their developmental trajectories. Even without such diverse influences on temperament, there is nothing intrinsic about temperament traits that would suggest that some people and not others should be entitled to preferred freedom, opportunity, or law.

Throughout the 1970s and 1980s, the uneasiness associated with the idea of temperament began to subside and it gained increased attention as a worthy topic of study. Part of the reason for this shift was likely the tremendous explosion of research that documented the biological underpinnings of behavior, both for "normal" personality traits and for pathological conditions such as schizophrenia and bipolar disorder. This surge of scientific investigation, exemplified by the National Institutes of Health naming the 1990s the "Decade of the Brain," coincided with a dramatic increase in the use of psychiatric medications to treat anxiety, depression, psychosis, and attention problems. Strangely, however, the synchronous appreciation regarding the neurobiology of both temperament and psychiatric disorders did little to change the public perception that the two domains were essentially separate. People both within and outside of the mental health community continued to view psychopathology primarily as an externally driven disease, with causes that were qualitatively rather than quantitatively different from those of even similar-sounding personality traits. Children's varying activity levels, for example, were essentially kept separate from the study of ADHD. Panic attacks were thought to "come out of the blue" rather than being related to an anxious personality type. Depressive episodes descended upon people like the flu, without any advance notice.

To some degree, the dichotomy between traits and psychiatric illness continues today, despite the fact that many of the core principles of temperament, as promoted by Chess and Thomas, are no longer considered to be particularly revolutionary. The idea that children are born with some inherent predispositions toward certain traits that can be shaped over time into more or less adaptive functions is unlikely to draw major protest from the scientific community these days. At the same time, major gaps remain in our knowledge regarding fundamental aspects of child temperament, the degree to which temperamental traits are linked to psychiatric disorders, and the mechanisms underlying those associations.

Goals and Principles of This Book

This book concentrates on what is known about temperament and its relations to psychopathology since the landmark research of Chess and Thomas. It is divided into two parts: Part 1 is a synthesis of what is currently known about temperament and its links with emotional-behavioral problems, and Part 2 is a practical guide to how this new knowledge can be applied by mental health professionals, educators, parents, and others.

Many fine books about temperament have been printed over the years, and a number of them are cited in this and subsequent chapters. The hope here, however, is to provide a bridge between the two prevailing types of volumes that have been produced—research-oriented publications and "how-to" books. The first type chronicles in great detail important studies, often carried out by the author. Such works can be tremendously helpful, especially to those interested in running their own studies at some point. During my training as a child psychiatrist with an academic interest in temperament, these books were often found on my coffee table. At the same time, readers with an interest in temperament but without a background in research or neuroscience might find that level of detail beyond what is necessary, and lacking in practical application. How-to books, on the other hand, offer a great deal of advice on incorporating temperament into everyday life. These works offer hands-on strategies that are readily applicable, yet may leave data-driven persons (like me) wondering whether such guidance comes from the solid conclusions of controlled studies or the inner workings of a single individual whose opinions have been shaped by his or her own dreams and disappointments. Thus, the goal of this book is to provide not only a readable summary of the current science of temperament but also a scientifically informed guide to applying temperament-based perspectives in real-life settings.

Throughout these chapters, efforts will be made to keep scientific jargon to a minimum and explain even complex neurobiological processes in plain English. While the book is written with a clinician as reader in mind, parents, teachers, and any other persons interested in the topic should have no trouble adapting the text to a different perspective. Another goal is to articulate the importance of these findings beyond their inherent scientific interest. Such value will not be difficult to explain, as the study of temperament and its relations to psychopathology may usher in a fundamentally new way of addressing psychiatric disorders that is potentially less stigmatizing and more effective. A full appreciation of these concepts also compels parents, clinicians, and educators to challenge many long-held beliefs.

Chapter 2 reviews some of the core principles of temperament including its definition, core dimensions and types, and overlap with the concept of personality. Chapter 3 then expands upon certain elements of temperament that have received study such as its degree of stability over time, differences between males and females, and factors such as birth order. Chapter 4 plunges into the neurobiology of temperament, including genetic and environmental influences, brain regions, neurotransmitters, and associated physiology. Attention will be paid here to putting together these different domains as much as possible into a synthesized process, with an emphasis on the idea that genetic and environmental factors impact not only temperament but also each other. After this solid foundation has been laid, the next two chapters get into the heart of the matter—which temperament traits are related to which psychiatric disorders and the critical issue of how these two constructs are inter-twined. It is here that we will address the search for boundaries that separate normally varying temperament traits and pathological psychiatric symptoms.

The second part of the book explores practical applications of this new knowledge of temperament and its associations with psychopathology. Chapter 7 examines how a new understanding of temperament and psychiatric disorders may alter the clinical approach in mental health settings. Case examples will be presented in this chapter but represent composites of many individuals rather than specific examples. Chapters 8 and 9 explore temperamentally based parenting strategies that can be used to add some needed complexity to the "one size fits all" parental advice that is so prevalent today. Then, in Chapter 10, I propose an approach to enhancing school environments and educational processes using a temperament-informed perspective. Finally, the last chapter addresses behavioral medications and how they alter temperament, both during the treatment of psychiatric illness and through the deliberate use of these agents to alter or augment certain human characteristics.

There is certainly a lot of ground to cover. By the end of this book, readers can expect to have a solid and current knowledge base regarding child temperament and the boundaries between traits and mental illness, as well as a new set of temperament-based perspectives and approaches for parenting, teaching, counseling, and treating our children.

Chapter 2

The Basics of Child Temperament

After more than 40 years of focused attention from scholars across the world, one might think that the fundamentals of child temperament would be worked out by now, including its proper definition, core dimensions, and relations to constructs such as personality. Unfortunately, this is not the case. One main reason for the delay is the fact that beneath the theories and models and logical arguments, temperament must ultimately boil down to brain activity. And while certain regions do specialize in certain functions, the operations of the brain are remarkably interconnected and seamless. Concepts such as temperament, personality, extraversion, and sociability are, in the end, just words that we have created, and searching for an organic line between temperament and personality is a bit like standing in the middle of a desert looking for a natural boundary between Arizona and New Mexico. Nonetheless, science does tend to progress most quickly when there is at least some consensus about what exactly we are studying. And while brain functions are indeed complex and interrelated, there are places where we can "carve at the joints" and separate constructs in a meaningful way.

Defining Temperament

One definition of temperament from a prominent researcher, Mary Rothbart, is "constitutionally based differences in reactivity and self-regulation" (Rothbart & Derryberry, 1981). Chess and Thomas (1996) described temperament as a child's behavioral style—the *how* or *way* of behavior, distinct from motivation or the *why* of behavior. This definition, as they viewed it, served to separate temperament from ability or motivation. Another distinguished temperament scholar, psychologist Jerome Kagan at Harvard University, defined temperament as "an inherited physiology that is preferentially linked to an envelope of behaviors and emotions" (Kagan & Snidman, 2004).

These various definitions share common threads but include and emphasize different points. Does temperament have to be inherited? Can ability really be excluded? During a "temperament roundtable" in which the participants attempted to achieve consensus about the definition of temperament (Goldsmith et al., 1987), the following core features were listed as requirements of a temperamental trait:

- Appearance early in life. How early is early enough continues to be a matter of debate, but certainly observable components during infancy should suggest at least the emergence of the trait. An extraverted toddler might not yet be able to make small talk smoothly with several friends from day care, but he could show a preference for the excitement of the playground over playing quietly with a puzzle. A regulated infant probably won't take 10 cleansing breaths when getting overstimulated by an intrusive grandmother, but she might have the ability to turn her head and look the other way.
- Genetic influence. When people talk about temperament, words like "innate," "constitutional," and "predisposition" are often used, conveying that it has been present from the very beginning of life. Our knowledge of genes and how they influence behavior has advanced quite a bit in the past few decades, as will be demonstrated in Chapter 4. For now, it is probably sufficient to say that temperament traits are influenced by one's genes but certainly not controlled by them.
- Stability over time. Temperament is considered to be enduring. The level of a particular trait at one point in life is predictive of levels of that trait at a later point, even decades later. Stability, however, is not synonymous with intractability, just as genetic influence should not be confused with genetic destiny. Kagan and Snidman (2004) have used words such as "envelope" or "retaining wall" to describe the idea that temperament influences the probability that certain psychological profiles will be attained later in life.

One of the best analogies I have come up with for temperament is in music. If a person's life is a symphony, then his or her temperament is the main key of that piece of music. This key, whether F major or A minor, does not restrict the endless possibilities that can arise in the symphony, but it is always there, influencing the tone of the music throughout the piece. The key of a composition is detectable to the discerning ear and intuitively perceived by nearly everyone. From time to time it may change, but eventually, it comes home.

Frameworks of Temperament

There are two main ways to carve up the overall concept of temperament. The most common, a *variable-centered approach*, divides temperament into a number of dimensions such as extraversion or novelty seeking. These dimensions are then subdivided into smaller and more specific components or facets, such as impulsivity or perceptual sensitivity. A contrasting, albeit related, strategy is to group people who have similar behaviors across a variety of dimensions into types or classes. These two approaches are not contradictory; rather, each perspective can inform the other. There are even statistical procedures, such as factor mixture models, that produce a hybrid between the two approaches. Before getting into that level of complexity, however, let us look at some of the primary dimensions of temperament that have been proposed, studied, and modified over the years.

Chess and Thomas

With the help of their colleagues Herbert Birch, British psychiatrist Sir Michael Rutter, and others, Chess and Thomas took the extensive data from the New York Longitudinal Study and hypothesized that child temperament could be organized into nine main dimensions, listed below (Thomas, Birch, Hertzig, & Korn, 1963). While considerable refinements have taken place since this structure was introduced, the nine dimensions have endured as a cornerstone of developmental psychology as it is taught around the world.

1. Activity level. Here the emphasis is on actual motor activity. Children with higher activity levels often prefer physical play in contrast to play that involves extended sitting.

2. Rhythmicity (regularity). Taking into account patterns of sleeping, eating, and elimination, this dimension reflects how predictable these functions are over time. For example, some young children get tired each night at nearly the same time, whereas others seem to have no regular pattern at all. Older children with high rhythmicity might have specific routines that involve snacking or sleeping habits.

3. Approach or withdrawal. This aspect examines a child's response to novelty such as a new person or a new place. A child with a high-approach temperament exhibits more exploration, whereas those on the withdrawn side show more negative emotions and avoidance of new experiences. The high-approach child might be excited to take vacations in new places, try the latest roller coaster, and meet the new student in class. The child with lower approach, by contrast, is likely to show restraint and caution and prefers predictable routines.

4. Adaptability. This dimension captures the ways in which a child can modify and be modified to function in a particular environment over the long term. In a school context, this trait can be related to the tendency for some children to do well from year to year regardless of the teacher, whereas others show marked variation across grades as they encounter new teachers and educational styles.

5. Threshold of responsiveness. Regardless of the actual type of response, this trait covers the amount of stimulus it takes to elicit a response in a child. People often talk about how easy it is to "push someone's buttons" or "rock their boat." This dimension also encompasses responses to sensory stimuli such as sounds, textures, and tastes.

6. Intensity of reaction. Once a reaction is triggered, this dimension captures the amplitude of the response, whether positive or negative. For children with high-intensity reactions, happy emotions are expressed with enthusiasm and joy, and negative reactions may be characterized by rage or panic. Youth with lower intensity tend to stay on a more even keel.

7. Quality of mood. The baseline emotional state is what is being discerned here, ranging from a generally happy and pleasant disposition to one that is generally negative and unfriendly.

8. Distractibility. This dimension refers to how easily external stimuli can interfere with a child's current activity. Kids with high distract-

ibility tend to bounce from one thing to another, especially when other children and activities are available, whereas low-distractibility children are not easily sidetracked.

9. Attention span and persistence. The attention span component reflects how long a child continues to focus on a particular activity. Persistence is a related concept but adds a degree of being able to overcome obstacles that might get in the way of an overall goal. This dimension can be observed across many settings, especially with older children, as they perform schoolwork, play board games, or try to learn a new sport or skill.

In addition to the variable-centered framework that breaks down temperament into specific dimensions, Chess and Thomas also proposed a person-centered scheme consisting of three temperament types that describe groups of children who possess a similar profile of several traits. The "easy" child group (roughly 40% of the sample) exemplified traits such as high regularity, positive quality of mood, high adaptability, and average to high levels of mood intensity. In contrast, the now-famous "difficult" children showed low regularity, low quality of mood, withdrawal, high intensity, and low adaptability. This group represented about 10% of the sample. Since the "difficult child" label emerged, the term has exploded into common language, now referring to all kinds of challenging behavior. Finally, there was a "slow to warm up" group. These children, especially in new situations, looked similar to the difficult group, although perhaps at a lower level of intensity. Like the difficult group, these kids generally showed low rhythmicity. However, if given the chance, they could become much "easier" with time, showing more positive responses as they became accustomed to the new situation. This group represented about 15% of the children studied.

For those doing the math, these groupings still leave 35% of the children uncategorized. Similar to the ancient Greek and Roman temperament scholars, Chess and Thomas also found a sizable segment of their sample who could not easily be placed in one of their boxes. Who are these people who keep coming up and why can't they be categorized easily? One reason a child might not fall into one of the main profiles or types is because he or she possesses a combination of traits that doesn't fit any of the major patterns, such as low regularity, low adaptability, and high mood. For others, however, the problem in categorizing arises not from the particular combination of traits that are displayed but rather from how inconsistently the traits are displayed across various settings. For example, certain children might be labeled as difficult at home but easy at a child care facility. The richness of the data that were collected in the NYLS compelled the researchers to acknowledge the fact that their data sometimes challenged one of the core tenets of temperament, namely that it describes the manner in which a child typically behaves and reacts. For many children, behavior is unpredictable and the word typical does not seem to apply. This understudied but potentially very important component of temperament is discussed in more detail in Chapter 3.

More Cooks in the Kitchen

The pioneering work of Thomas, Chess, and their colleagues put child temperament back onto the radar screens of countless mental health professionals who had previously given little thought to the topic. Their work brought in new followers, new enthusiasm, and, inevitably, new skeptics. Among the questions from challengers was whether or not the framework of these nine proposed dimensions was indeed the best way to conceptualize temperament. One criticism pointed to the fact that the nine dimensions were derived without the application of modern statistical procedures to determine empirically which types of traits hold together as discrete entities. In the 1960s, many of the statistical procedures used today, such as factor analysis, principal component analysis, cluster analysis, and latent class analysis, were still in their infancy. Some of the analyses had been described, but in the absence of computers, their applications were tedious and esoteric. Although observation and good clinical judgment are critically important (and many now consider them dying arts), they are prone to bias. In addition, there is always the possibility that Chess and Thomas missed including some important elements of temperament that would therefore not be part of their final model.

Steadily, the nine-dimension framework was put to the test, even utilizing data from Chess and Thomas themselves. While many of the dimensions seemed to hold up well to scrutiny, some refinements appeared to be warranted (Martin et al., 1994). Dimensions such as attention span and distractibility were thought to be better conceptualized as being part of the same factor rather than separate dimensions (which may be why both dimensions became criteria for disorders such as ADHD). Other dimensions such as rhythmicity looked as though they might need to be subdivided, as many children were rhythmic in some parts of their life (e.g., sleeping) and less so in others (e.g., eating). Sensitivity was another dimension that seemed prone to losing coherence. Some children with autism, for example, are incredibly sensitive to the tactile sensation of clothing tags against their skin while at the same time have remarkable tolerance for pain.

Throughout the 1970s and beyond, more and more researchers were studying temperament and personality and coming up with classification schemes, or taxonomies, that bore some resemblance to that of Chess and Thomas but often departed from it in important ways. Hans Eysenck proposed three main higher-order dimensions of personality: neuroticism, extraversion, and psychoticism (Eysenck & Eysenck, 1975). In the temperament arena, researchers such as Buss and Plomin, Cloninger, and Rothbart proposed systems of their own. The temperament dimensions proposed by these scholars and the instruments designed to assess them provide the basis for much of the research that is reviewed in this book.

To this day, there remains no universally agreed-upon structure or framework for child temperament (Rothbart, 2004). The renewed interest in temperament has spawned new generations of researchers who have proposed their major dimensions of temperament, as well as new ways to measure them. Readers of child temperament studies now commonly encounter different taxonomies from article to article. Those who conduct their own temperament research and plan their own studies must decide between choosing an existing framework (and the accompanying rating scales that typically go along with them) versus coming up with their own structure and assessment scales, an endeavor that can take quite a bit of effort.

On the one hand, the coexistence of many different ways to understand and categorize temperament dimensions adds richness to the field. The question of which taxonomy is most accurate is also, to some degree, a testable question that can be addressed in research studies and then generate lively discussions at conferences. One the other hand, competing frameworks can make it very difficult to interpret and compare studies across different research groups. When that happens, the progress of the entire field can decelerate.

Consider, for example, two studies trying to find genes that are related to a particular trait. Both studies focus on the famous serotonin transporter gene, a gene that is involved in the proper flow of the brain neurotransmitter serotonin (more about that in a later chapter). Both studies are interested in the relations between that gene and a temperamental propensity to experience negative emotions like sadness or anxiety. Furthermore, let's assume that both studies also chose a sample of children around the same age and measured temperament by having the child's mother fill out a questionnaire. One study, however, adopted the framework of one prominent temperament researcher and used a scale that measures the trait of negative affectivity, while the other chose a different instrument that measures the trait of harm avoidance. While both of these dimensions do indeed get at the tendency to experience negative emotions, they are not identical with regard to the wording of the questionnaire items, the relative number of items that refer to sadness versus anxiety, or the inclusion of other subcomponents like how easily someone becomes fatigued.

Now assume that both studies are published and one of them finds a statistically significant link to the serotonin transporter gene and the other does not. This very common scenario in science is called nonreplication and, if it happens enough, can lead to researchers and funders of researchers to abandon particular areas of investigation. The question is, however, whether these studies are truly similar enough to call this disagreement a nonreplication or whether the disparity has more to do with the fact that their dimensions of interest, while similar in many ways, are different enough to cause these varying results. Without further investigation, it is very difficult to know.

This situation has led some leaders in the field of temperament to call for consensus building and at least a trimming of the number of different frameworks used. There seems to be some agreement that such efforts are worthwhile until the process gets down to which frameworks should be used and which should be dropped. Then it gets complicated. Researchers who have proposed particular taxonomies for temperament and have developed instruments in their service have invested a lot of scientific capital in them. Having their scheme devalued could result in a loss of prominence, reputation, academic momentum, and, in some cases, royalties. While everyone agrees in theory that we need to let the data decide these debates, separating the human element is not always simple.

Major Dimensions of Child Temperament

Before getting too discouraged about the roadblocks to categorizing temperament traits, it is worth noting that the field has definitely moved forward since Chess and Thomas opened the door. Many of the major and minor temperament dimensions that have emerged from multiple classification frameworks are now generally accepted. Debate and refinement will undoubtedly continue, but the following represents what to many are the core dimensions of temperament as they are understood today. A summary of these dimensions can be found in Table 2.1.

TABLE 2.1. Major Temperament Frameworks Since Chess and Thomas						
Founder	Negative Emotionality/ Withdrawal	Extraversion/ Approach	Sociability	Activity	Regulatory Ability	Scales
Rothbart	Negative Affectivity	Extraversion/ Surgency			Effortful Control	Infant Behavior Questionnaire; Child Behavior Questionnaire; Early Adolescent Temperament Questionnaire
Cloninger	Harm Avoidance	Novelty Seeking	Reward Dependence		Persistence	Temperament and Character Inventory (and Junior version)
Gray	Behavioral Inhibiting System	Behavioral Activating System				
Buss and Plomin	Emotionality	Shyness (R*)	Sociability	Activity		EAS Temperament Schedule
Kagan and Snidman	Behavioral Inhibition	Behavioral Disinihibition				Laboratory Observation Protocol

*R = reversed

- Negative emotionality. Nearly every temperament taxonomy contains a dimension related to how easily a child experiences negative emotions such as anxiety, sadness, or anger. Some have labeled this dimension neuroticism, in deference to some of its historical roots, while others have used the term emotionality (Buss & Plomin, 1984) or negative affectivity (Rothbart, Ahadi, & Evans, 2000). In temperament schemes that are less focused on the outward manifestation of traits and more aligned with underlying motivational systems, this dimension has been labeled harm avoidance (Cloninger, Przybeck, & Svrakic, 1991), which is described as a reflection of a person's sensitivity toward cues of punishment or part of the behavioral inhibition system (Gray, 1987). It has further been suggested that this broad dimension can be broken down into two main areas that operate somewhat independently of each other, namely negative responses to being limited (frustration, irritability) and negative responses to novelty (shyness, fearfulness) (Rothbart, Ahadi, Hershey, & Fisher, 2001).

- Extraversion. Another dimension with good consensus but a few wrinkles to work out refers to approach behavior and the tendency to engage the world and other people. Versions of this quality have been called extraversion, surgency, novelty seeking, and approach. It is thought that extraversion reflects the functioning of an individual's behavioral activating system (BAS) (Gray, 1982). Components of this broad dimension include qualities such as impulsivity, sensation seeking, spontaneity, dominance, and exuberance. There is often but not always a social component to the dimension as well, with highly extraverted people being gregarious and gaining enjoyment from being the center of attention.

- Regulatory ability. The ability to control the output of the previously mentioned dimensions is often considered to be a trait in itself. Across different theoretical frameworks, the trait has been called effortful control or persistence. Like the other broad dimensions, it can be further broken down into interrelated but somewhat separate domains, such as the regulation of attention, emotion, and behavior (Althoff et al., 2010).

Some temperament schemes don't specifically include regulatory processes as a separate major dimension, under the idea that it is already incorporated into other dimensions. For example, a child with high levels of negative emotionality can be presumed to have difficulty regulating that emotion. According to other perspectives, however, the *experience* of the emotion of anger is distinct from its *expression*, and a child with high negative emotionality and high regulatory ability could well feel anger intensely but not show it. Developmentally, regulatory abilities progress rapidly throughout childhood. Not many 2-year-olds can powerfully feel an emotion without expressing it; however, the same cannot be said for many teens. Thus, the inclusion of this dimension as a separate major player may depend somewhat on age.

One perhaps oversimplified analogy that illustrates the complexity of the relations between regulatory ability and other traits is the observed speed of a car as a function of the accelerator and the brake. Consider two cars coming to a stop at an intersection, both at 30 miles per hour. The first car is moving slowly because the driver is pressing only very gently on the accelerator and the brake is not being applied. The driver of the second car is actively stepping on the brake after having used the accelerator more aggressively. Negative affectivity and extraversion would be considered accelerator-type systems, while regulatory ability is the brake, and one cannot judge the degree to which both systems are being engaged simply by looking at the speed of the car.

The accelerator and brake, like most analogies, falls short with additional scrutiny. In cars, the accelerator and brake systems operate independently, with the accelerator delivering force to the axles and the brake applying friction to the wheels. In the brain, however, things aren't divided up so cleanly, and the accelerator and brake regions are connected both anatomically and physiologically. The output of one system thus modifies the other from the very start.

Other Proposed Dimensions

Beyond the "big three" above, several other dimensions have been proposed as major traits and have found their way into the scientific literature.

- Activity level. This trait is sometimes included as a stand-alone, higher-order trait in frameworks such as the Buss and Plomin (1984) model. In their system, activity refers to a hurried, fast-paced lifestyle and the experience of bursting with energy. In other frameworks, the dimension is seen as a component of extraversion.
- Sociability. When the activity or extraversion dimension is kept distinct from social qualities, sociability can emerge as a major independent dimension on its own. Think here of the difference

between a lion and a tiger—two animals with comparable activity levels but very different levels of sociability. Lions live in prides. They hunt together, look after one another's cubs, and hang out in groups, while tigers are much more solitary creatures, usually coming together only to mate.

- Shyness. In many ways, shyness would seem like the prototypical temperament trait. Going back to the three required criteria of a temperamental trait, shyness does often emerge very early in life, tends to be stable over many years, and has been shown to be under at least moderate genetic influence. Shyness refers to the tendency to be timid, withdrawn, and uncomfortable in social situations. It differs from traits such as sociability because most people who are shy enjoy and even crave social contact, but find it very difficult and anxiety provoking. Further study of shyness, however, has revealed it to be a bit more complex. One study from Norway found that among children between the ages of 18 months and 9 years, those characterized by their mothers as being shy fell into two main groups: those whose shyness was driven by high levels of general anxiety (high negative emotionality) and those whose shyness was a function of low approach behavior accompanied by lower sociability and activity (Janson & Mathiesen, 2008).

- Behavioral inhibition. The term *behavioral inhibition* was coined by Jerome Kagan and his colleague Nancy Snidman. The researchers followed a group of subjects from infancy into adulthood, and many other scientists such as Dina Hirshfeld-Becker have continued the investigation with other groups of people. Behavioral inhibition (or BI for short) refers to the tendency to show restraint and fear when presented with novel situations or people. Studies have shown this trait to be present in about 10–15% of 2-year-olds, with approximately the same percentage showing an opposite pattern of behavioral disinhibition—children who are bold and approach novelty (Kagan, 1994).

There is a great deal of research surrounding BI and its association with particular genes and patterns of brain function. BI has been described as a risk factor for later psychopathology, in particular anxiety disorders (Chapter 5 explores this association in more detail). Here I discuss how BI fits into other temperament frameworks. Unlike the majority of personality and temperament researchers, Kagan and his colleagues have focused their research efforts on this one trait rather than trying to organize an entire temperament structure. Relative to some of the dimensions recently described, BI might also be understood as the combination of high negative emotionality and low extraversion or approach. The overlap between BI and plain old shyness has certainly been noticed, although certain distinctions exist between the two labels.

Our research group in Vermont applied a statistical analysis called latent class analysis to a group of children (average age 11) whose mothers completed a temperament questionnaire about them that contained items related to the construct of BI (Rettew et al., 2004). The analysis was used to examine patterns of children's scores, and then to divide the children into a small number of groups on the basis of their scores. The results showed that while most children manifested no excessive reticence and fear of novel people and situations, there was a small group that did. In this way, the analysis supported the construct of BI. However, the procedure also found evidence of groups of children who were restrained in the face of novel people or novel situations, but not both. Thus, our analysis suggested that analyzing BI as a single trait may be lumping together two distinct traits that can also exist independently. Regardless of whether BI is its own entity or a combination of other traits, important work continues with behavioral inhibition and disinhibition, which will be covered as we explore the neurobiology of temperament and its relations to emotional and behavioral problems.

Temperament Types and Profiles

Whether the research community settles on three, nine, or ninety main temperament dimensions, there are even more ways in which the traits can mathematically combine in an individual to form an overall temperamental profile. For researchers who use person-centered approaches, the unit of study is not a temperament dimension but an individual person. Given that brain connections are both extensive and nonrandom, however, there is probably good reason to suspect that there is a relatively small number of temperament profiles within a population.

Chess and Thomas attempted to define some of these groups with their designation of the difficult, easy, and slow-to-warm-up categories.

As mentioned, they arrived at these particular groups through careful observation. Since then, other researchers have also tried to characterize groups of children with a similar clustering of traits. In a long-term investigation known as the Dunedin Study, based on the sample's location in New Zealand, researchers have been following a large group (more than 1,000 individuals) from early childhood into adulthood (Caspi et al., 1995). Using a statistical procedure called cluster analysis on three temperament dimensions—lack of control, approach, and sluggishness—the researchers identified five temperament types: undercontrolled (high lack of control and high approach), inhibited (high lack of control and high sluggishness), confident (high approach), reserved (high sluggishness but moderate lack of control), and well-adjusted (average levels across dimensions).

More recently, two Norwegian researchers studied a group of nearly 1,000 children across multiple time points from 18 months to 9 years of age (Janson & Mathiesen, 2008). Using a person-oriented procedure called I-States as Objects Analysis applied to the Emotionality, Activity and Shyness (EAS) Temperament Survey (Buss & Plomin, 1984), they also identified five groups, although the composition of these groups differed somewhat from those in the Dunedin Study. The researchers labeled their groups undercontrolled (high emotionality, sociability, and activity), confident (low shyness and emotionality with high activity and sociability), unremarkable (moderate to low levels of all dimensions), inhibited (low activity and sociability with high shyness), and uneasy (moderate to high shyness and emotionality).

In a study from our research team that involved 200 Vermont families and 447 children with an average age of 11, we attempted to identify profiles of temperament on the basis of the mothers' ratings. The sample contained a higher percentage of children with significant behavioral problems than is normally found in a community sample (Rettew, Althoff, et al., 2008). Rather than relying on our observations to determine the groupings, we used a statistical procedure called latent profile analysis. This procedure takes data from a number of different variables, in this case the child's score on the four temperament dimensions of the Junior Temperament and Character Inventory (Luby et al., 1999), and tries to identify groups of kids with similar profiles. The procedure does this by trying different groupings of numbers until it finds a good "fit" with the actual data. When we applied this procedure to our data, three groups or classes provided the best fit. The profiles of those three classes are shown in Figure 2.1.

FIGURE 2.1

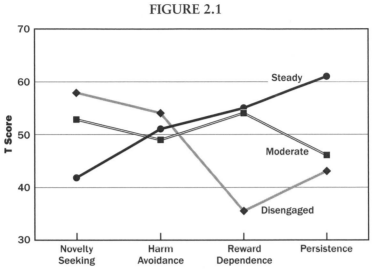

Figure 2.1. Profiles of temperament as determined though latent profiles analysis. The moderate group shows average levels across all dimensions; the steady group is characterized by low novelty seeking and high persistence; and the disengaged group shows moderately high levels of both novelty seeking and harm avoidance with low levels of reward dependence (adapted from Rettew, Althoff, et al., 2008, and used with permission).

The largest class, representing 45% of the sample, was the "moderate" class. They tended to have average levels of the four temperament traits. (Incidentally, one of the trickiest and least scientific parts of these kinds of studies is giving the profiles meaningful names, as the computer only labels them class A, B, etc.). The "steady" class was characterized by low novelty-seeking scores and high persistence scores (36% of the sample). This group showed the highest performance of the three groups when it came to school achievement, social functioning, and involvement in activities. The last and smallest group (19% and mainly boys) we called the "disengaged" class, as their profile featured relatively high scores for novelty seeking and harm avoidance (the latter trait similar to negative emotionality and behavioral withdrawal) and relatively low scores for persistence and reward dependence (the latter trait similar to sociability and seeking others when stressed). This group was not doing well, as measured by their school and social functioning and by their levels of problem behavior. Other important aspects of this group are further described in Chapter 5.

Unlike Chess and Thomas, we were not left with a large number of children who didn't fit into any class, because our particular statistical procedure classified everyone as well as possible. If individuals within a class are too heterogeneous, the procedure indicates that more classes are needed to describe the sample. Nevertheless, one can argue that the analysis can "force" a conclusion of more structure than there actually is. Other procedures such as configural frequency analysis don't classify the entire sample (Aksan et al., 1999) and there is legitimate debate about which statistical technique is best.

It is easy to get lost in all the different studies, with their various methods, samples, and types of profiles. The partially overlapping names for the different types or profiles generate the same sorts of problems when comparing one study to another that are encountered comparing similar-sounding temperament traits. From the confusion, however, some general trends are beginning to arise. Many studies have successfully grouped most of the child participants into a relatively small number of temperament profiles. Table 2.2 summarizes these temperament groups.

- Moderate. This group shows moderate levels across traits and encompasses what other researchers have called average or "unremarkable," a word that seems to have an undeserved negative connotation.
- Mellow. Individuals in this group may or may not be low on stimulus seeking but show relatively high frustration tolerance and can be persistent and focused in working toward their goals. In our own research, we called this group "steady," given their high persistence and low novelty seeking.
- Agitated. This group shows low distress tolerance and low regulatory abilities, with high levels of approach and activity.
- Confident. This group similarly shows high approach or extraversion, but in contrast to the agitated group possesses better regulatory skills and lower anxiety.
- Anxious. This group manifests low approach and high negative emotionality. Like the mellow class, these children tend to avoid the spotlight but are nervous and fearful and can become dysregulated in the process.

	TABLE 2.2. Temperament Types	
Group Name	Description	Approximate Frequency in General School-Age Population (%)
Moderate	Average levels of the main dimensions with no prominent outliers	35
Mellow	Lower levels of approach and energy but not particularly anxious and with good regulatory skills	20
Agitated	High energy but also prone to experience negative emotions that can be hard to regulate	10
Confident	High extraversion and sociability with low anxiety and good regulatory skills	20
Anxious	High negative emotionality but lower regulation ability and lower extraversion	15

In hearing these assignments, many readers may now be trying to fit themselves or their children into one of the groups. Thus, it is a good time to mention that some children will appear to cross two or more categories while for others no group will seem particularly characteristic. While imperfect, the use of profiles is an important development in temperament research because it keeps the focus of study on the individual rather than on the more abstract temperament dimensions. How particular combinations of traits fit together could also offer clues about underlying brain function and the way in which one region may exert regulatory control over others. Finally, a grouping by temperamental type may set the stage for customized guidance and intervention programs that are tailored to the unique features of each class. For these reasons, a profile approach can work well for both scientific research and practical applications, and we will use these five temperament types as the primary groupings in Part 2 of this book.

Measurement and Assessment

The most widely used tool for assessing child temperament in both research and practice is a questionnaire given to a parent. Older children and adolescents sometimes complete questionnaires themselves. These questionnaires usually tie into one of the prevailing temperament frameworks shown in Table 2.1. In some systems, different questionnaires are used for children of different ages. For example, Rothbart and her colleagues have developed distinct instruments to be used for infants, young children, adolescents, and adults (Capaldi & Rothbart, 1992; Gartstein & Rothbart, 2003; Rothbart et al., 2001). Other instruments are designed for wider age ranges such as the Junior Temperament and Character Inventory (Luby et al., 1999), although a preschool version has also been developed (Constantino et al., 2002).

These rating scales typically contain a number of statements (the number of items can range from as few as 20 to more than 200) that the informant rates as being characteristic or uncharacteristic of their child's usual behavior. Most rating scales allow for a graded response from "very uncharacteristic" through "very characteristic," with a neutral middle option. The responses then get converted into numbers, say 1 for "very uncharacteristic" through 5 for "very characteristic." Each item is usually designed to tap into just one of the major dimensions that the scale assessed. The total score for a dimension such as negative emotionality is then calculated as the sum or average of the scores for all the items that "load" onto that dimension. Because responders often tire of the process and start making quick responses without thinking them through, study designers tend to randomly scatter questions for each dimension throughout the questionnaire rather than having, for example, all the negative emotionality items first then all the extraversion items, and so on. In addition, the wording of many of the items is reversed, which requires another step in converting the reverse-scored items to accurately reflect the trait. For example, an extraversion item might read "does not like being the center of attention at a social gathering." The mother of a very extraverted child might rate that item a 1 for "very uncharacteristic," which in the scoring algorithm would convert to a 5 to reflect higher levels of extraversion.

Proponents of the questionnaire method point to a number of advantages over other types of temperament assessment strategies. Perhaps the strongest advantage is that people who know the child best are involved in the assessment. Kids often act in atypical ways in new settings like a doctor's office or a research lab. Having a parent do the instrument allows for a broad perspective on the child's behavior across time and multiple settings.

Another reason parental questionnaires are so widely used is, frankly, because they are easy to administer. Short questionnaires can be done in about 10 minutes. They can even be completed online or on paper at home, enabling researchers to collect information on large samples of people they may never meet.

Research evidence shows that this assessment strategy yields fairly reliable results. When investigators create a new questionnaire that they would like others to use in their studies, they are obliged to examine the instrument's psychometric properties, such as its internal consistency, test-retest reliability, and validity. Test-retest reliability can be assessed by having parents fill out the same questionnaire twice over a brief period of time. Interrater reliability can be measured by having two raters assess the same behavior using the same instrument.

Cross-informant agreement refers to the level of correspondence between two qualified raters, such as the mother and father, or a parent and a teacher. This type of agreement is a bit more complex than simple interrater reliability (e.g., when two researchers look at the same video of a child and then rate what they saw). Although a mother and a father are likely to see much of the same child behavior, different adults may evoke different responses in the child (more on that later) or tend to see the child in different contexts.

When it comes to ratings of child temperament, cross-informant agreement between two people who know the child well is often good but not great. A correlation coefficient (or r value) reflects the amount of association between two variables, and can range from 0 (no relation whatsoever) to 1 (perfectly aligned association). The correlation coefficient can also be negative if the value of one variable goes up when that of the other variable goes down. The correlation between a person's height and weight, for example, tends to be around 0.4. For behavioral ratings between a mother and father, the average correlation is around 0.3 (Achenbach & Rescorla, 2000), which is enough to be considered "statistically significant" but indicates that there certainly are some discrepancies between the two informants. Why these associations are not stronger is a matter of interest to scientists and is discussed in more detail later in the book. For now, it may be enough to say that the sources of disagreement go beyond simply the flaws of the instruments themselves.

The questionnaire method is not without critics, and those skeptical of relying on parental questionnaires point to a number of possible problems. First, observing behavior is not as easy as it sounds. Parents are not trained to assess behavior and they certainly aren't objective. As a result, all kinds of factors can get in the way of accurate reporting, including a tendency to rate the behavior you want rather than the behavior you see, a difficulty in separating your own temperament from that of the person you are trying to observe, and allowing preconceived notions to dominate the actual data coming in (Rettew et al., 2009). For example, a father may have formed the concept that his son is extraverted on the basis of a few dramatic examples. When he fills out a temperament questionnaire about his son, that attitude could shape his responses, even in the face of contradictory evidence. A further complication, called a *contrast effect*, can arise when a parent is asked to rate the temperament of multiple children within the same family. Jim Hudziak, director of the Child Psychiatry Division at the University of Vermont, uses the hypothetical example of a lucky mother of two boys: the most active child in town and the second most active child in town. When she completes a temperament instrument for the two kids, she might well rate her most active child as quite active and her other son as not particularly active because of the relative difference between her sons. In studies involving twins, similar effects can arise. For these reasons and more, some researchers prefer to rely on trained observers rather than questionnaires.

Observational scales and protocols in child temperament are surprisingly scarce in the temperament literature. One protocol that has been developed is called the Laboratory Temperament Assessment Battery or LAB-TAB (Goldsmith et al., 1993) and an observational measure called the Infant Behavioral Record can also be administered, usually as part of the widely known developmental assessment called the Bayley Scales of Infant Development (Bayley & Shaefer, 1963).

Perhaps the best-known observational assessment methods for temperament were developed by Kagan's group, and they have now been further adapted by others such as Nathan Fox (Fox et al., 2001; Kagan, 1994). Instead of using rating scales, Kagan's method involves children performing standardized activities that are video recorded in the laboratory and then coded by trained research assistants. During my child psychiatry training, I was one of those coders. The laboratory protocols, which were adjusted for a child's age, involved a series of short activities designed to elicit certain traits. One of the procedures for 4-year-olds was called the "risk room," which sounds a lot scarier than it was. A child entered a room with his or her mother to find a number of new things to explore. There was a box with a hole in it where the child could insert her hand, a balance beam just a few inches off the ground, a Halloween mask, and things that made noise when shaken. Some children came in and immediately went through every piece of equipment in rapid succession. Others stayed close to their mother, who was instructed to be as neutral as possible, before making a tentative attempt with one or two pieces. After a few minutes, a research assistant, usually a friendly young woman, came into the room and tried to prompt the child to interact with all the pieces of equipment. The presence of an encouraging adult was enough for many kids to leave their mother's side and demonstrate their prowess on the various apparatuses. In other cases, however, the presence of a new adult signaled even more danger and the child froze or refused to participate.

After the risk room, a research assistant took the child into a different room for more activities such as a vocabulary test, or to take the child's pulse and blood pressure. There was also an exercise in which the child was instructed to perform very low-level crimes, such as scribbling in a textbook or pouring a small amount of juice on the table. At one point, the door to the room opened and a gloved hand set a box on the floor. (This event replaced a clown coming into the room, which was scratched after creating quite a bit of anxiety for some children.)

While these activities took place, the coders were instructed to observe the children for signs of distress and events such as smiles and spontaneous comments. All of these data points would then go into a final determination of how inhibited the child was, ranging from very uninhibited to very inhibited. With some practice and instruction, my ratings of behavioral inhibition became quite reliable with other raters and with Kagan himself.

This type of protocol, involving trained observers, has some advantages over parental questionnaires. The fact that the children were engaged in roughly the same activities while their temperament was being measured was a major plus in terms of reliability. On the other hand, it is difficult to know how much of a child's behavior in the lab is truly reflective of typical reactions rather than an artifact of the testing procedures. Since the goal of this particular protocol was to assess a child's temperament specifically with regard to new situations and people, a stronger case could perhaps be made for this observational method compared to assessments designed to measure other traits.

In summary, both types of assessment thus have relative advantages and disadvantages and offer important windows into a child's temperamental style. There is also no law against using both questionnaires and observational methods within a single study. Indeed, a striking difference seen between a temperament questionnaire as completed by a parent and a child's behavior as observed in a laboratory setting can reveal valuable clues about what might trigger some kids to act so differently in different settings.

Temperament and Personality

As long as researchers of temperament focused their efforts on very young children and researchers of personality focused on adults, there were few territorial disputes about the boundaries between the two constructs. However, as personality researchers began looking at younger people, and as temperament studies began to include adults, debate was bound to ensue.

As in temperament research, multiple frameworks have been created for understanding personality structure, each with accompanying instruments such as the Myers-Briggs Type Indicator (MBTI), the Minnesota Multiphasic Personality Inventory (MMPI), and the NEO Five-Factor Inventory (NEO-FFI). Unlike in the world of child temperament research, however, there are fewer classification systems that pervade the academic literature (although quite a few exist in clinical and commercial practice). Arguably the most-utilized framework for personality structure is known as the Big Five and corresponds to what are considered to be the five main higher-order personality traits: neuroticism, extraversion, openness to experience, agreeableness, and conscientiousness. The neuroticism and extraversion dimensions have obvious counterparts in temperament, and the conscientiousness dimension maps closely to the regulation domain in temperament. The agreeableness dimension also has good correspondence with sociability as well as some ties with certain definitions of extraversion, depending on the degree to which social aspects are included. Perhaps the only Big Five dimension without a clear home in temperament is the dimension of openness to experience, which does not replicate well, especially in samples of younger children (Shiner, Masten, & Tellegen, 2002). This trait refers to an individual's tendency to embrace new ideas and conventions versus being more conservative. The prominent cognitive components of openness may make it more difficult to connect clearly to a temperament trait present in infancy.

Another prominent personality structure that remains widely used was developed by Robert Cloninger and colleagues at Washington University. The original system, as measured by the Tridimensional Personality Questionnaire for adults, consisted of three main personality dimensions: novelty seeking, harm avoidance, and reward dependence (Cloninger, Przybeck, & Svrakic, 1991). When the structure was modified to form the Temperament and Character Inventory (Cloninger et al., 1994), these three dimensions became temperament dimensions onto which three "character" dimensions were added. Personality, in this theoretical context, includes temperament but requires additional elements, regardless of a person's age. This system is consistent with the common conviction that temperament is a narrower construct that forms the foundation upon which the more complex notion of personality is built.

Some prominent temperament and personality researchers have concluded that there really is no clear distinction between the two domains. Costa and McCrae, who developed the NEO-FFI on the basis of the Big Five, declared that their instrument could in many ways be considered to be a temperament instrument (McCrae et al., 2000). The boundaries can get particularly blurry as the age range of the various instruments expands to include the assessment of personality in children and the assessment of temperament in adults. Scientists in Belgium, for example, have tried to drop the age floor of the Big Five framework down into adolescence using an instrument called the Hierarchical Inventory of Personality in Children, which utilizes the Big Five structure but adapts the questions to be more developmentally appropriate (Mervielde & De Fruyt, 1999). Rothbart and her colleagues, meanwhile, have developed scales such as the Adult Temperament Questionnaire that push the construct of temperament well beyond childhood years (Evans & Rothbart, 2007).

In the end, it is unlikely that any clear boundary will be discovered that separates temperament traits from personality traits on the basis of actual behavior. What may continue to distinguish them, however, are the driving forces behind the behaviors. For example, an individual's personal narrative—the conscious understanding of who we are and how we got to our particular place in life—may have a causal role for personality but not temperament. Consider, for example, a youngest sibling born into a highly extraverted family. This boy may well have inherited a tendency to be somewhat more extraverted than average, but compared to his older brothers and sisters, he seems positively restrained. In fact, he begins to acquire the label of "the cautious one" or the "rational kid" from his parents and siblings until, over time, it becomes part of his identity. If this boy is asked to fill out a temperament or personality scale as an adolescent, his extraverted scores would likely be lower than those an observer outside the family would choose. Even more insidiously, his self-concept might begin to modify his actual behavior and cause him to behave in less extraverted ways. This influence of a person's narrative or self-concept on behavior would likely be considered a component of personality but not temperament, even though it relates to the same observable behavior.

One theory of temperament and personality held that temperament was the genetic aspect of personality (Buss & Plomin, 1984). Indeed, Kagan (1997) wrote, "the environment acts on that temperament to produce personality." Rothbart and Bates have also proposed that temperament is a bit more limited in comparison to personality, which includes aspects such as values, attitudes, skills, and social cognitions (Rothbart & Ahadi, 1994). There may indeed be qualitative differences between temperament and personality, but the precise boundary between the two domains seems as difficult to define as the point at which a boy becomes a man.

Temperament in Nonhuman Animals

The concept of temperament has been studied in several species, most notably rats, dogs, and monkeys. Temperament assessment batteries, based on human infant protocols, have been developed for species such as rhesus macaque monkeys and have revealed traits analogous to human temperament dimensions, such as behavioral inhibition (Schneider et al., 1991). The orientation of temperament research in animals often relates to evolutionary questions such as how different traits are adapted to particular environments. For example, among animals that live in groups, does having members with different temperaments confer an advantage to the whole group? Certainly temperaments differ between species of similar types of animals. Birds such as mallard ducks and Canada geese stick together in huge flocks and can become habituated to human beings, whereas species like the common loon shun human contact and often swim alone. Even within a species, there can be dramatic temperamental differences as well. Dogs, for example, have been specifically bred not only for physical features but for temperament. Guides to dog breeds are full of descriptions of temperament. Some breeds are more aggressive, some more excitable, and some more docile. These predispositions, however, do not preclude the possibility that individual differences within a breed can be striking, especially under varying environmental conditions.

While few would have a hard time accepting the idea that primates or dogs have well-established temperamental variation, its establishment in sheep, birds, and guppies may come as more of a surprise. Canadians Denis Réale at the University of Québec and Marco Festa-Biancet at the University of Sherbrooke studied wild Rocky Mountain bighorn sheep in Alberta. They found consistent behavior over a period of years in how individual ewes approached a large corral that the researchers created and baited with a salt lick. They characterized the sheep as either bold or shy and found that this categorization related to other behaviors, such as the ability to wean lambs (Réale et al., 2000). The bighorns' temperament did not seem to be related to survival until a cougar showed up and started preying upon the herd. Then, the bolder ewes seemed to have an advantage, perhaps due to their ability to stand their ground against the predator (Réale & Festa-Bianchet, 2003). Interestingly, the reverse was found in guppies. In a captive and safe environment, the bold guppies are more dominant and have a reproductive advantage. The tables turn, however, when a larger fish enters the tank. Then, the bolder guppies tend to be easier prey than the tentative ones, who spend more time hiding in cover (Dugatkin & Alfieri, 2003). There is evidence that individual birds select mates on the basis of having similar temperamental traits (van Oers et al., 2008), perhaps our most direct evidence to date that birds of a feather really do flock together (sorry, I just couldn't resist).

In summary, quite a lot of temperament research has been done since the seminal studies of Chess and Thomas, which has refined our understanding of what the core temperamental traits are and how they tend to fit together in groups of individuals. Despite the multitude of investigations, however, uncertainty and debate still surround the most basic tenets of child temperament and its boundaries with related concepts such as personality. The next chapter builds upon some of these core principles and goes into more depth about temperament traits as they relate to gender, age, and culture. Chapter 3 also explores the scientific debates that pervade the research community in its continuing effort to understand the fundamental ways in which children differ from one another.

Chapter 3

Features of Temperament

Now that the core elements of temperament have been "settled," a series of questions ensue. Is temperament best conceptualized as a dimension or as a category? Are certain traits good and others bad? Do the temperaments of boys and girls differ? How stable are temperament traits across years of development, or from one situation to another? These and other issues related to temperament are addressed in this chapter.

Dimensions Versus Categories

Most temperament models treat each dimension as a quantifiable trait, similar to height or intelligence. For something like negative emotionality, for example, a child can possess levels that are very low, very high, or anywhere in between. If the trait is being measured with a rating scale, a numerical score is derived for each dimension. Scientists can then use those scores to address a particular research question, such as the temperament differences between children with and without depression.

Temperament may also be conceptualized in a binary or categorical framework. In a binary format, a child either possesses or does not possess the trait in question. A child could also fall into a high or low group, with regard to a trait. A categorical structure could also include more than two groups, such as low, moderate, and high. Promoters of such an approach generally believe that important biological distinctions exist between the categories.

Kagan has been one of the strongest proponents of a categorical approach to temperament and in particular the trait of behavioral inhibition, which involves fear and avoidance of the unfamiliar. Furthermore, he has argued that the dominance of the dimensional or "continua" approach to temperament is due, in part, to the fact that the most popular statistical techniques require this perspective (Kagan & Snidman, 2004). His support for a categorical framework seems to come not from the idea that outward behaviors exist categorically, but that the underlying causes, namely genetic variations that lead to very high or very low levels of behavioral inhibition, are themselves categorical. He and Snidman, authors of *The Long Shadow of Temperament*, wrote, "we view temperaments as categories because we believe that the origin of each is a distinct genetic profile" (2004, p. 56).

Whether the root causes of temperamental differences between children are categorical or simply a matter of degree needs to be studied much more directly. Unfortunately, even a clean finding of differing genetic profiles, as Kagan predicts, would probably not end the debate because the more proximal causes of temperament could still be quantitative in nature. If, for example, extreme levels of behavioral inhibition were found to be caused by allele X on gene A, allele Y on gene B, and allele Z on gene C, this very distinct genetic profile still needs to be translated into brain structure and activity—perhaps reduced neuronal growth and thus fewer connections between two brain regions. Measuring the amount of connectivity would then bring us back to a dimensional framework. Further, the likelihood that other factors, such as environmental ones, are additionally influencing temperament via the same pathway potentially adds even more quantitative variation to the mix. Chapter 5 delves into this critical issue in more detail.

An important point to make here, however, is that a dimensional approach to temperament does not preclude the study of individuals who are at the extremes—those whose behavior may be the most clinically important to their overall mental health. What is needed, however, are data-driven techniques to establish these very high and low groups within a particular trait rather than imposing arbitrary cutoff points. If a researcher designates, say, the top 10% of children on a social anxiety questionnaire as being categorically "shy," then there should be some sort of justification for choosing that threshold rather than, say, 1%, 5%, or 20%.

It is worth pointing out again that despite the efforts of some temperament researchers to conceptualize temperament categorically, the exercise often yields large numbers of children who don't seem to fit into any particular box. As you may recall, Chess and Thomas found that over one-third of their sample didn't fit neatly into the easy, difficult, or slow-to-warm-up categories. Even Kagan found that a significant minority of the children in his sample did not clearly fit into high-reactive, low-reactive, inhibited, or disinhibited categories. In total, there does not seem to be scientific justification for defining temperamental behavior in terms of meaningful categories with well-established boundaries between them. At the same time, as Kagan and Snidman suggest, we need to be on the lookout for the very real possibility that embedded within the quantitative distribution of a particular trait are distinct, rare, and qualitative causes that should be identified and could be driving some of the more extreme temperamental variation in the population. Indeed, it could be argued that a dimensional approach to temperament might enhance our ability to find naturally occurring temperament categories through improved statistical power. When groups are created from quantitatively distributed scores, some important variation is lost. Dividing a group at the mean, for example, leaves no distinction between the person who scores just above the mean and the person with the highest score of the entire group, and such differences may be very important. Especially as we begin to focus on the line between "normal" traits and mental illness, these classifications and boundaries take on additional importance.

One related question that arises within a dimensional structure has to do with the degree to which a dimension is viewed as unipolar or bipolar. In other words, is a lack of one thing something else? Most frameworks tend to be more unipolar in their conceptualization, with each dimension standing independently of others. On the EAS questionnaire (Buss & Plomin, 1984), for example, a child's emotionality (E) score doesn't influence his or her activity (A) score. Further, a child who scores low on emotionality would be labeled "low emotionality" rather than, say, "high tranquility" (I made that one up). Other measures of personality such as the Myers-Briggs instrument incorporate more of a bipolar structure: one can be labeled as more "thinking" or more "feeling" but cannot receive a high score in both (Briggs-Myers et al., 2009). In most academic research on temperament, a unipolar approach is used and integrated into the rating instruments.

The "Yet" Problem

Temperament dimensions are not inherently good or bad, and scientists who describe these traits take pains to avoid attaching positive or negative judgments to them. Someone high in a trait such as novelty seeking, for example, might show characteristics such as exuberance and spontaneity, which are considered positive qualities in most societies. At the same time, this person could also have a tendency toward more negatively associated traits such as impulsivity and extravagance. Other dimensions may start out as being viewed positively but become more negative as the level rises toward the extreme (e.g., one who is careful versus one who is incapacitated by anxiety). One trait can also accentuate or mitigate the effects of another. Being highly energetic and animated, for example, may work extremely well for a child who also has enough regulatory ability to modify that behavior when appropriate versus an otherwise similar child who is incapable of turning it off.

Evidence shows, however, that both the positive and negative aspects of a trait usually go together in a person (which is, of course, why they are considered part of the same higher-order dimension in the first place). Personal experience generally confirms this. The person you admire for punctuality and responsibility may not be the first person you expect to be the life of the party. Conversely, the exciting and adventurous spirits who captivate others with their energy and charisma may struggle, at times, with losing their cool.

Herein lies the rub. When most people are asked to describe their ideal partner or child or friend, the word "yet" often sneaks into the description. We want someone who can be spontaneous yet responsible, sensitive yet assertive, a good talker yet a good listener too. From the perspective of temperament, these "yets" are usually splitting off the positive aspects of a temperamental trait while attempting to leave behind the negative components. Such a profile can be extremely difficult to find in the real world (present company excluded, of course). High levels of sociability, for example, may be a wonderful trait in a friend but not uncommonly can be associated with a certain degree of dependence or even "neediness." Examining this issue from a clinical perspective, the prospect of treating or changing a more negative dimension runs the risk that the associated positive features will be diminished as well. Ironically, the end result could well be a person with very average levels of temperament dimensions that may strike many as being somewhat "vanilla."

Wise souls who have learned about succeeding in relationships have come to understand that people generally come "prix fixe" rather than "à la carte." While celebrating a person's passion and zest for life, one may have to accept that person's occasional over-the-top behavior. While applauding a child's ability to be conscientious and responsible, one should expect that he or she may not be as wildly exuberant as some other children. This truth does not preclude the promise of self-improvement that can come with hard work and honest insight, but hopefully it does offer some relief to those who find their attempts to "fix" someone else similar to swimming against an outgoing tide. The balance between accepting a child's entire temperamental profile while trying to smooth out some of the rough spots that may be holding the child back is not just a philosophical discussion but has real practical implications. These issues are discussed in more detail in Part 2.

Sex Differences

If men are from Mars and women are from Venus (Gray, 1992), it would seem a foregone conclusion that men and women have major temperamental differences. While treading into these waters can be quite treacherous politically, popular culture exploits these perceived differences in countless movies, television shows, and comedy routines, where women are usually portrayed as more emotional and social than the adventurous, physically active, and aggressive men.

Case closed? Hardly. In addition to the question of whether these societal stereotypes are indeed based in fact, there remain questions regarding how robust these differences are, when in development they occur, how well preserved they are across cultures, and what causes them to be present. Matters are further complicated by the nagging problem of how we define specific dimensions of temperament. As mentioned previously, extraversion can have more or less of a social component, depending on the temperament scheme that is used to measure it. If it is true that males tend to seek out new experiences and sensations more often, and females tend to have stronger social affiliations, then sex differences in extraversion might vary according to which system is used to assess it.

In 2007, a review and meta-analysis (a study that combines data from many previous studies into a single database) aggregated 32 studies on sex differences in adults from across the globe, all of which used Cloninger's temperament dimensions (Cloninger et al., 1991) as their basis of study. In total, over 21,000 subjects were assessed, with an average age of 34. Overall, women showed higher levels of reward dependence and harm avoidance than did men, while novelty seeking and persistence were found to be roughly equal between the two sexes (Miettunen et al., 2007). The authors examined how big the differences actually were by calculating an effect size for each study, which relates to the mean difference between men and women on a given dimension, relative to the standard deviation. Conventionally, effect sizes of 0.2, 0.5, and 0.8 are deemed small, moderate, and large effects, respectively, but this determination is fairly arbitrary (Cohen, 1992). In the meta-analysis, the magnitude of increased harm avoidance for women was somewhat small (0.3 effect size), whereas for reward dependence it was categorized as moderate to large (0.6 effect size). The country of origin was not found to be a major factor, except in reward dependence, where the difference was smaller (0.3 effect size) among studies from Asia. It should be further noted that some of the studies reported results that were exactly opposite the overall trend found in the meta-analysis. Indeed, the results of a previous investigation by some of the same authors showed higher novelty-seeking scores among men, which was not replicated in the meta-analysis.

In a similar study, the researchers looked at studies of children using Rothbart's temperament structure (Else-Quest et al., 2006). Effortful control was found to be higher in girls, surgency was higher in boys, and negative affectivity was comparable between the two sexes. Previously found interactions with age, such that gender differences were more apparent during one developmental period than another, were not as apparent in this analysis. Activity level, which is a major dimension in many temperament schemes, has been found to be higher in boys on average, with the difference growing with age (Campbell & Eaton, 1999; Eaton & Enns, 1986). Table 3.1 summarizes sex differences that are generally reported in the literature.

Some sex differences are also found when temperament is examined according to types or profiles rather than mean levels of a single trait. In the previously cited study from Norway (Janson & Mathiesen, 2008), more 8- to 9-year-old boys fell into the "confident" group, and more girls fell into the "unremarkable" group. Otherwise, few differences were found. In our own study of temperament types (Rettew, Althoff, et al., 2008), we found that the moderate (average levels of most traits) and

TABLE 3.1. Sex Differences in Temperament Traits*			
Dimension	Higher in Males	About Equal	Higher in Females
Negative emotionality			X
Thrill and novelty seeking	X		
Sociability and affiliation			X
Activity level	X		
Regulatory ability			X
Extraversion (broadly defined)		X	

*Note that some of these differences are more prominent at different developmental periods of life.

steady (high persistence and low novelty seeking) groups did not show prominent sex differences, with 57% and 43% of those groups, respectively, being boys. Members of our disengaged group, who showed high levels of both novelty seeking and harm avoidance and lower levels of reward dependence and persistence, were predominantly (85%) male.

There is an ongoing lively discussion regarding whether or not individuals who perceive their gender to be different than their birth sex (referred to as gender identity disorder, or GID) should be considered to have a psychiatric disturbance. This debate is beyond the scope of this book, but the discussion has included arguments and research related to child temperament (Rettew, 2012). Some proponents of retaining the diagnosis have pointed to data indicating that children diagnosed with GID have biological features that are more akin to their perceived than their assigned gender. In particular, the temperament trait of activity level, which is generally higher in boys than in girls, has a flipped pattern among gender-variant youth (Zucker et al., 2012). Compared to a control group of the same assigned sex, girls with gender dysphoria have higher activity levels, while boys have significantly lower activity levels. In fact, girls who meet criteria for GID have higher activity levels than boys who meet criteria for GID (Zucker & Bradley, 1995). The intriguing question that remains here is whether the gender identification arises from some sort of rationalization process (i.e., a boy concludes that since he is more like a girl than a boy, he is a girl) or whether the identification reflects a brain that is fundamentally more similar to the affirmed rather than the assigned gender, in a manner that we do not yet understand.

Overall, then, differences in temperament between girls and boys can be readily found in studies that are equipped to find them. Girls tend to have higher levels of self-regulation, attention, sociability, and (during adolescence) negative emotionality while boys, by contrast, tend to show higher levels of activity and novelty seeking. Studies that measure temperament using temperament types also frequently find differences between males and females. These differences often parallel the sex differences that are found when looking at rates of various types of corresponding psychiatric disorders. ADHD and autism, for example, are more common in boys, while anxiety and depressive disorders, particularly when looking at adolescents, are more prevalent in girls. It is important to remember, however, that the magnitude of these temperament differences tends to be smaller than what someone might expect after being immersed in popular media, and there are many children who buck the trend. These differences measured at a single time point also say nothing about the possibility of children changing their levels of temperament traits over time: the topic that we turn to next.

Stability

Temperament traits, as defined in Chapter 2, are stable across time. Anecdotally at least, that is exactly what many parents describe. In my clinical work, I have certainly heard mothers tell stories of their hyperactive boys, for example, who were noticeably active in utero and "never stopped moving." Temperament dimensions that become apparent in older children and adults, such as irritability, shyness, and thrill seeking, can also in some cases seem prewired from the start. We watch television biographies of Olympic divers and freestyle skiers doing back flips off the living room sofa at age 3, or of career criminals who showed explosive anger and were cruel to animals from a young age. Yet are these publicized outcomes the inescapable destiny of temperamental momentum, an artifact of selective storytelling, some kind of self-fulfilling prophecy, or a combination of multiple factors working together?

The answer depends a lot on one's perspective. From a mathematical viewpoint, the level of a temperament trait at one point in time usually has a statistically significant association with the level of that trait at a future time, even across a span of decades (Rothbart, 2011). In their 2000 review, researchers Roberts and DelVecchio found evidence of increasing stability in temperament as a function of age. That is, the older one gets, the more stable traits seem to become. The well-known Dunedin Study from New Zealand reported statistically significant correlations between temperament scores at age 3 and those at age 9 (Caspi et al., 1995). In general, studies that use temperament questionnaires instead of observational methods to assess temperament stability tend to report higher stability coefficients (Rothbart, 1986; Saudino & Cherny, 2001).

Studies that span several years or longer also report significant stability in temperament. The amount of stability is often modest, but these studies are remarkable given the number of years that have elapsed and the inherent imperfections in measuring temperament at any point in time. Some of the most basic dimensions of temperament, such as the tendency toward approach behavior (novelty seeking, surgency, extraversion) or the tendency toward withdrawn and inhibited behavior (introversion, shyness, social inhibition) have been found to be quite steady in individuals from infancy all the way into adulthood (Bayley & Shaefer, 1963; Caspi, Harrington, et al., 2003; Gest, 1997; Pfeifer et al., 2002). The ability to regulate and control one's impulses and emotions, a trait that fully emerges a bit later than many other dimensions, also shows considerable stability from preschool onward. This dimension is captured within the effortful control dimension, but it has also been described as an ability to delay gratification as one pursues a long-term goal. It seems to be fairly well preserved from the preschool years into adulthood (Caspi et al., 1995; Rothbart, Ahadi, & Evans, 2000) and, as we shall soon see, it may have tremendous implications for the development of or protection from emotional-behavioral disorders.

Researchers often use the term *rank-order stability* to refer to the type of continuity being measured in these studies in which the scores within each individual are compared over time. It is, however, just one of several ways that temperament stability can be conceptualized and measured (De Fruyt et al., 2006). Another type of continuity, called *mean-level stability*, refers to the way in which overall levels of a particular dimension increase or decrease in an entire population (Roberts, Walton, & Viechtbauer, 2006). A mean-level stability approach is conducive to studies involving adults because the same instrument can be used across all subjects, covering the entire age range. Levels of negative emotionality or neuroticism, for example, are generally found to decrease slightly, especially in women, from early to late adulthood (McCrae & Costa, 2003;

Viken et al., 1994). In pediatric studies, however, one cannot use the same questionnaire to assess the temperament of an infant and an adolescent. The items of the instrument must change to reflect the marked developmental differences that are present. Consequently, it is somewhat difficult to investigate whether 3-year-olds have higher levels of extraversion, on average, than do 15-year-olds. Another complexity relates to the different elements that make up a dimension. Sociability, as measured by the level of affiliation with a parent, may peak fairly early in childhood and then trail off in adolescence as the child moves toward greater independence; sociability as measured by interactions with friends and other acquaintances, however, changes in the opposite direction. If negative emotionality is measured by indicators such as frequency of crying, then the level of this dimension will certainly decrease for most people throughout childhood; however, adolescents can brood and ruminate with anxious thoughts for days or weeks at a time without any crying episodes. Despite these methodological and developmental complexities, it is probably fair to say that levels of effortful control increase with age from early childhood into adolescence, and negative emotionality and surgency, by contrast, tend to decrease throughout the school-age years (Sallquist et al., 2009).

It is also possible to examine temperament stability on the basis of types rather than dimensions. In the previously mentioned Dunedin Study, children fell into one of five categories at age 3, and the researchers found predictable continuity in personality traits even 23 years later (Caspi, Harrington, et al., 2003). In the study by Janson and Mathiesen, nearly 1,000 children were tested at four time points (18 months, 30 months, 4–5 years, and 8–9 years), and the prevalence of the different types changed a great deal over time. The two most common types among 18-months-olds, confident and undercontrolled, were the least common at 8–9 years old. From 18 months to 9 years, the percentage of children in the undercontrolled group dropped from about 25% to 8%, and the proportion of children in the confident group dropped from nearly one-third of the sample to about 10%. One-third to one-half of the individuals in the sample stayed in the same group assignment throughout the study, and those individuals who did change groups tended to do so in a somewhat predictable manner. Children in the uneasy profile typically moved into the inhibited one, and migration from the outgoing to the unremarkable group was also fairly common.

Far more unusual was a shift from the undercontrolled to the confident group or vice versa.

In Kagan and Snidman's (2004) cohort of youngsters with behavioral inhibition, somewhat more stability was observed in their temperament status. The subjects' temperaments were assessed several times between the ages of 4 months and 11 years. Infants completed a short protocol that included looking at a mobile, smelling a cotton swab dipped in alcohol, listening to nonsense syllables, and hearing a balloon pop behind them. About 30% of the group tended to get upset, cry, and show a lot of motor activity—they were labeled high-reactive. About 40% remained relatively calm and were labeled low-reactive; the rest were somewhere in between.

These children were assessed again at age 11, when they participated in a longer protocol involving a number of physiological (heart rate, EEG, finger temperature) and behavioral tasks. Among other things, they received a global rating of 1 through 4 to describe their level of inhibited behavior (1 = relaxed, smiling, talkative; 4 = nervous, rarely smiling, soft-spoken). A total of 21% of the children received a rating of 4, while 35% received a rating of 1. Looking at the stability across more than a decade, a full 50% of the low-reactive infants received a rating of 1, and one-third of the originally high-reactive infants were rated as a 4. Only 22% of the low-reactive infants were in the more inhibited group at age 11 (i.e., a rating of 3 or 4). A fair proportion (45%) of the originally high-reactive infants, however, were rated in the less inhibited groups (rating of 1 or 2) at this follow-up assessment. Overall, then, the authors reported that up to half of children, as they approach adolescence, possess a temperament (at least in this domain) that is well predicted by their behavior as young infants, and only about 10% behave in a manner that is "seriously inconsistent" with their infant profile.

One important point to consider when it comes to studies of temperament stability is that most are naturalistic in design, meaning that they study the development of children as it occurs, without specific interventions. As is covered in more detail later, the environment can often conspire to accentuate temperament traits that exist and make them more prominent, thereby increasing the trait's stability. Temperamental irritability can breed hostility, and shyness can lead to increased social withdrawal. Such patterns, however, should not be seen as evidence that the solidifying of those traits is predetermined or inevitable. Steps can be taken by parents, schools, and clinicians to address some of the more problematic aspects of a child's temperament, and this is the focus of the second part of this book. In addition, the seemingly intuitive idea that temperamental change is dictated by environmental factors and temperamental stability is driven by genetics is newly challenged by findings in developmental neuroscience, as we will see in Chapter 4.

In summary, we are left with a wholly unsatisfying conclusion that temperament is stable and it is not stable. Studies that have tracked temperament over time sometimes show stunning continuity over spans of decades and starting from very early in life. More extreme levels of a trait seem to show more stability over time, yet many children show significant change as they develop. Perhaps one way to reconcile these apparently divergent findings is to imagine that an early-appearing trait generates some momentum to carry itself forward, but forces can act upon that momentum to speed it up, slow it down, and in some cases change its direction completely.

Birth Order

In the world of popular psychology, there is a long-standing belief that temperament and personality are a function not only of one's innate predispositions but also of one's birth order in relation to other siblings. Some of the statistics can be quite impressive, such as the fact that 21 of the first 23 astronauts and the vast majority of U.S. presidents were firstborn sons. Birth order has also been suggested to play an important role in a person's tendency to rebel against authority (Sulloway, 1996). Although the importance of birth order is commonly accepted in public discourse, most temperament and personality investigators have dismissed it as urban legend, unworthy of rigorous study.

As the story goes, firstborns and especially those who are only children are the achievers. They tend to be responsible, motivated to excel, and driven to please their parents. Last-borns, in contrast, are more social and outgoing, but also more prone to be disorganized and irresponsible. Middle children can wind up as the peacemakers of the family but may also feel somewhat resentful of their undistinguished place.

From a scholarly perspective, researchers have pointed out legitimate problems with the birth order literature, including the fact that most studies confound birth order with family size. As pointed out by Hartshorne (2010) in *Scientific American Mind*, children in smaller families have a higher chance of being born first. Therefore, if achievement is associated with higher socioeconomic status or the availability of more parental resources (both of which are related to smaller families), then the birth order findings may be quite spurious. Another problem is that people are often aware of the birth order predictions, which could influence their ratings on questionnaires. Finally, some birth order differences may exist within a family relative to one's siblings, but not relative to one's peers in general.

In 2007, two Norwegian epidemiologists published in the prestigious journal *Science* their study of more than 250,000 17–18-year-olds (Kristensen & Bjerkedal, 2007). They found a small but statistically significant positive effect on IQ (about 2 points) for being an older sibling. Interestingly, however, the effect seemed to be mediated by social order more than birth order. If a second-born was raised as a firstborn in the unfortunate case of an older sibling's death in childhood, the slight difference in intelligence was not found. Another study that examined possible mechanisms for birth order differences (Hartshorne, Salem-Hartshorne, & Hartshorne, 2009) showed that firstborns tend to associate with firstborns, last-borns with last-borns, and so on, suggesting that any effect may be driven by social factors rather than something intrinsic to birth order per se. In summary, the lore surrounding birth order appears overblown relative to the available evidence, although small effects may be driven by social factors related to birth order.

Temperament in Hiding

One question that arises in the study of temperament in older children and adults relates to the possibility that a person might have temperament characteristics that an observer can't see. This is less of an issue in studies of infants and toddlers, but as development continues, people get better at regulating or holding back feelings and behaviors, opening a potential space between inward sensations and outward expressions. Most people are familiar with those who self-describe their temperament or personality in terms that seem to bear no resemblance at all to their outward behavior. A domineering and gregarious man might report feeling shy and anxious much of the time; a placid and pleasant woman might reveal that she is bursting with rage on the inside. Furthermore, self-report instruments have an inherent measurement gap between actual behavior and the way people would like to see themselves.

Given the marked differences that might arise between a person's temperament profile as assessed by self-rating versus an observer's rating, which of these profiles should be viewed as "correct"? From the perspective of a brain researcher, the question becomes whether it is possible, on a biological level, to detect a deeper temperamental trait, regardless of whether or not the individual is able to acknowledge its existence. If a person feels one way but acts another, can the emotional pull, or the part fighting against those inclinations, be revealed?

An analogy that I have found useful is what I call the "dry paint" versus "wet paint" models of temperamental impressions. Consider the task of painting a wall. In the dry paint model, a person paints the color blue over a red wall that was painted long ago. While the wall now looks unmistakably blue, the red color is still there, hiding beneath the blue layer and readily detectible using the proper technology (in this case, a good scraper). Covering over wet paint, however, is a different story. If you start with red when it is wet and then add blue, you wind up with purple, and the red undercoat is no longer detectable.

Which way does the brain work when it comes to temperamental leanings that a person may sense but not enact? In many ways, the wet paint model seems to be most logical, with the outward "color" being a reflection of current brain architecture and activity. How could someone, after all, be biologically shy when they're not behaviorally shy? The brain is a living, dynamic organ and not an old field that can be excavated to find hidden artifacts. On the other hand, feelings, not just outward behaviors, must have brain correlates too. From a neuroscience perspective, brain activity must be associated with both observable behaviors and internal states of emotion or tension.

While there has been little direct study on this subject, a temperament stability study produced some findings. Carl Schwartz and colleagues brought back a small subset of behaviorally inhibited or uninhibited toddlers from Kagan and Snidman's cohort who were now about 22 years old (Schwartz et al., 2003). These subjects underwent a brain scan, and while in the scanner, they were shown pictures of familiar or unfamiliar faces. While viewing unfamiliar faces, the adults who were found to be behaviorally inhibited as toddlers showed more activation in the amygdala, a region involved in the signaling and processing of fear, than did those who were previously labeled as uninhibited. The finding itself is noteworthy, but what is even more remarkable is that most of the previously inhibited toddlers did not continue to be anxious as adults. When the few inhibited subjects who remained clinically anxious were removed from the analysis, the results of the study remained, suggesting that what was being measured by the brain scan reflected an inward temperamental tendency that was not necessarily evident in the adult subjects' outward behavior. These results were published in the journal *Science* and provided evidence that neuroimaging can be used to reveal underlying temperament, even in the absence of observable behavior.

The study brought up the interesting question of whether or not it is possible to detect a physiological "footprint" for a temperamental trait that may not be directly visible. The authors of this study contended that people can have an anxious brain without being apparently anxious. Indeed, many adults do describe feeling emotions just as intensely as they did when they were younger, but they have developed an improved ability to control those feelings. What is likely happening neuroanatomically to account for this developmental phenomenon is that the regulatory parts of the brain, such as the frontal cortex, mature more slowly than other areas. The emotion driving regions within the limbic area of the brain remain active over time (and sensed by the individual), but their output is better modulated by these regulatory areas that come more fully online later in life. Thus, the adult subjects in the Schwartz (2003) study who showed behavioral inhibition as toddlers may still possess overactive amygdalas but now have better-developed regulatory centers to handle that activity. From a clinical perspective, this study would suggest that a useful strategy for more extreme traits might be to strengthen our temperamental "invisibility cloak"—an ability to regulate our thoughts, emotions, and behaviors. As previously discussed, such an ability may be seen as a temperament trait itself, whose manifestations can be evident early in life but requires additional development and environmental nurturing before it is able to override other temperamental leanings.

Temperament Variability

At first, the term *temperament variability* seems to be an oxymoron, as the concept of temperament is built upon the premise that there is a consistent pattern in a child's behavior that can be measured and described. But what if certain children are more like chameleons who change their colors in different environments? Since the work of Chess and Thomas, it has been clear that such children are around and at some point the experts are going to have to deal with them.

Although I have tried not to use my own children as examples, this particular concept was nailed home by one of my sons when he was around the age of 5. It was becoming abundantly clear that he really did not like going to get his hair cut. In addition to resisting the undertaking altogether, he would squirm, cry, fuss, and complain about being uncomfortable, despite being in the hands of a seasoned child barber. Further, to the best of my knowledge, he had never experienced any haircut trauma in the past. If his temperament were assessed based upon his experiences at the barber, his negative emotionality levels would have been off the charts, especially in comparison to other boys his age who seemed to have no trouble at all with haircuts.

Around the same time, however, he also started going to the dentist. While in my mind the degree of actual physical poking and prodding in sensitive areas is decidedly higher at the dentist, my son sailed through these appointments in good spirits. In the waiting room, I observed the anxious faces on many other children and heard the wails of similarly aged boys against the whirring of dental equipment. My son, meanwhile, made no protest and was complimented repeatedly as a brave and model patient. Here, I would have rated his level of negative emotionality as decidedly low.

These experiences made me wonder what response I would give on a temperament questionnaire that asked something like, "Please rate on a scale of 1 to 5 how much distress your child experiences when going to appointments like the doctor, dentist, or barber." Such a question would seem like a very apt one to include in building a score for negative emotionality, yet the proper rating for the question was difficult. Marking an intermediate score like 3 seemed to remove the very essence of the question. My son wasn't moderate; he varied between the extremes based on the specific context. The child who habitually gets mildly upset versus the one who becomes very upset under some stressful circumstances and not at all in others are quite different. Furthermore, this hidden difference could well reflect differences in underlying genetics, brain regions, or intervention strategies.

Temperament researchers have tried to avoid the problem of situational variability as best we can. Those who use questionnaires to assess the temperament of their subjects usually include instructions on the form for the informant, such as a parent, to rate how the child "usually" behaves. Researchers who measure temperament observationally by having kids go through procedures or protocols don't necessarily fare any better. These assessments are generally done in one setting at one time point, thus removing the quandary of what to do with inconsistent behavior across contexts. Furthermore, when such questions do arise, the raters of these observational protocols are instructed, just like parents, to provide a general score across the entire protocol that takes variability out of the equation as much as possible. If a child became extremely upset in having his blood pressure taken but then showed a lot of approach and spontaneous speech when talking to a new research assistant, the child would probably receive an overall medium score, just as if he had responded consistently in both situations with moderate behavior.

This complicated notion of temperamental variability likely demands a more rigorous investigation than it has received to date. The topic is beginning to find its way into animal studies (Sussman & Ha, 2011), yet we are a long way from being able to capture the phenomenon well. While its measurement is tricky, it is not impossible, especially if we allow parents simply to tell us how much variability is present across situations. Indeed, temperament variability may be best understood as a component of temperament itself. Furthermore, understanding the concept of temperament variability may also have very important implications. If a little boy gets very afraid in some situations but is not afraid at all in similar circumstances, perhaps there is something important to understand about these different situations that could help him feel better. Perhaps this child is born to be more reactive to subtle environment cues than other children. There is much to learn about this important aspect of temperament that has somehow evaded our spotlight for decades.

Summary

Debate remains about whether the core temperament dimensions are best conceptualized as quantitatively distributed or categorical in nature. While there is strong evidence supporting temperament dimensions as continuous traits, the possibility remains that qualitative and categorical factors underlie temperament traits in individuals at the extreme ends of the distribution. Sex differences are common when it comes to temperament traits, but they are modest in size and can change across developmental periods. Temperament traits can persist over years or decades, yet a great deal of change remains possible. Despite the definition of temperament pertaining to a characteristic pattern of behavior, the degree to which a child's behavior can vary across situations is an understudied and underappreciated phenomenon. These questions have more than an academic interest, as they each carry strong clinical implications that could potentially challenge some of our core beliefs about temperament and what distinguishes these traits from psychiatric symptoms. In the next few chapters, we will shift the focus to some of the factors that underlie temperamental traits, before applying this knowledge to understanding the boundaries between "normal" traits and symptoms of a mental illness.

Chapter 4

Neurobiology:
The Brains Behind Temperament

Ultimately, temperament and all of its related concepts must translate into brain function. Although it may seem obvious, this simple fact often gets lost in the debates over whether particular behaviors belong to temperament, personality, disorder X, or disorder Y. All of these phenomena are mediated by neuronal activity between different regions of the brain. Moreover, these intricate operations underlying all traits and disorders are influenced by mutually interacting genetic and environmental factors. Gradually, we are coming to understand more about these factors and their complexity—in the process leaving antiquated debates such as the famous "nature versus nurture" question in the proverbial scientific dust. In the same way, territorial claims that a particular brain region or neurotransmitter belongs exclusively to a single temperament trait or a psychiatric disorder are increasingly dismissed. In a healthy brain, regions are physically connected to one other and in constant communication through electrical impulses and the chemical transfer of neurotransmitters across synapses—the microscopic gaps between brain cells.

Advances in our knowledge of the neurobiology of temperament have exploded in the past few decades, riding the same wave as other areas of neuroscience. The technology available for studying living human brains has progressed dramatically since the days of Chess and Thomas. Magnetic resonance imaging (MRI), a neuroimaging tool that can provide detailed images of the brain, is commonly used to estimate the volume of specific brain regions, as well as the thickness of the outer cortex. A newer technique called diffusion tensor imaging is now available for viewing the white matter connections between brain regions. Furthermore, functional MRI (fMRI), in addition to providing volume and thickness measurements, allows researchers to estimate how active a brain region is at rest, during a specific activity, and even in relation to the activity of other brain regions.

Genetic research has also expanded our knowledge of temperament in the last few decades. The human genome has now been fully sequenced, and over 1 million genetic differences can now be analyzed at once. Beyond analyzing the DNA code, we can also peer into the mechanisms through which that code is transformed into functional proteins. More and more, research is also linking the worlds of genetics and neuroimaging. This chapter explores current research on the neurobiology of temperament, particularly with regard to neuroimaging and genetics. A full rendering of the topic could easily fill a book by itself, but what is contained here should provide a good taste of the methods that are now being used to unlock some of the mysteries surrounding the way temperament traits are manifested in the brain.

Brain Function and Anatomy

The brain regions that are involved in temperament are widely dispersed and highly interconnected. Some of the key players, such as the nucleus accumbens and the hypothalamus, are located deep within the brain. Other areas, such as the orbitofrontal cortex and the anterior temporal lobe, are part of the outer layer of the brain. Figure 4.1 highlights some of these key areas, and Figure 4.2 demonstrates how widely (some might say hopelessly) interrelated brain regions are.

The region that has probably received the most attention with regard to temperament, and negative emotionality in particular, is called the amygdala. This rather small, almond-shaped structure is found deep within a region of the brain called the limbic area, which is very important in the processing of emotions (LeDoux, 2000). The amygdala itself is divided into even smaller subregions, each with specialized functions.

Jerome Kagan and his team have long hypothesized that behavioral inhibition is strongly related to the amygdala and its projections to other areas such as the ventral prefrontal cortex, an area above the eyes that

FIGURE 4.1.
Major areas of the brain involved in temperament

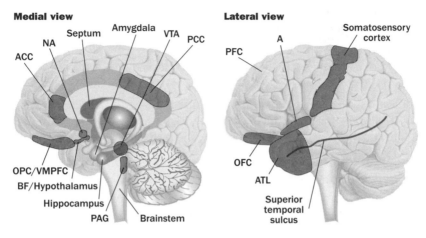

ACC, *anterior cingulate cortex; AI, anterior insula; ATL, anterior temporal lobe; BF, basal forebrain; NA, nucleus accumbens; OFC, orbitofrontal cortex; PAG, periaqueductal gray; PCC, posterior cingulate cortex; PFC, prefrontal cortex; VMPFC, ventromedial prefrontal cortex; VTA, ventral tegmental area (adapted from Pessoa, 2008, and used with permission).*

includes the orbital frontal gyrus (Kagan, Reznick, & Snidman, 1988). The amygdala is also involved in triggering the body's sympathetic nervous system (SNS), the network that underlies our "fight or flight" stress response. Kagan's general hypothesis has been that in some people, this region is hyperreactive due to genetic influences, leading to a quick triggering of the brain's danger alarm. The 4-month-old infants categorized as "highly reactive" because of the degree of distress and motor activity they showed when confronted with unfamiliar stimuli are likely candidates for having a hyperreactive amygdala (Kagan, 1994). Later as children, they commonly showed behavioral inhibition, as well as physiological evidence of increased SNS arousal: higher resting heart rate, pupillary dilation, and increased cortisol levels and vocal cord tension (Kagan et al., 1988). The SNS activation that seems to underlie the trait of behavioral inhibition may also relate to a host of other features, from blue eyes to increased rates of allergies to a narrower face with a more ectomorphic body (i.e., thinner build). By contrast, significantly decreased autonomic nervous system arousal, characterized by a low resting heart rate, seems to be related to the enjoyment of highly stimulating activities (Dietrich et al., 2009).

FIGURE 4.2

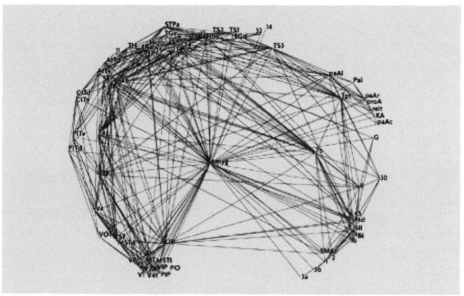

An illustration of the degree of connectivity in the brain, utilizing the amygdala as an example. Research shows that the amygdala is connected to most cortical centers of the brain (adapted from Pessoa, 2008, and used with permission).

In 2005, Lukas Pezawas and his colleagues at the National Institute of Mental Health used MRI to measure the volume and activity of the amygdala and other regions of interest in adults. What separated this study from many earlier ones, however, was that rather than just looking at volume or brain activity in a region by itself, it examined the degree to which activity in one region was related to activity in another. This type of "functional connectivity" analysis represents an important addition to the neuroimaging literature because it better captures what brain regions do—namely, talk to other brain regions. The researchers found that the amygdala was functionally connected to a region above it called the anterior cingulate cortex (ACC). However, the degree of connectivity differed among subjects. Those who were temperamentally more anxious, as manifested by higher harm avoidance scores, had weaker connections between the two regions. Furthermore, the degree of uncoupling was related to different versions, or alleles, of a particular gene called the serotonin transporter.

Why would that matter? In animals, regions of the ACC have been found to be important in regulating amygdala activity through negative feedback loops (Stefanacci & Amaral, 2002). Under normal circumstances, activity in the amygdala leads to activity in the ACC, which then feeds back to diminish the activity of the amygdala. If these two regions are not adequately coupled, then amygdala activity goes unchecked, perhaps leading to further anxiety.

In a study of brain anatomy in adolescents from Australia, the volumes of subregions within the ACC were found to have correlations with temperament (Whittle et al., 2008). Negative emotionality was related to a smaller volume of one part of the anterior cingulate gyrus relative to another part, thus showing some correspondence to the Pezawas study. The sizes of ACC subregions were also related to the trait of sociability or affiliativeness and, interestingly, some of these associations were significant only in females. Volume of a particular ACC subregion was also related to the trait of surgency, which has many parallels to extraversion. Lower levels of surgency were associated with a smaller right-side amygdala, but only in adolescent girls.

In this study, the regulatory dimension known as effortful control was found to be related to a region in the front of the brain called the orbital frontal gyrus (the same area implicated in the cortical thickness study among low-reactive infants). The larger the volume, the better the regulatory ability was. Effortful control was also related to the volume of the left hippocampus. The hippocampus is a region that is famously involved in memory function, but it also helps modulate the hypothalamic-pituitary-adrenal (HPA) axis, a series of interconnected areas that trigger the release of circulating stress hormones in the body (Hyman, 2009).

Structural brain differences can be reflected not only in a region's volume but also its thickness, especially with regard to the outer cortex, which does not have easily demarcated boundaries. In 2010, researchers studying behavioral inhibition found significant associations between reactivity levels as infants and cortical thickness as adults (Schwartz et al., 2010). Adults who were originally categorized as low-reactive had greater cortical thickness in the orbitofrontal cortex, and those previously designated as high-reactive had greater thickness in the right ventromedial prefrontal cortex.

These studies illustrate that temperament dimensions can be related to measurable brain differences in volume, thickness, and connectivity. Although the differences are detectable with modern technology, it is important to note that the magnitudes of these differences are typically small, usually less than about 10%, and they tend to be inconsistent from person to person. Therefore, a radiologist cannot look at an MRI image and declare that it comes from someone who is extraverted or shy.

It is also important to remember that associations between brain regions and temperament traits should not be misinterpreted as evidence that the trait is "housed" in a certain part of the brain. In the 1800s, the field of phrenology ascribed particular mental functions to very specific and circumscribed regions of the brain. Many people have seen the elaborate drawings of a person's scalp divided into sections, with names of emotions or abilities scribbled in small letters to show where that function was controlled. Although these "maps" are now the domain of comic artists, some aspects of that thinking remain today. Yes, different areas of the brain do specialize in particular functions, as we know from people who experienced very localized brain damage that resulted in well-demarcated deficits. Most of our day-to-day brain activity, including the expression of temperament traits, however, requires the networking of multiple regions. Regions such as the ACC play a role in more than one dimension, and each dimension, in turn, has associations with more than one brain area.

Neurochemical Substrates of Temperament

Another line of research within the neurobiology of temperament focuses on neurotransmitters in the brain, substances that are released by one neuron and picked up by receptors on a neighboring neuron. This process, which occurs at the synapses, either activates or inhibits the receiving neuron. Certain neurotransmitters tend to cluster in specific brain regions and others are found ubiquitously. Acetylcholine, norepinephrine, dopamine, and serotonin are examples of neurotransmitters, and some of these names are widely known because of their association with particular psychiatric disorders or treatments. Direct marketing of medications to the public sometimes involves little cartoons that explain how the medication corrects these "imbalances" in the levels of neurotransmitters. However, saying that depression is due to low levels of serotonin or that ADHD is due to low levels of dopamine would be vastly oversimplifying the causes of those disorders.

In studies that use animals as subjects, the actual levels of neurotransmitters or receptors can be measured in brain tissue. In studies involving living humans, however, the by-products of these substances must be detected in the blood or in the cerebrospinal fluid that surrounds the brain. Although most research studies focus on psychiatric disorders rather than temperament or personality traits per se (e.g., ADHD instead of overall attentional abilities), results from such studies offer important clues about the neurotransmitter systems that underlie various temperament traits.

The neurotransmitter dopamine, for example, is thought to have important roles in reward, attention, and motivation. It is therefore a logical player in dimensions such as extraversion, novelty seeking, and attention regulation (DiMaio, Grizenko, & Joober, 2003; Lakatos et al., 2003). Individual differences in dopamine transmission, influenced partially by genetic factors, could be related to individual differences in these traits. Activities that increase dopamine levels in brain regions such as the nucleus accumbens, especially those that increase dopamine levels quickly, can be highly reinforcing. Indeed, some illegal drugs such as cocaine owe their addictive qualities to their ability to rapidly increase dopamine levels in the synapses.

Serotonin and norepinephrine are important chemicals in mood and anxiety (Charney et al., 1990) and are thus associated with traits such as negative emotionality, shyness, and, to some degree, extraversion. An older but well-known study revealed low levels of serotonin metabolites in the cerebrospinal fluid of adults who died by suicide (Asberg, Traskman, & Thoren, 1976), which many interpreted as an association between low serotonin levels and both impulsivity and depression.

The hormone oxytocin is known for its important role in lactation, but it also seems to be related to social affiliation and bonding. Some of the best-known work in this area was performed by Tom Insel (2010), the current director of the National Institute of Mental Health, who studied two types of voles (a type of rodent) that differed in their degree of affiliation and social bonding as well as in the level and distribution of oxytocin in their brains.

Much of the neurochemical research is now closely tied to genetics, as optimal functioning of neurotransmitters relies on the genes that encode the neurotransmitters themselves as well as the genes that encode related molecules that support neurotransmitter formation and functioning. The importance of nongenetic factors in regulating neurotransmitter function is also becoming clearer, such as the role of the intrauterine environment. The developing fetus is exposed to varying concentrations of hormones, which may, in turn, be related to certain traits seen in the child. For example, attention problems and aggression in boys were found to correlate with increased exposure to prenatal androgens (Liu, Portnoy, & Raine, 2012). While genetic factors certainly play an important role in determining prenatal hormone exposure, other events can also alter the makeup of the uterine environment. In a fraternal twin pregnancy, for example, in which one twin is male and the other female, the female twin may be exposed to higher levels of testosterone than is typical for nontwin girls. One study reported lower levels of disordered eating and anxiety among female twins who had a male cotwin rather than a female cotwin (Culbert et al., 2008), although another study did not replicate the results.

Genetic and Environmental Influences

Initial conceptualizations of temperament up through the work of Chess and Thomas and beyond reflected an understanding that it represents the "inborn" component of personality and is determined almost exclusively by one's genes. This section describes some of the data collected over the past 30 years indicating that both genes and the environment contribute to the formation of temperament traits. Quine and later Kagan (Kagan & Snidman, 2004, p. 43) used a gray fabric analogy to describe the roles of these two important forces: behavior is comparable to the overall shade of the fabric, with the biological and environmental influences represented by the many individual black and white threads.

This analogy acknowledges the combined effect of genetics and experience and as such represents a major advance to earlier theories that held that behavior must be dominated by either genetics or experience. Where the fabric analogy falls short, however, is in portraying the idea that genetic and environmental components are distinct, if only we could look closely enough. Recent investigations illustrate how richly interconnected the worlds of genetics and the environment actually are, and how these effects combine to influence brain structure and function to the point where the search to separate their effects seems nearly impossible and prone to misinterpretation.

Twin and Adoption Studies

While the statistics involved in calculating the heritability of a particular trait can be complex, some basic principles guide these estimates. One first needs research samples that include families. Many biological variables cluster in families, including diseases as well as temperament and personality traits. In the past, people have used the finding that traits run in families as evidence that they are genetically influenced. The problem with such reasoning when it comes to children is that parents have a strong influence on both the child's genes and environment. To separate these influences, researchers have to find children within the same family who have been exposed to similar environments. In addition, research studies should include relatives who are genetically different from each other, to a known and measurable degree.

Enter twin and adoption studies. Twins are either identical (monozygotic; they share all of the same genes) or fraternal (dizygotic; they share roughly 50% of the same genes). Regular nontwin siblings also share 50% of their genes, but fraternal twins tend to be preferred as control subjects because they are the same age and share the same uterine environment before birth. Establishing whether twins are monozygotic or dizygotic is not always obvious and can require DNA testing. Once zygosity has been established and the variable of interest has been measured, then the fundamentals are in place. In essence, the degree to which monozygotic twins are more similar on a particular variable than are dizygotic twins is the most common basis on which heritability is calculated.

When many people think back on their studies of genetics, the image of pea pods manipulated by Gregor Mendel comes to mind. Mendel's plants had two copies of each gene, and one allele (e.g., wrinkly pods) could be dominant over another (e.g., smooth pods). If allele A was dominant over allele B, then plants that possessed two A alleles looked the same as plants with a single A and a single B allele. Since this one gene determined the trait, other genes were not needed to predict the overall appearance or phenotype being examined. In medicine, and especially when it comes to brain function and human behavior, however, there are few behavioral phenotypes that operate under straightforward Mendelian principles. A complex dimension such as extraversion is not influenced by one gene; more likely, dozens or hundreds of genes contribute in some way to the trait. The more of those genes an individual possesses, the stronger the trait will be. This phenomenon is called additive genetic influence. When a trait operates according to additive genetics, monozygotic twins are predicted to be very similar because they share all of their genes. Dizygotic twins or regular siblings, on the other hand, would likely have moderately similar levels of such a trait because they share about 50% of the same genes. Thus, when researchers encounter high trait correlations in monozygotic twins and moderately high correlations in dizygotic twins, they suspect a strong additive genetic component.

Getting back to Mendel's peas, however, the effect of one gene might trump the effect of another so that their influences do not add up in a linear fashion. In this scenario, monozygotic twins tend to be very similar in a trait (just like with additive genetics), but dizygotic twins might not be similar at all, despite the fact that they share half of the same genes. This indicates the presence of genetic dominance, or a phenomenon called *epistasis*—when one gene moderates the effects of a completely different gene.

There are also environmental factors operating within a family that tend to make children in the same family behave similarly to one other. When these *shared environmental effects* are strong, genetic influences become less apparent. In a scenario of strong shared environmental effects on a trait, both identical and fraternal twins would be very similar to each other because the environmental factors would be acting on both types of twins equally. If a young child's attendance at religious services were a trait, for example, it would have a strong shared environmental component since twins of both types tend to be brought to services by their parents, regardless of their degree of genetic relatedness.

Environmental influences can also, of course, lead to temperamental differences between siblings or twins in the same family. This type of influence is called an unshared environmental effect. A trait with a strong unshared environmental influence would cause neither monozygotic nor dizygotic twins to be that similar. If a child's temperament is heavily influenced by the temperament of a friend, for example, then the effect might be considered a large unshared environmental effect.

Temperament traits tend to be influenced by both genetic and environmental (and both shared and unshared) factors. Using statistical modeling techniques that utilize heavy doses of matrix algebra, researchers in behavioral genetics can look at the patterns of a trait among monozygotic and dizygotic twins, and calculate the relative amounts of genetic, shared environmental, and unshared environmental influences for that trait.

Adoption studies can be used to address the same question using similar logic. Biological siblings share approximately 50% of the same genes, while the genetic relationship between a biological child and an adopted sibling is close to zero. Similarities in temperament between the adoptive and biological sibling, therefore, would be due mostly to shared environmental influences. If little similarity is seen between the two children with regard to a given trait, then genes may be more important. Adoption studies tend to be less powerful than twin studies, as they have more complicating factors. Adopted children come into families at different ages, a variable that can be difficult to account for but may affect the child's receptivity to traits modeled in the adoptive family. The knowledge that he or she is adopted may also influence the child's behavior in a manner that is not predictable. There are also studies in the past of even more unusual situations, such as twins who are reared apart. While these designs are certainly interesting to consider, the circumstances under which such a situation would occur today are much more limited.

Magnitude of Genetic and Environmental Influences on Temperament

Many twin and adoption studies have concluded that temperament dimensions are significantly influenced by genetics, but to a degree that is less than expected. Heritability estimates, calculated as the percentage of variance that can be attributed to genetic factors, generally range between 20% and 60% for the major temperament dimensions (DiLalla & Jones, 2000; Gillespie et al., 2004; Saudino, 2005) and often hover around 50% in studies of school-age children and adolescents. The remaining variance is usually due to unshared environmental effects (or measurement error). Heritability estimates above 60% are unusual, and some dip below 20%, especially in studies of younger children. Table 4.1 summarizes the magnitudes of genetic and environmental effects across various developmental stages. The table combines studies that used different temperament instruments, different informants, and slightly different dimensions. Consequently, it may be difficult to draw firm conclusions regarding changes in the magnitude of genetic and environmental influence across development.

Nonetheless, some general statements are probably safe to make. The changing heritability coefficients across different age groups reveal a common myth about genetic influences, namely that they are constant. This is an easy misconception; after all, a person's DNA code doesn't change across his or her lifetime. However, the relative magnitudes of genetic and environmental influences vary over time as gene expression

TABLE 4.1. Summary of Genetic (G) and Environmental (E) Effects on Temperament			
Trait	Infants	Children	Teens
Negative emotionality	G: 44	G: 25	G: 43
	E: 56	E: 75	E: 57
Extraversion	G: 35	G: 24	G: 53
	E: 65	E: 76	E: 47
Activity level	G: 21	G: 41	More research needed
	E: 79	E: 59	
Sociability	G: 41	G: 14	More research needed
	E: 59	E: 86	
Regulatory ability	G: 9	G: 29	More research needed
	E: 91	E: 71	
Shyness	G: 50	G: 24	More research needed
	E: 50	E: 76	
Persistence	G: 37	G: 18	More research needed
	E: 63	E: 82	

Sources: Gillespie et al., 2004; Krueger et al., 2008; Rettew, Rebollo-Mesa, et al., 2008; Rettew, Vink, et al., 2006; Saudino & Cherny, 2001.

turns on and off and different types of environmental factors exert their effect on the developing brain.

In the MacArthur Longitudinal Twin Study of more than 200 twin pairs (Saudino et al., 2001), temperament was assessed by observers at multiple time points, from 14 to 36 months of age. As shown in Table 4.1, the heritability estimates often were small and could vary quite a bit between the infancy and toddler years. The genetic effects for sociability, for example, dropped from 41% to 14% during that transition while for activity level it rose from 21% to 41%.

Perhaps even more surprising is the finding that genetic effects can increase with age. For many traits, the strongest genetic effects are not detected in the earliest phases of development, as one might expect. (As the environment has more and more time to make its mark, the relative contribution of genetics should diminish, right?) Although this very logical assumption may indeed have influenced some researchers to use very young infants as subjects in studying the genetics of temperament, the data indicate that this hypothesis is not always correct. Rather, genetic effects can sometimes reveal themselves slowly, even into old age. Diseases such as Alzheimer's disease and type 2 diabetes, as well as physiological processes such as puberty, are under fairly significant genetic influence, yet the biological processes do not begin until later in life. People often joke about becoming more and more like their mother or father as they get older. This expression may have some scientific validity; similar to the story of the tortoise and the hare, our genes, like the tortoise, keep plugging away until they inexorably cross the finish line. Furthermore, genetic influences can conspire to stack the environment deck, as it were, and to cause certain environments to be more likely to occur (Krueger et al., 2008), thereby expanding what may be initially small genetically mediated differences through a process called gene-environment correlations, to be discussed a little later.

Another finding that comes up frequently in these studies is that shared environmental effects, those environmental differences that contribute to making children within the same family similar to each other, usually show the smallest effects (Keller et al., 2005). This result, which is commonly reported in twin studies that examine many types of behaviors, has initiated quite a bit of discussion. One interpretation is that factors long considered to belong to a shared environment, such as parenting practices and socioeconomic status, may be less important than we thought. Another line of thought, however, advocates that perhaps we shouldn't dismiss the importance of these variables altogether but rather alter the way we think of them (Plomin, 2011). Maybe factors like parenting do matter, but they affect different children unequally. A parental divorce, for example, might hit one child harder than another, leading siblings to diverge temperamentally as a result of the environmental stressor rather than becoming more alike. In the Nonshared Environment in Adolescent Development (NEAD) project, more than 700 sibling pairs were assessed in adolescence and early adulthood, and the findings demonstrated that environmental factors are crucial in the expression of many genetically influenced behaviors (Reiss et al., 2000).

Extraversion and the tendency to experience positive emotions are dimensions that seem to show a moderate effect of shared environment, particularly among infants and younger children (Goldsmith, Buss, & Lemery, 1997). Our own laboratory, working with Dorret Boomsma's group in Amsterdam, who run the Netherlands Twin Registry, examined the trait of extraversion in an older adolescent sample (Rettew, Rebollo-Mesa, et al., 2008). To increase the power of our mathematical models, we examined extraversion in adolescent twins ranging in age from 12 to 18 as well as their parents. We found that genetic effects accounted for slightly more than 50% of the variance for adolescent extraversion. The genetic effects showed both additive and nonadditive patterns, and the additive genetic effects increased with age.

The relative strength of genetic and environmental effects can also vary as a function of sex. Males and females have genetic differences, starting with the X and Y chromosomes in males versus the two X chromosomes in females. These genetic differences trigger a number of neurodevelopmental differences, including the levels of male hormones, or androgens, that are present in the intrauterine environment and onward. Since temperament has an important genetic component, then, it is reasonable to ask whether or not the magnitude of genetic effects differs between the sexes.

The appropriate calculations can be done with large twin samples and the right statistical software. Although most studies have reported similar magnitudes of genetic effects between males and females, that finding alone is not necessarily the end of the story. Even when the amount of genetic influence is similar, different genes might be the source of those effects in males and females. That is, the heritability coefficient for Trait X could be 50% for both girls and boys, but the genes responsible for that 50% may be different. One way to get at this information in twin studies is to compare temperament similarity between dizygotic twins of the same sex with dizygotic twins of the opposite sex.

We examined this question in our study of genetic and environmental effects in adolescent neuroticism (Rettew, Vink, et al., 2006). We found the correlations in neuroticism scores among dizygotic twins were .32 for males and .36 for females, but only about .18 for opposite-sex twins. While there was no evidence that the overall amount of genetic influence (about 59%) was different for girls and boys, the correlation results and subsequent statistical analyses indicated that some of the important genes for neuroticism were different between the sexes.

A provocative twin study by Bob Krueger and coworkers from the University of Minnesota showed that the magnitude of genetic influences on positive and negative emotionality could also vary as a function of the family environment (Krueger et al., 2008). Specifically, adolescents who felt more highly regarded and came from families with lower levels of conflict tended to show stronger genetic effects on these personality traits, as compared to adolescents who felt less well regarded by their parents and came from higher-conflict families. These findings may indicate the presence of gene–environment interactions (discussed in more detail later in this chapter).

Molecular Genetic Studies

Twin and adoption studies can provide a lot of information about the factors at play in temperament, but they suffer from important limitations. For one thing, the mathematics behind these studies tends to refer back to the idea that genetic and environmental effects are constants and operate independently of each other (Krueger et al., 2008). Another difficulty is that large numbers of subjects are needed to draw meaningful conclusions, which means that practical considerations will often dictate that child temperament is assessed as easily as possible, namely, by having parents fill out questionnaires for multiple children in the family. This situation can induce the problem of contrast effects—the tendency to accentuate differences between siblings when they actually may be quite similar to each other relative to other children their age. Additionally, parents of twins may be inclined to overrate similarities between identical twins (knowing they are identical) or overrate differences between fraternal twins. Some studies have found that parents rate monozygotic twins as being quite similar while rating dizygotic twins as being no more similar to each other than unrelated children (Saudino, 2005). Lastly, without examining the genetics directly (i.e., DNA sequences) and the presence of particular genes and alleles, twin studies can't speak to which specific genes are involved for a certain trait.

Genetic studies of psychiatric disorders several decades ago used to operate according to the one gene, one disorder (OGOD) principle. A search was on to find the single gene responsible for autism, or for schizophrenia, or for neuroticism. After these searches failed to yield answers, scientists began to shift their perspective. Rather than looking for one or a few genes with a large effect, researchers began looking for many genes that were related to the same temperament or personality dimension, each with a very small effect (e.g., 1% of the variance).

Fortunately, technological advances developed alongside this shift in approach. In particular, the application of the microarray chip ushered in the possibility of looking at huge numbers of genetic variations simultaneously. Microarray chips can contain millions of DNA probes, and each probe is designed to detect a single base pair difference (single-nucleotide polymorphism or SNP) in a gene. Yet despite the impressive technology, the huge sample sizes, and the firm knowledge that genetic effects are important, researchers have become increasingly disappointed in the results, or rather the lack thereof.

In 2010, an international group of scientists published the results of a study analyzing the genetics of temperament dimensions, as proposed by Cloninger: novelty seeking, harm avoidance, reward dependence, and persistence (Verweij et al., 2010). The study included more than 5,000 adult participants who completed temperament questionnaires about themselves. The genetic analyses tested more than 1 million genetic markers spanning all 23 chromosomes for associations with temperament, but they couldn't find any significant links.

Despite disappointing results in some studies, many others have discovered evidence of associations between particular genes and dimensions of temperament and personality (Van Gestel & Van Broeckhoven, 2003). Ironically, studies that set out to test the association between temperament or personality and a small set of candidate genes often find more positive results than studies that test thousands, if not millions. A partial list of genes that have been linked to traits is shown in Table 4.2.

Many of the genes that have been associated with temperament are "usual suspects" in that they code for proteins that are involved in the functioning of brain neurotransmitters. As mentioned earlier, the effective functioning of neurotransmitters relies on a whole support network of receptors, promoters, and metabolizers, all of which are also encoded by genes.

Perhaps the two most famous molecular genetic associations with temperament are the gene that encodes one of the receptors that binds to the neurotransmitter dopamine and the gene that produces a transporter for the neurotransmitter serotonin (Keltikangas-Jarvinen et al., 2004; Munafo et al., 2008; Schinka, Busch, & Robichaux-Keene, 2004; Schinka, Letsch, & Crawford, 2002). Sometimes these genetic effects are detectable only under specific environmental conditions (Sheese et al., 2007). As we will see later, these two genes have also been implicated in psychiatric disorders or symptoms.

TABLE 4.2
A Partial List of Specific Genes That Have Been Associated
With Temperament and Personality Traits

Gene	Function of Gene Product	Trait	Comments
5HT1A and B	Part of family of several serotonin receptors (1D)	Aggression, compulsiveness	
5HT2A	Serotonin 2 receptor	Neuroticism, persistence	
5HTTLPR	Promotes the genetic expression of the serotonin transporter that takes serotonin back into the neuron after its release	Negative emotionality	One of the most widely studied genes in neuropsychiatry
Beta-1 adrenergic receptor	Beta-1 adrenergic receptor	Extraversion	
BDNF	Brain-derived neurotrophic factor	Trait anxiety	
COMT	Catechol-O-methyltransferase gene involved in the metabolism of neurotransmitters	Multiple	Plays a role in degradation of many substances found to be involved in temperament
CRHR1	Corticotropin-releasing hormone receptor 1	Anger	Involved in regulation of hypothalamic-pituitary-adrenal axis
DAT1	Dopamine transporter	Novelty seeking	
DRD2	Dopamine 2 receptor	Novelty seeking	
DRD4	Dopamine receptor 4	Novelty seeking/approach, attention span	Most focus of the 7 repeat allele in the variable number of tandem repeats (VNTR) region
MAO-A	Monoamine oxidase A	Neuroticism, reward dependence	Involved in degrading multiple brain neurotransmitters
RGS2	Regulator G-protein signaling 2	Behavioral inhibition	
TYH	Tyrosine hydroxylase	Anger, aggression	

Gene–Environment Interactions

For years, genetic researchers of behavior would pay their respects to environmental causes while those interested in environmental causes would do the same for genetics. Yet despite these perfunctory homages to each other, measurement of both genetic and environmental variables within the same study was uncommon. In 2002, however, a seminal article was published by Avshalom Caspi and coworkers in the highly prestigious journal *Science* that clearly demonstrated that the effect of a gene could depend on a particular environment and vice versa: a gene–environment interaction (Caspi, 2002). These data came from the Dunedin Study in which a large group of subjects in New Zealand were studied from childhood into adulthood. The goal was to predict which individuals would later display antisocial behavior such as aggression or criminal acts. At the time, it had already been shown that being the victim of maltreatment as a child was a risk factor for later antisocial behavior, as was having a particular version of the gene that encodes monoamine oxidase A (MAOA). MAOA is important in metabolizing neurotransmitters such as dopamine and serotonin. Studies of both of these risk factors, however, yielded somewhat inconsistent results, leading the researchers to wonder if there might be more to the story.

Indeed there was. The link between child maltreatment and antisocial behavior, as Caspi's team discovered, depended on a person's genetic status with regard to the MAOA gene. People with one allele of the MAOA gene were very likely to show antisocial behavior if they were mistreated as children, and those with a different MAOA allele were relatively insensitive to the negative behavioral effects of maltreatment.

This study and another similar one that followed (Caspi, Sugden, et al., 2003) generated a tremendous amount of attention, despite the fact that most people had been expecting this type of result for years. Indeed, the most popular conceptual model for the origins of emotional behavioral problems at the time was the diathesis-stress model, which posits that psychopathology results from stressors acting upon people who have a predisposed vulnerability to the negative effects of those stressors. What was novel wasn't the overall concept of combined genetic and environmental factors, but rather the finding of a specific environmental factor (childhood maltreatment) that interacts with a specific mutation in a single gene (MAOA) whose function is clearly related to brain function.

The central idea in gene–environment interactions is that the genetic and environmental factors in question don't always have major effects on their own, but when combined, they can heavily influence a temperament trait or a specific behavioral disorder. These interactions (sometimes referred to as G × E) have become a central focus in behavioral research and in many ways represent a true advance in the field. This advance is perhaps the third major progression in our process of understanding the genetic and environmental influences on behavior since the research of Chess and Thomas.

1. Behavior is due to genes or the environment.
2. Behavior is due to genes and the environment, operating through different mechanisms.
3. Behavior is due to genes and the environment operating though mutually causative pathways.

As cool as G × E sounds, however, the concept is neither new nor specific to child development. Seasonal allergies, for example, operate through a classic gene–environment interaction. The predisposition to a particular allergy is strongly influenced by genetics; however, if a person doesn't happen to live in an area that contains the allergen, then he or she won't experience allergic symptoms. Similarly, an individual living in an area that contains the allergen won't be affected unless he or she has the genetic predisposition. G × E studies remain popular today, although a new dose of skepticism has arisen due to the failure of genome-wide studies (those efforts to look at massive numbers of gene variants across all chromosomes within a single study) to find robust genetic effects of single genes. In a Spanish study (Ivorra et al., 2010), the authors assessed infant temperament (irritability) at 8 and 32 weeks of age, and they also measured the mothers' levels of anxiety and confidence in caretaking. A few genes were analyzed using DNA samples from both mothers and infants, including the serotonin transporter gene, which has "short" and "long" alleles. The level of irritability among infants with at least one copy of the short allele was strongly correlated with maternal anxiety; infants with two long alleles stayed relatively mellow regardless of how anxious the mother was. The same gene was implicated in another study that examined children's regulatory ability and whether or not the child was securely or insecurely bonded to the mother or "attached" at age 15 months (Kochanska, Philibert, & Barry, 2009). Again, the children with two copies of the long allele seemed to function fairly well regardless of their attachment status, while those with the short allele fluctuated more in their regulatory ability, depending on their attachment status as an infant.

Gene–Environment Correlations (rGE)

Gene–environment interaction studies teach us that the effects of genes depend on environmental factors and the impact of certain environments varies according to one's genetic makeup. As important as this concept is to both our academic understanding of temperament and our attempts to modify problematic behavior, we are still far from having a complete picture of how genetic and environmental influences get tangled up with each other.

Until recently, an assumption underlying many studies that examined how various environmental factors affected behavior was that the probability of those environmental factors taking place is independent of genetic effects. In other words, if you measured an environmental factor at one time point and a behavioral outcome at a later time point and found a significant association, you were safe in concluding a causative role of that environmental factor even without expressly taking genetics into account.

The logic behind this design can be sound if the investigator does one important thing, namely, randomize subjects so that some receive the environmental factor and some don't. Otherwise, however, there can be trouble; and unfortunately, many studies of human children don't lend themselves to randomization very easily (it is much easier with rats). Consider, for example, a researcher who is interested in the age-old question of whether or not spanking children makes them more aggressive in the future. As wonderful scientifically as a study might be that could flip a coin and tell half the parents to spank when appropriate, and others not to spank, finding a sufficient number of parents willing to let a coin toss determine an important parenting decision would be quite challenging.

But without randomization, a number of other potentially important variables can sneak into the study and exert an effect that makes it look like your variable of interest is the important player when it isn't. These confounders are the bane of all investigators trying to understand the origins of complex behaviors like temperament when (1) you can't randomize and (2) you can't measure everything.

Genetic researchers have complained for years that hidden genetic effects can masquerade as environmental effects because the environmental events are not occurring independently but are instead associated or correlated with genetic effects. These gene–environment correlations can be abbreviated as rGE (r is the correlation coefficient, G and E are genes and environment, as before). Without taking into account the genetic effects, a researcher can be led astray and draw the wrong conclusions.

Gene–environment correlations come in three main types: passive, evocative, and active (each described below). While these terms have been in existence for decades (Plomin, DeFries, & Loehlin, 1977), it has taken quite a bit of time for these types of mechanisms to become operationalized in the field, probably because they add complexity to searches for the causes of child behavior. Understanding and appreciating them, however, opens windows into potential places for productive intervention.

Passive rGE

Throughout the latter part of the 20th century, studies of parenting and other environmental influences on child behavior often went something like this. The investigator would recruit a group of families to participate in a research study. Then, since randomizing families into experimental groups wasn't an option, the researcher would measure what families do already, by using a questionnaire or perhaps bringing families into the lab to observe them doing something together. The investigator would find a range of parenting behaviors in their sample—some parents were warm and encouraging; others tended to be harsher and exert more overt power over their children. Then the researcher would look for associations between parenting styles and some outcome variable, such as child aggression or defiant behavior, either at the time of the study or at a later point in time. If a correlation was found between, say, hostile comments by the parent and disruptive behavior in the child, the investigator made a casual inference that harsh parenting caused disruptive behavior.

Most researchers, being aware of confounding factors such as socioeconomic status or family structure, would try to account for the effects of as many of these variables as possible in their statistical analysis. A variable that was usually missing in the accounting, however, was genetics. Why was this omission particularly problematic? Biological parents contribute not just a particular environment to their children but also half their genes. Furthermore, the same genes that influence their child's behavior may also be contributing to the creation of a particular environment—a phenomenon known as passive rGE.

In the example above, it is quite possible that some of a child's aggression is partially influenced by genes inherited from his or her parents. Those same genes may also be a source of the hostile parenting environment, via their effect on the parents' behavior. Without measuring those genetic effects directly, however, it is difficult to know how much aggression would be present in those genetically at-risk children, even in the absence of the hostile environment. As a result, it is likely that many of these kinds of studies have overestimated environmental effects.

Evocative rGE

The best way to explain evocative rGE with regard to child behavior is to use a mountain analogy. Kids, like large mountains, can create their own weather. When genes influence a child to be more irritable or less socially interactive, for example, the environment can respond in kind. In this way, what may look like the effect of some environmental variable might actually be the result of some genetically influenced trait. As complex as this concept may sound at first, just about everybody has encountered this idea in day-to-day language. When a person "brings out the best (or worst) in us," an evocative gene–environment correlation may be at work, to the extent that the other person's behavior is genetically influenced.

If child temperament is partially influenced by genetics, as most studies seem to suggest, then let us consider how this setup may affect a family environment. The classic Chess and Thomas difficult child is quite a challenge for most new parents, and perhaps even more so for parents who themselves may have some difficult traits such as being quick to become angry or irritable. These parents are very easily going to be set off or have their buttons pushed. With a temperamentally easy infant, alternatively, the parents can look like stars. But a difficult infant, with his irritability and resistance to being soothed, may exhaust the abilities of the parents and trigger a number of negative parenting responses that, in turn, can reinforce the difficult tendencies of the child. Simply looking at the parenting environment and the associated child behaviors, therefore, does not seem to capture the dynamic processes that might be at work in a family. Research studies equipped to identify these effects have demonstrated both positive and negative effects of child personality on the parent-child relationship (South et al., 2008).

Most parents report that they treat all of their children very similarly. Yet most children, when asked, will readily complain that their parents treat them quite differently from their siblings (with the child being asked usually claiming to get the short end of the stick). Available evidence suggests, not surprisingly, that the truth is somewhere in the middle: general principles hold true for the whole family while some differences are seen in the parenting of different siblings (Reiss et al., 2000). More scientific data would be very welcome in this area.

In our Vermont Family Study (Hudziak et al., 2003), mothers and fathers completed a questionnaire about their parenting behavior, and were asked to fill out a separate questionnaire for each of their kids. This simple but relatively unique configuration allowed us to examine parenting differences within the same family. In looking at parenting practices associated with ADHD, we found that the diagnosis was associated with an inconsistent pattern of discipline in mothers, and that the mothers were more consistent in their parenting of non-ADHD siblings (Mebust, Rettew, & Hudziak, 2010). A study from the NEAD project found additional evidence of this effect: challenging child temperament traits were associated with more evoked negative parenting (Ganiban et al., 2011).

Active rGE

A third mechanism through which genetics can be involved in making certain environments more likely is called an active gene–environment correlation. This correlation reflects what self-help authors have been telling us for years, namely that things don't just happen to us but rather that we, as individuals, play an essential role in selecting and promoting the likelihood of certain situations in our lives. If an evocative rGE correlation is a large mountain that inadvertently creates its own weather, then an active rGE is a bird that migrates south for the winter.

In child development, an example of an active rGE might be a child's selection of his or her peer group. That choice, especially as the child gets older, is likely to be based on that child's genetically influenced traits and tendencies. Active children often prefer to play with other active children, and kids prone to defy authority and break rules unfortunately also tend to congregate. Once these peer groups are formed, the environmental effects of being in a particular group often work in the same direction to amplify the child's initial predispositions.

These types of interplay demonstrate how quickly and deeply genetic and environmental components get intertwined, making it very difficult to separate or compare them. Child temperament studies that are equipped to measure different types of gene–environment relations tend to involve unusual groups of subjects, such as the offspring of twins or adoptive families. As molecular genetic studies progress, it may become easier to directly measure the effects of particular genes. Nonetheless, the age-old question of whether a behavior has a genetic or environmental cause has lost much of its meaning. Not only do both types of influence exert important effects on all major temperament traits, but they also influence one another at the same time. When parents ask whether genes or the environment is responsible for a trait in their child, I often say "yes."

How the Environment Changes Genes

Gene–environment interactions and correlations make a lot of intuitive sense. Indeed, after reading about them, many people may wonder how there could have ever been such controversy in the first place. The idea that a child's genetic makeup is tied to both the probability of certain environments showing up and the magnitude of those environments' effects on behavior is not hard to imagine. More difficult to picture, perhaps, are the mechanisms through which the environment can actually change brain function and, even more abstract, how the environment can change genes. After all, a person's DNA sequence doesn't change, right?

Right. However, there are several steps involved in translating a gene into the protein it encodes. Different cells in our body, although they contain the same DNA code, have drastically different functions. This is because each cell regulates which proteins it makes, which proteins it doesn't make, and how much of each protein it makes. The study of genetic effects that go beyond the actual DNA code, called *epigenetics*, is an area of rapid growth and exciting new findings. Epigenetics is concerned with the expression of genes, rather than the underlying sequence of nucleotides itself. One process that seems to be important in turning genes on and off is called methylation—a methyl group (CH_3) attaches to a segment of DNA, thereby altering the ability of RNA to translate that gene into a protein. A leading epigenetic research group at McGill University in Montreal, led by Michael Meaney, has been studying how this process relates to behavior and the HPA axis, which plays a major role in the body's regulation of stress. In rats, increased maternal licking, a marker for good rat mothering, led to a diminished stress response and lower levels of the stress hormone adrenocorticotropic hormone (ACTH) in young rat pups (Weaver, 2007). This response appears to be related to serotonin-containing neurons in the brain's hippocampus. More serotonin leads to less DNA methylation in the gene that increases or "promotes" the expression of a receptor in the hippocampus. That receptor binds to glucocorticoid stress hormones, which turns up a negative feedback mechanism in the HPA axis and thus turns down the overall stress response. (If you think that process is complicated, you may be dismayed to know that I left out several intermediate steps.) A study in humans comparing people who died by suicide and were victims of child abuse versus those who died suddenly by accidental causes showed similar changes in methylation and gene expression (McGowan et al., 2009). Compared to controls and individuals who died by suicide but had no history of child abuse, suicide victims with a history of child abuse showed increased methylation and reduced gene expression of this important glucocorticoid receptor that helps regulate the body's response to stress.

The McGowan study and those described previously in this chapter highlight the complexity of the neurobiology of temperament. From this perspective, broad statements about temperament traits being due solely to genes or to simple levels of particular neurotransmitters in the brain just seem silly. There is strong evidence showing that temperament traits are neither the automatic outcome of a DNA code nor the product of a particular style of parenting. With an ever-expanding set of technological tools for investigating brain function, neurotransmitters, and genes, the list of important determinants and mediators of temperament seems to be growing. Many of the "old friends" that have been implicated in abnormal brain function and psychiatric disorders are turning up as factors in normal functioning as well. This observation leads us to question how temperament and other brain-mediated entities such as psychiatric disorders are related to each other, both at a surface level of description and with regard to their underlying neurobiology.

Chapter 5

Temperament and Psychopathology

At what point does active become hyperactive? Where does shyness end and social anxiety disorder begin? When should we start talking about autistic spectrum disorders in place of terms like *quirky* or *eccentric*?

These basic but critical questions have challenged parents, clinicians, and scientists for decades, and we still have a long way to go before reaching definitive answers. Perhaps we've been in trouble since the time of Chess and Thomas. With temperament dimensions such as "attention span" and "quality of mood" existing alongside ADHD (which was called minimal brain dysfunction at that time) and major depression, there was bound to be some confusion about the relations between traits and disorders. Today, it is one of the central issues that arise when parents bring in their child for a mental health evaluation.

In child psychiatric assessment, it is widely recognized that most behaviors labeled as pathological exist at lower or "subthreshold" levels, with the line between normality and pathology a moving target across development. Nobody would expect a 3-year-old to be able to focus on a simple cognitive task for very long, but the bar changes for a 15-year-old. How much it should change becomes our task as "experts" who have seen hundreds or thousands of children and have at our disposal questionnaires and rating scales that are standardized according to a patient's age and sex. Yet despite the evidence and tools available, the boundary between normality and abnormality is still the subject of much speculation and controversy.

As we saw in Chapter 1, the study of temperament and personality has existed largely apart from clinically oriented research. This separation widened as the field of psychiatry became increasingly focused on the biological factors that underlie mental health disorders. But with studies such as those from Chess and Thomas, coupled with the increasing evidence that all thoughts and behavior are the result of brain function and are therefore "biological," it has become more and more difficult to keep the two worlds of temperament and clinical medicine apart. Still, in many ways, our society clings to the idea that psychiatric illness strikes out of nowhere and exists in all-or-none form. ADHD is commonly thought of as something a child "gets," like an infectious illness, and depression is described as a cloud that descends without warning. Certainly such cases exist, and perhaps not all psychiatric disorders work in association with temperament, but for most people who suffer from the most common behavioral disorders, there is a connection with temperament. And that connection should not be ignored.

In an effort to strengthen our image as real doctors who treat real illnesses, practitioners in psychiatry and child psychiatry may have, ironically, helped perpetuate this all-or-none idea of mental illness, thus increasing the stigma attached to mental illness. Television, of course, plays its part. People with everyday struggles related to their thoughts, feelings, and behaviors don't look like the people on talk shows who were suddenly overcome with crushing symptoms. In this way, the first group is easily dismissed as just being lazy, difficult, emotional, and so on, rather than having a valid brain-based condition. *Just* could very well be the most dangerous word in the field of mental health. That one syllable implies a lack of true substance and a process wholly under the control of the individual (who is probably acting that way just to annoy you). As we saw in Chapter 4, nothing could be further from the truth when it comes to temperament traits.

This chapter is devoted to studies that have attempted to evaluate and measure the degree to which temperament is linked to various psychiatric disorders. It addresses the question of whether and how much various temperament dimensions are associated with corresponding disorders. This area of study is now quite popular, so for readers who are interested in a comprehensive summary of the available literature, additional books on the subject are available (Cloninger, 1999; Kreuger & Tackett, 2006).

Attention-Deficit/Hyperactivity Disorder

In the *Diagnostic and Statistical Manual of Mental Disorders, Fourth Edition With Text Revision* (DSM-IV-TR), ADHD is described as "a persistent pattern of inattention and/or hyperactivity-impulsivity that is more frequent and severe than is typically observed in individuals at a comparable level of development." The DSM-5, which is in press at the time of this writing, is not expected to have major changes to these criteria. Symptoms of ADHD are divided into two types: those that reflect problems with inattention (difficulty with focus and organization, forgetfulness, and distractibility) and those that relate to hyperactivity and impulsivity (an inability to stay in one's seat, excessive running or talking, impatience, and acting before thinking). A person can meet criteria for an ADHD diagnosis on the basis of having inattentive symptoms alone (inattentive subtype, often referred to as ADD), hyperactive or impulsive symptoms alone (hyperactive/impulsive subtype), or both types of symptoms together (combined subtype).

A number of research groups have investigated temperamental associations with ADHD. As expected, ADHD seems to be related to low levels of effortful control and high levels of approach—dimensions such as novelty seeking, extraversion, and surgency (Nigg, 2006). The temperament associations with ADHD can vary somewhat depending on who (parents, teachers, or trained observers) does the assessments (Martel & Nigg, 2006; Martel, Nigg, & von Eye, 2009). Table 5.1 summarizes these links for ADHD and several other disorders.

A high level of extraversion or surgency is more strongly related to the hyperactive subtype of ADHD than it is to the inattentive subtype of ADHD. Despite the similarities between ADHD symptoms and a low effortful control/high extraversion temperament profile, the degree of association is modest, with correlation coefficients (r values) between ratings of ADHD symptoms and selected temperament dimensions around 0.2 to 0.3.

Another trait that is frequently linked to ADHD is negative affectivity. Oppositional and angry behavior is certainly common among children with ADHD, but it is not part of the disorder per se. The correlation between ADHD and negative affectivity tends to weaken once symptoms of other disorders, such as oppositional defiant disorder (ODD), are controlled for statistically. We examined temperament traits in approximately 300 children from approximately 200 families in Vermont

TABLE 5.1.
Temperament Traits Associated With Common Psychiatric Disorders

Disorder	Negative Affectivity	Extraversion/Approach	Sociability	Regulatory Ability/Effortful Control
ADHD, combined	+/−	++	+	—
ADHD, inattentive	+	+/−	+/−	—
ODD	+	+/−	+/−	—
CD/psychopathy	+/−	++	+/−	+/−
General anxiety	++	+/−	+/−	—
Depression	+/−	—	+/−	-
Bipolar disorder	+	+	+/−	—
Autistic spectrum	+	—	—	—
Substance abuse	+	+	+/−	-
Psychotic disorders	+/−	-	-	-
Eating disorders, "undercontrolled"	+	+/−	+/−	—
Eating disorders, "overcontrolled"	+/−	—	+/−	+/−

ODD, oppositional defiant disorder; CD, conduct disorder. ++, increased levels of trait strongly associated with the disorder; +, increased levels of trait moderately associated with the disorder; +/−, trait not associated with disorder; −, decreased levels of trait moderately associated with the disorder; —, decreased levels of trait strongly associated with the disorder.

(Rettew, Copeland, et al., 2004). The trait of harm avoidance, which has features similar to negative affectivity, was commonly found among children who also had an internalizing disorder, such as a mood or anxiety disorder. The dimension of low persistence, as assessed by the Junior Temperament and Character Inventory and related to effortful control, was linked to ADHD whether or not other disorders were present.

Overall then, effortful control and traits similar to it appear to correlate broadly with ADHD, whereas high extraversion and surgency are linked more specifically to the motor symptoms of ADHD (i.e., hyperactivity). High levels of negative affectivity are often found in parallel with ADHD, but this is likely related to other disorders found alongside ADHD, rather than being part of the disorder itself.

The current scientific and public debate regarding the apparent rise of ADHD in the population may be related to the association between ADHD and temperamental traits. According to a 2004 epidemiological study, the prevalence in U.S. youth was about 6.7% (Woodruff et al., 2004), and a more recent study showed an overall prevalence of 8.7% for all adolescents, with a remarkable 13.0% for teenage boys (Merikangas et al., 2010). Hypotheses about why the rate of ADHD appears to be increasing include sources from artificial food additives to video games and television. There was even a theory that the disorder was invented by the pharmaceutical industry to make money, which led to several lawsuits that were dismissed in court.

Like many health dimensions, from height to blood pressure to cholesterol levels, a child's activity level and attentional abilities exist along a broad continuum. When population data are charted, the distribution often forms a bell-shaped curve. However, the distribution curve for scores on traditional psychiatric rating scales often looks like the right half of a bell-shaped curve because most individuals have "no problems" and their data points therefore clump together at the left side of a curve, with the various degrees of problematic behavior falling in a long tail toward the right (top graph in Figure 5.1). Binary distributions, with a clump of individuals at both extremes, are very rare in child psychiatry.

Left with this reality, there is no obvious cutoff that marks the point at which a particular behavior becomes clinical. For medical conditions such as high cholesterol and high blood pressure, it is relatively easy to obtain objective measurements of the variable of interest, and experts typically reach consensus on threshold levels. For example, blood pressure above 140/90 or total cholesterol above 200 are classified as disease states. For ADHD, however, we do not have universal measures of attention or activity level, so the appraisal of these dimensions tends to rely on the subjective judgment of parents, counselors, or psychiatrists. In this way, the threshold between clinical and subclinical can become a moving target, subject to the collective opinions of the mental health community and society at large.

Making matters more complicated is the fact that attentional abilities and activity levels do extend across the full spectrum of a normal bell-shaped distribution. Some rating scales, such as the Strength and Weakness of ADHD Symptoms and Normal Behavior Scale (SWAN; Swanson et al., 2006), were designed to consider that full range. They go beyond the "no problems" rating to differentiate children with very high attention spans, for example, or very low activity levels. A study published from our lab in Vermont, in collaboration with researchers from the Netherlands Twin Registry, showed that among a group of 12-year-old twins the SWAN scores were indeed normally distributed (Polderman et al., 2007). A graph of these distributions is shown in the bottom section of Figure 5.1.

FIGURE 5.1

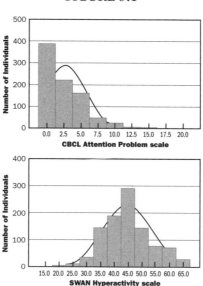

Distributions of traits measured through clinical versus temperamental rating scales. Top graph shows the distribution from a clinically oriented rating scale, which includes a "no problem" category. This results in a positively skewed (or right-tailed) distribution with a large number of individuals on the left edge of the curve and a long, gradual tail toward the right that reflects smaller numbers of people with higher levels of problems. The bottom graph shows the distribution of ADHD hyperactivity symptoms using a rating scale more closely aligned to temperament. Here, the "no problem" group is expanded to differentiate between those with average and low levels of activity. The result is a much more bell-shaped distribution (adapted and used with permission from Polderman et al., 2007).

It is very likely that the "speed limit" for ADHD has slowly decreased over the past several decades, contributing to the trend of increasing diagnoses. Thirty years ago, an attention-deficit diagnosis was reserved for the most extremely inattentive and hyperactive behavior—behavior that was readily recognized as different from others'. Over time, however, more and more children with high but perhaps not extremely high levels of inattention and hyperactivity have been diagnosed and thereby qualify for treatment. This trend causes both relief and horror, depending on whom you ask; the ongoing debate about medications is discussed in more detail in Chapter 11.

Oppositional Defiant Disorder and Conduct Disorder

Symptoms of ODD include high and pervasive levels of negative, hostile, and defiant behavior. Children with ODD often lose their temper, argue, resist and defy rules, and then blame others for their problems. They are quick to react negatively and may look to exact revenge. Some children with ODD may seem to act this way in a deliberate manner, as is described in the DSM-IV-TR criterion "often deliberately annoys people," whereas others' hostility tends to be more reactive than proactive, a distinction that is important in conduct disorder as well.

Designing temperament studies of children with ODD is a challenge, as the condition is so heterogeneous. In the Avon Longitudinal Study of Parents and Children (ALSPAC), temperament was assessed at around 3 years of age using the Emotionality, Activity, and Sociability (EAS) questionnaire, and then the same children were screened at age 7 or 8 for psychiatric disorders (Stringaris, Maughan, & Goodman, 2010). The researchers found that an ODD diagnosis was most strongly related to high emotionality and high activity, but the associations depended on other disorders that the children also displayed (i.e., comorbid disorders). For example, high activity levels in the EAS questionnaire showed a correlation with an ODD and ADHD (combined type) diagnosis, but not with an ODD and ADHD (inattentive type) diagnosis.

In contrast to the reactive type of oppositional behavior, which is linked to high levels of emotionality or negative affectivity, another group of children tend to appear more deliberate with their transgressions. These children do act aggressively and defy rules, but instead of extreme outbursts, the offenses tend to be more calculated attempts to exploit others to their advantage. These children and adolescents not only break family rules but can commit criminal acts and are known to initiate aggression and cruelty toward others. The diagnosis of conduct disorder (CD) in the DSM-IV attempts to capture this behavioral profile and often does so, although more reactively defiant children can also meet criteria for CD. Another term, *callous-unemotional traits*, developed by psychologist Paul Frick, might capture this group more fully (Frick & Morris, 2004).

Those who meet criteria for CD or for callous-unemotional traits have a temperament that resembles the classic description of psychopathy or sociopathy. They tend to be very cool customers in general, with low rather than high levels of temperamental anxiety. These individuals also tend to have average or high levels of regulation and very high levels of approach or thrill-seeking behavior, with low baseline levels of arousal and low resting heart rates (Dietrich et al., 2009). Finally, their famous lack of empathy is reflected in low levels of sociability or reward dependence. Some studies have reported different findings, however. For example, a community sample assessed at age 3 for temperament and at age 28 for psychopathic traits found elevated autonomic activity and sociability in children correlated with higher psychopathy scores in adults (Glenn et al., 2007). These differences may be related to how temperament was measured, the composition of the various dimensions that were studied, or how psychopathy was assessed.

Mood and Anxiety Disorders

Mood and anxiety disorders are considered to be separate categories of illness, according to the DSM system. They are grouped together here, however, because there is strong evidence showing that mood and anxiety problems often exist together in youth. Thomas Achenbach and colleagues (2001) collected data from thousands of children and looked at which types of behavior problems occur together statistically. Their results did not always align with the DSM system, which incorporates data into its process but ultimately arrives at final diagnostic categories through committee consensus. By contrast, Achenbach employed a more bottom-up approach, and he assigned the names of the various types of emotional-behavioral problems by examining the group of individual behaviors that were found to cluster together in children naturally. The family of instruments he used to make these categories, the Achenbach System of Empirically Based Assessment (ASEBA), is now arguably the most widely used set of child behavior rating scales in the world. According to their taxonomy, there is both an "anxious/depressed" domain and a "withdrawn/depressed" domain. In considering the links between mood, anxiety, and temperament, the Achenbach symptom clusters may be as important as the DSM-defined disorders.

The work of Lee Anna Clark and David Watson at the University of Iowa suggests that depression, characterized by low mood, lack of interest, loss of energy, and feelings of worthlessness, may reflect a combination of low approach (low extraversion/surgency) and high negative emotionality (Clark & Watson, 1991; Watson, Gamez, & Simms, 2005). High levels of negative emotionality are also linked to anxiety disorders, particularly conditions such as generalized anxiety disorder—high levels of pervasive, day-to-day worries. This shared temperamental feature of high negative emotionality explains the common overlap between depressive and anxiety disorders. However, generalized anxiety and depression differ from each other in the extraversion/surgency dimension: it remains low in depressive disorders but not in chronic anxiety conditions. One exception may be social anxiety disorder or social phobia, which involves intense concern about negative evaluations from others. People suffering from social anxiety disorder are often extremely shy and reticent in social situations, despite wanting to be around people. The temperament profile of social phobia, like that of depressive disorders, consists of high negative emotionality and low extraversion/surgency. And, as expected, the comorbidity between major depression and social anxiety disorder is quite high.

Further work with children has emphasized the role of regulatory domains in anxiety disorders (Lonigan et al., 2004). When high negative emotionality is accompanied by low effortful control, it is a recipe for anxiety disorders. Lonigan's work with anxious children has also included the measurement of cognitive domains such as the tendency to perceive more threats in the environment than other children do. Higher effortful control enables some children to shift their attention and reappraise their initial threat alert, thereby putting the brakes on a full anxiety response in uncertain or stressful situations.

One of the most extensively studied associations between temperament and psychopathology concerns the relations between behavioral inhibition (BI) and anxiety disorders, and social anxiety disorder in particular. As mentioned in Chapter 2, this work was begun decades ago by Jerome Kagan and Nancy Snidman. Since then, many other researchers, including Dina Hirshfeld-Becker, Joseph Biederman, and Carl Schwartz have made important contributions to the neurobiology of BI and its links to child psychiatric disorders. Children with BI, perhaps 10–15% of 2-year-olds, tend to be very restrained when faced with new people and new situations. They show distress easily and talk and smile less than their non-BI peers. Groups of children with BI have been followed in a few studies, and increased rates of psychopathology have been found. An early study that followed BI children for three years found elevated rates of avoidant disorder (an older DSM-III-R diagnosis that is no longer used and had a description extremely similar to BI) and multiple anxiety disorders (Biederman et al., 1993). It should be noted, however, that most of the behaviorally inhibited children did not manifest clinical anxiety disorders. As these children moved into adolescence, the association with BI appeared to become more specific to social anxiety (Schwartz, Snidman, & Kagan, 1999).

These findings of a relatively robust association between temperament traits and anxiety disorders have been generally accepted by the mental health community, who recognize not only the surface similarities between the two domains but also their shared features such as stability over time. Similarly, some depressive disorders such as dysthymic disorder, characterized by more chronic and less severe depressive symptoms in comparison to major depressive disorder, also bear good resemblance to the aforementioned temperament profile of low approach and high withdrawal.

Major depressive disorder and bipolar disorder are somewhat more challenging with regard to finding ties to temperament, as both conditions are, by definition, cyclic. Individuals with these diagnoses tend to move in and out of "episodes." In bipolar disorder, depressive and manic episodes appear diametrically opposed to each other: manic episodes are characterized by elevated moods and high energy, and depressive episodes manifest the reverse pattern. Such oscillations seem to weaken the case for associations with temperamental traits, which by definition should be enduring. As discussed in Chapter 3, most temperament assessment measures don't address the question of temperament variability and the degree to which a child's temperament can change from day to day or even moment to moment. Nonetheless, the question of temperamental associations with bipolar disorder has received some attention. Hagop Akiskal, a psychiatrist at the University of California–San Diego, has been studying bipolar disorder for decades with an interest in a potential link with a "hyperthymic" temperament—energetic, talkative, and easily bored (Akiskal et al., 1995). In many ways, this description is quite similar to the confident type described in Chapter 2.

The matter is further complicated by the intense debate related to the definition of pediatric bipolar disorder. Specifically, the debate is about whether or not children who tend to be nonepisodically irritable and explosive should be included in the diagnosis. Some researchers have argued that these children are better understood as having severe and comorbid disruptive behavior disorders, such as ADHD and ODD (Carlson, 2009). Indeed, it has been shown that children with pediatric bipolar disorder share temperamental characteristics with ADHD children (high novelty seeking, low persistence and reward dependence) relative to controls (Tillman et al., 2003). If the bipolar "not otherwise specified" (NOS) children are pulled out of the bipolar disorder category and diagnosed perhaps with new DSM-5 disruptive mood dysregulation disorder, it is quite likely that strong temperament associations will be found with this specific group of children. In the end, what may be different in the case of major depressive disorder and bipolar disorder, in contrast to less cyclic disorders, is not existence of links to temperament but rather the mechanisms that underlie this association.

Obsessive-Compulsive Disorder

Obsessive-compulsive disorder (OCD) is an anxiety disorder that contains some unique features, including specific rituals such as checking or washing that are performed to diminish the anxiety associated with reoccurring thoughts. Although obsessive-compulsive behavior is not typically designated as a temperament trait in and of itself, obsessive-compulsive personality is currently described as one of the core personality disorders in DSM-IV. Another characteristic of OCD that suggests some temperament links is that many individuals who do not qualify for an OCD diagnosis manifest moderate levels of obsessive-compulsive behavior (Althoff et al., 2009; Apter et al., 1996; Rettew, 2007). Young children in particular tend to show high levels of compulsive behavior (Zohar & Felz, 2001), as anyone who has let a 3-year-old's peas touch the macaroni and cheese would know.

Surprisingly, few studies have actually investigated the association between OCD and the major temperament dimensions. In a mixed study of adolescents and younger children, Ivarsson and Winge-Westholm

(2004) found high levels of shyness and negative emotionality, with low levels of activity, among those diagnosed with OCD. Studies of adults with OCD have also demonstrated associations with the dimension of harm avoidance (Ettelt et al., 2008; Kim, Kang, & Kim, 2009). All of these elements lead us to suspect strong links between temperament and OCD, but the topic requires further research.

Substance Abuse

The connections between substance abuse disorders and temperament might be less apparent than they are for other disorders. Whereas most psychiatric disorders are described in terms of behavioral traits (e.g., social anxiety disorder sounds a lot like extreme shyness), substance abuse disorders are typically described in terms of concrete behaviors.

The commonly heard "self-medication hypothesis" posits that individuals use substances in an attempt to regulate emotional states that are difficult to manage, and these states are usually described as psychiatric symptoms rather than temperament or personality traits. From the self-medication hypothesis, it follows that individuals with extreme levels of temperament dimensions or psychiatric symptoms would be more prone to use substances that help shift that emotional state to a more tolerable level. Moreover, one might expect there to be a logical connection between a person's temperament and the choice of substance that is used. More anxious individuals, for example, would be predicted to use anxiety-reducing substances like benzodiazepines, whereas less energetic people would choose stimulating drugs. While there is ample evidence that individuals with psychiatric disorders are at higher risk for substance abuse, there is little evidence supporting the second part of the hypothesis related to substance choice (Chutuape & de Wit, 1995). In keeping with the self-medication hypothesis, there is good evidence that a high level of negative emotionality is predictive of later substance use, especially alcohol use (Kuntsche et al., 2006). The Dunedin Study from New Zealand also found that children classified as inhibited at age 3 (in a way slightly different than Kagan's definition) were more likely to have alcohol problems as young adults (Caspi et al., 1996).

At the same time, there is also strong evidence that people with disinhibited temperament profiles are at greater risk for substance use. In these cases, the underlying mechanism may not be an attempt to diminish internal feelings but rather to enhance them (Cooper et al., 1995). High approach behavior, as measured by traits such as extraversion, novelty, or thrill seeking, has been found to predict later substance use (Cloninger, Sigvardsson, & Bohman, 1988; Jackson & Sher, 2003).

In an attempt to refine our understanding of the links between temperament and substance use, many researchers are trying to look beyond simple associations and test for more complex interactions between temperament and environmental variables such as stressful life events, socioeconomic status, and demographic factors such as age and sex. In a study published in the *Journal of Addictive Behaviors*, we examined whether the link between certain profiles of adolescent personality and young adult alcohol use depends on socioeconomic status (Ayer et al., 2011). Results revealed that dysregulated (high disinhibition and high boredom susceptibility) and extraverted (low neuroticism, high extraversion) profiles were related to later drinking, but the associations were not correlated with average neighborhood income.

The term "addictive personality" gained popularity after a National Academy of Sciences report in 1983 that was authored by psychologist Alan Lang. Over the years, the term has survived more in the popular media than in scientific circles, where it continues to be controversial. Components of an "addictive personality" include characteristics such as impulsivity, nonconformity, insecurity, and feelings of isolation. Most researchers interested in this area prefer to use updated personality terminology and instruments in their investigations.

The story of temperament and substance use is likely to become more complicated in the future, due to the varied effects of different substances on the brain, the increasing complexity of environmental variables such as poverty and culture, and changing aspects of the substances themselves such as their legality at different ages. For example, teenagers with higher levels of negative emotionality and effortful control might be tempted to drink alcohol but don't because they fear getting into trouble and because it's illegal. These individuals might therefore show little association between the trait of negative emotionality and drinking until adulthood, when alcohol becomes legal and this barrier is eliminated. Further research will hopefully illuminate pathways that could provide methods for early intervention.

Eating Disorders

Individuals with eating disorders are preoccupied with their body image and often have distorted perceptions of how they look. The two main categories of eating disorders are anorexia nervosa and bulimia nervosa. In an effort to be thin, people with anorexia may restrict their food intake to the point of becoming malnourished; those with bulimia do compensatory behaviors such as self-induced vomiting to avoid absorbing calories that have been consumed, sometimes in large binges. Although the public perception of the main difference between the two conditions is the presence or absence of purging behavior, the actual primary difference according to diagnostic criteria is body weight. A diagnosis of anorexia, but not bulimia, requires that a person be markedly underweight. For the many individuals who struggle with eating disorder symptoms but don't fit neatly into the anorexia or bulimia categories, there is also a DSM-IV diagnosis called "eating disorder not otherwise specified." Eating disorders are much more common in females, and they carry a fairly high mortality rate due to suicide or to medical complications resulting from excessive food restriction or purging.

As with many psychiatric conditions, the current diagnostic structure for eating disorders is unsatisfying to many, and efforts are underway to classify eating disorders in more meaningful terms. The fact that patients often switch between anorexia and bulimia suggests to some that the two labels may be phases of the same illness (Eddy et al., 2002). One approach to improving the validity of eating disorder diagnoses has been to use personality profiles (Westen & Harnden-Fischer, 2001; Wonderlich et al., 2005). Although findings are not entirely consistent, three different personality profiles tend to be associated with eating disorders (Wildes et al., 2011). The "undercontrolled" subtype is characterized by high impulsivity and low regulatory abilities; the "overcontrolled" subtype is characterized by low impulsivity and behavioral restraint; and the third subtype does not manifest particularly high or low degrees of any of the major personality dimensions. Grouping patients with eating disorders along these three personality-based categories, rather than using DSM-based divisions, leads to stronger associations with clinical parameters such as risk of hospitalization and likelihood of relapse (with the undercontrolled group having the worst prognosis).

Psychotic Disorders

It is difficult to imagine a continuum of psychosis, or some kind of spectrum of psychotic symptoms that would lend itself to strong temperament or personality correlations. An auditory hallucination, for example, is either present or not present. Psychotic disorders tend to affect older individuals, with typical symptom onset in late adolescence or early adulthood. Because this is beyond the age range of most temperament studies, relevant literature on the subject must be found in the realm of personality research.

Despite these limitations, however, associations between psychotic disorders and temperament/personality are a worthwhile pursuit. First, the debilitating nature of schizophrenia and other primary psychotic disorders has led to large research investments on the part of the National Institute of Mental Health and other public and private funding organizations. This research has revealed some important clues about the causes of psychotic disorders—information that could provide a backdoor approach to a deeper understanding of the biological underpinnings of personality. Second, although symptoms such as hallucinations or delusions are often the most salient part of psychotic disorders (the so-called positive symptoms of schizophrenia), elements such as affective flattening and lack of motivation often exist side by side with the positive symptoms. These elements could have important links to personality and temperament.

One clue that certain aspects of psychotic disorders lie on a continuum comes from studies that assessed first-degree relatives of individuals with psychotic disorders such as schizophrenia. The Roscommon Family Study carried out by Ken Kendler and colleagues 20 years ago examined relatives of people with schizophrenia. They found that although most relatives did not meet criteria for schizophrenia themselves, many did show somewhat odd, eccentric, or avoidant behavior, consistent with various personality disorders (Kendler et al., 1993). A more recent study reported that the monozygotic cotwins of individuals who later developed schizophrenia had more abnormal personality traits than controls, even though these individuals did not develop psychotic illness themselves (Picchioni et al., 2010). This was not found among dizygotic twins. A recent study that used statistical models to test categorical, continuous, and hybrid models of psychotic symptoms in a large Australian epidemiologic sample also found evidence that the continuum perspective provided the best fit to the data (Wright et al., 2013).

Some evidence indicates that individuals who later develop psychotic illnesses begin to struggle years before overt symptoms develop, particularly with regard to social functioning and relationships (Malmberg et al., 1998). Less is known about temperament links in childhood, due in part to the relative rarity of schizophrenia and the difficulty in prospectively assessing a large enough cohort of children who will develop the illness later in life. One fascinating study found a way around this difficulty by having the families of patients with schizophrenia bring in home movies taken during the first five years of life (Walker & Lewine, 1990). Videos were also obtained from control families, and the films were coded by raters blind to the subjects' clinical status. Although personality or temperament was not measured directly, statistically significant differences were found in the behavior of children who later developed schizophrenia: girls showed less frequent expression of joy, a sign of lower extraversion or surgency perhaps, while boys displayed increased expressions of negative emotions, potentially indicating higher levels of negative affectivity. A subsequent study using similar methods in an older group reported similar findings (Schiffman et al., 2004).

In summary, accumulating reports point to temperamental differences between people with and without psychotic disorders. Some of these traits may appear in childhood, sometimes decades before the onset of full psychotic symptoms. This line of research would be enhanced through the use of actual temperament or personality instruments. The nature of these associations, specifically the question of whether these early traits represent a cause or an early effect of later illness, is addressed in the next chapter.

Autistic Spectrum Disorders

Autism, like psychotic disorders, does not suffer from a public perception that the disorder lacks substance. Even the harshest skeptics of child psychiatry recognize that autism is something real. Indeed, certain groups have advocated that it be recategorized as a neurological disorder rather than a psychiatric diagnosis. While such a switch would be scientifically meaningless, the sentiment does suggest that autism might be an arena where the distinction between illness and nonillness would be well defined and where true separations between a disorder and a trait could be found.

Autism spectrum disorders are developmental conditions that involve significant social, communication, and behavioral challenges. They are much more prevalent in boys than in girls, with symptoms typically beginning before the age of 3 and generally lasting in some form throughout a person's life. The diagnosis for DSM-5 now consists of a single autism spectrum disorder category that replaces more distinct conditions such as Asperger's disorder and pervasive developmental disorder not otherwise specified. When scientists quantitatively measure core autistic symptoms such as social skills, reciprocal communication, and preoccupied thoughts using instruments such as the Social Responsiveness Scale, the spectrum is found to continue even further into the nonpathological range, similar to results in children with ADHD (Constantino & Todd, 2003). Thus, even here, there is no obvious boundary to guide a clinician in defining where true autism begins. Indeed, various features of autism, including a lack of interest and anxiety in social situations, strong need for routine and predictability, and a tendency to become easily upset, sound very much like extremely low levels of sociability and novelty seeking, with high levels of negative emotionality. These associations have led some researchers to propose, provocatively, that autism reflects an "extreme male brain" and that the different patterns of brain organization seen in autism may result from excess male hormone exposure in utero (Baron-Cohen, Knickmeyer, & Belmonte, 2005). There are surprisingly few direct studies of temperament and autism, although those that have been published are consistent in showing a temperament profile that includes low approach and low positive affect, high negative emotionality, low sensitivity to social rewards, and low emotional and attentional regulatory abilities (De Pauw et al., 2011; Garon et al., 2009).

Summary

There is quite strong evidence that the majority of psychiatric symptoms exist in a dimensional form (Hudziak et al., 2007; Krueger, Watson, & Barlow, 2005). Once we allow for the possibility that psychiatric disorders might be related to a child's intrinsic nature, the results of many studies seem rather obvious: Anxiety disorders are related to high negative emotionality; autism is related to low sociability; depression is related to low extraversion/surgency; and virtually every diagnosis, it seems, appears to be related to low effortful control. This overwhelming amount of scientific evidence, however, does not end the discussion; it merely takes it to another level. Rather than asking whether temperament is related to psychopathology, the challenge going forward is to discover how temperament is related to psychopathology when it comes to development, neurobiology, and early intervention. Is social anxiety disorder really just shyness turned up high, or is there something meaningfully different between the two entities that may not be detected by a simple questionnaire? Are the genetic and environmental factors that make one child somewhat active the same factors that are amplified in children who are very active, or do a few different ingredients make the key difference in developmental trajectories? These questions about the relations between temperament and psychopathology constitute a new frontier in psychiatric research that could change not only how we define illnesses but also how we treat or even prevent them.

Chapter 6

Spectrums, Risk Factors, and Scars

With the link between temperament and psychiatric disorders well established, the next step is to understand the mechanisms through which these two domains are intertwined. One possibility is that the difference between a temperament trait and a psychiatric symptom is only a matter of degree. If this is the case, then our task as experts in the field is to find a reasonable threshold between traits and disorders, which would serve as a basis for making decisions such as whether or not to prescribe medication. Another possibility is that traits and symptoms look similar on the outside but actually have clear differences when it comes to their underlying neurobiology. In this scenario, a psychiatric disorder could easily be misdiagnosed as just a temperament trait (e.g., "She isn't clinically depressed, she's just a miserable person"). This process could also work in the other direction, with psychiatric disorders masquerading as temperament or personality traits.

Careers have been made arguing these angles. On the one hand, many child temperament specialists condemn the application of psychiatric labels and spread the reassuring message that most so-called disorders are actually variations in temperament. On the other hand, pharmaceutical companies are now marketing drugs directly to the public with warnings that what you think is just your personality or temperament may actually be a clinical condition with a readily available remedy, so "ask your doctor." After one company's antidepressant medication, Zoloft, was approved for treating social anxiety disorder, Pfizer ran an advertisement showing a timid woman in a hat that covered her eyes. The caption read, "Is she just shy, or is it something else?" This appeal to the public illustrates that the seemingly academic discussion of temperament-psychopathology boundaries actually has quite profound practical implications. Not only does the temperament-psychopathology link get at the very heart of what a psychiatric disorder actually is, but there is also the critical issue of intervention. A psychiatric disorder, unlike a personality or temperament trait, is considered something we must treat, not something we accept. Lowering the bar for a disorder even slightly can lead to the sudden appearance of millions of new people with a psychiatric condition requiring clinical attention.

Item Overlap: Method Problem or Theory Problem?

In many of the studies cited in Chapter 5, including some from our own lab, the researchers took a sample of individuals, asked them to fill out one instrument that measures temperament and another that measures psychiatric symptoms, and then calculated the degree of association between the two scores using statistics like a correlation coefficient. A variation on the theme might be to take one group of youth with one particular DSM disorder and another group of youth with a different DSM disorder (or no disorder at all), give them all a temperament scale, and then look at the mean difference in temperament scores.

Most of these studies reported very strong associations and arrived at the conclusion that temperamental traits and psychiatric disorders are separate but related entities. The reports invariably describe and cite the particular instruments that were used to measure both traits and symptoms, but due to space and copyright limitations, the actual questionnaires and scales are rarely published. Therefore, it is difficult for a reader to challenge the overall conclusion.

Getting into the fine print, however, one begins to notice that the language used on the items of the temperament scale bear a remarkable similarity to the items on the psychopathology scale. Could this simple fact be a source of the associations? According to some estimates, the descriptions of more than one-third of psychiatric symptoms overlap directly with language used to describe temperament traits (Lemery, Essex, & Smider, 2002). For example, the phrase "losing one's temper" appears in questionnaire items that load onto the temperament dimension of novelty seeking, in quantitative psychopathology scales of aggression, and in the DSM-IV criteria for oppositional defiant disorder.

In 1993, Joseph Biederman and his colleagues published one of the first clinical follow-up reports for children with behavioral inhibition (BI). The study measured BI (but not psychiatric disorders) when the subjects were toddlers and psychiatric disorders (but not BI) around three years later. After finding high rates of psychiatric disorders at follow-up, the researchers concluded that children with BI are at high risk for developing childhood-onset anxiety disorders. To recap, BI is a temperament trait that involves a predisposition to be fearful and avoidant of new people, objects, and situations. In Biederman's analyses, avoidant disorder was found at elevated rates at follow-up. The diagnosis called avoidant disorder is now subsumed under other diagnoses in DSM-5, but the DSM-III-R (American Psychiatric Association, 1987) definition was "excessive shrinking from contact with unfamiliar people." This similarity then begs the question of whether avoidant disorder truly was something that developed from BI, or simply a new name for BI behavior three years later. From this study alone, it is difficult to tell whether or not these different labels relate to meaningful differences or are simply semantic variations of the same thing. In an editorial on the subject in the *Journal of the American Academy of Child and Adolescent Psychiatry* (Rettew, 2010), a food analogy seemed apt. At what point does fudge require enough flour to become a brownie and then a cake?

In one attempt to disentangle the content overlap between temperament and psychopathology rating scales, the investigators calculated the association between traits and symptoms after removing from the analyses any items that overlapped too closely (Lengua, West, & Sandler, 1998). In general, the links between temperament and behavioral problems persisted, indicating that the associations tend to go deeper than semantics. However, the theoretical problem is not solved. First, such procedures end up gutting items from both temperament and psychopathology scales, which then leaves their structural integrity in doubt. Second, the act of removing items with similar language does not necessarily prove that the remaining ones map onto a distinct construct.

The issue of item overlap presents not simply a methodological problem; it is a theoretical problem as well. How can we insist two entities are really distinct when common language is used for them both? Simply calling one area temperament and another psychopathology based upon the title of the instrument being used is not going to be enough. To be able to say confidently that we are or are not talking about a single entity requires looking beyond the names of our rating scales.

Separating Temperament From Clinical Disorder: Impairment

The complexities of item overlap and gradually increasing levels of symptoms haven't stopped intrepid psychiatrists from delivering a firm message on the distinction between traits and disorders. During my psychiatry and child psychiatry training, we were told that the difference comes down to a single word: *impairment*. If a particular behavior or set of behaviors leads to a reduction in the individual's functional ability or leads to significant distress, then it's a disorder. Without impairment or significant distress, it's only a trait.

Take obsessive-compulsive behavior, which shows a broad range of intensity across the population. As discussed in Chapter 5, many individuals show at least some degree of obsessive-compulsive behavior. Common manifestations are the need for items to be in a very particular arrangement and excessive thinking about germs, cleanliness, or bad things that might happen. Compulsive behaviors emerge from these obsessions: frequent washing or cleaning, elaborate checking and rechecking rituals, scrupulous arranging of objects in a very particular way, and so on. For some, the obsessive-compulsive behavior is isolated to a particular arena (e.g., handwashing), while others have a more generalized need for order, routine, and repetition throughout all aspects of life. The latter group has been casually called "anal," referring to the now-antiquated theory that such behavior resulted from overly aggressive toilet training. Many of these individuals are quite functional and seem perfectly happy the way they are, so they do not meet the disorder criteria (the presence of impairment or distress) and their obsessive-compulsive behavior is considered a trait. A diagnosis of obsessive-compulsive personality disorder, a sort of compromise between a trait and a disorder, still requires a clear demonstration that the behaviors are maladaptive.

From a practical standpoint, the system seems to work pretty well. A person who needs help to overcome washing rituals that consume hours of his day and prevent him from working or having friends receives the

OCD diagnosis, whereas eccentric Aunt Susie, who is employed and quite content to continue checking all the windows and locks exactly 17 times before going to bed has some obsessive-compulsive traits.

Unfortunately, using impairment and distress to separate trait from disorder is not a complete solution, especially when children are considered. The first big problem has to do with the concept of impairment. Even when particular behaviors are acknowledged to exist along a continuum, impairment is binary: it is either present or absent. Upon closer examination, however, impairment too exists dimensionally, and the degree of impairment often moves in lockstep with the severity of the behavior or symptom of concern. People who are very happy with no depressive symptoms have no impairment, those with some depressive symptoms have a little impairment, and so on, all the way up to people who become completely incapacitated by overwhelming degrees of depression (Judd, Schettler, & Akiskal, 2002). In this model, both the symptoms and the impairment are moving targets, and one is left with the choice of allowing any degree of impairment to "count" diagnostically, which means a huge increase in the number of people who qualify for a psychiatric diagnosis, or the choice of having to make a highly subjective judgment of when there exists enough impairment to be clinically meaningful.

Another important question is who gets to decide whether or not impairment exists: the patient, the parent, the clinician, all of the above? Is it valid for a college student in an honors English class with an average attention span to claim impairment and the need for a stimulant medication because he can't sit down and read for several hours at a stretch? When it comes to children, many behaviors that severely bother a parent or a teacher don't inconvenience the child in the slightest.

Finally, the environment can be manipulated to minimize impairment and distress. In a famous cartoon, a patient tells his doctor, "It hurts when I do this." The doctor replies, "Stop doing that." The removal of certain expectations or requirements can eliminate the presence of impairment. If a child is not required to stay in his or her seat at school, for example, then the impairment associated with the ADHD criterion of being unable to stay in one's seat will be hard to meet. Does that mean that the diagnosis of ADHD is simply the product of an outdated approach to school? Likely not, but the reliance on impairment as the gatekeeper between traits and illness appears shakier with each close examination.

Separating Temperament From Clinical Disorder: The Usual State
Another strategy that clinicians use to separate traits from disorders is the "usual state" clause. That is, behavioral tendencies that exist as part of a person's baseline mode are considered traits, whereas thoughts, feelings, and behaviors that depart from this usual state are considered disorders. Many mood disorders, as defined in DSM-IV, involve symptoms that occur during a distinct time period that represents a clear "change from previous functioning." Certain psychotic disorders may be exceptions to this rule, but even these diagnoses usually require a specific onset after which the patient began acting differently.

Once again, however, the usual state strategy becomes fragile with additional scrutiny. Some disorders do not have the usual state clause in their diagnostic criteria, including common conditions that affect children such as ADHD. Many anxiety disorders such as OCD also do not require the demarcated onset. Furthermore, the "change from the usual state" criterion has been challenged in pediatric psychiatry, most famously in bipolar disorder, where many clinicians have relaxed the requirement of a sustained shift in mood that lasts for several days because mood may change for only hours or even minutes. As reviewed in Chapter 3, the idea that temperament traits always persist across time and across situations has also been challenged. Study after study have shown that temperament and personality dimensions are generally stable but can fluctuate a fair amount, especially during childhood and adolescence. Moreover, there is accumulating evidence that behavior can change markedly from situation to situation in response to the qualities and demands of different environments. These fluctuations do not seem to be a simple artifact of informant bias in which observers of child behavior underreport or overreport certain traits. Instead, many children are truly different in different situations (Rettew, van Oort, et al., 2011). While some temperament purists might argue that some situations represent an artificial state and children will later return to their "temperamental equilibrium," it is becoming difficult to deny the level of behavioral variability that occurs across different settings.

Models of How Temperament and Psychopathology Are Related
A number of models have been proposed to explain the relationship between temperament and psychopathology that do not rely on impair-

ment or changes from the usual state (Clark, Watson, & Mineka, 1994). The four most common mechanisms have been labeled continuum, risk or vulnerability, scar, and pathoplastic (Rettew, 2009), and each will be summarized in turn.

The Continuum Model

As old ideas about the separations between temperament and disorders crumble, some mental health professionals are left with the conclusion that the only thing that really distinguishes a trait from a disorder is the level of the behavior in question. Quite simply, the continuum model holds that a trait becomes a disorder if there is too much or too little of that trait, according to a somewhat arbitrary threshold.

Attention has been viewed as a quantitative trait that crosses into the territory of a disorder (i.e., ADHD) at some threshold; this ability and ADHD thus appear to fit the continuum model quite well. In conjunction with the Netherlands Twin Registry, researchers examined more than 15,000 Dutch twins at 7, 10, and 12 years old (Lubke et al., 2009). After obtaining attention scores using the Child Behavior Checklist (Achenbach & Rescorla, 2000), the data were analyzed using two types of statistical grouping models: latent class models that assume discrete categories of individuals, and factor mixture models that incorporate dimensional differences in severity. The factor mixture models were found to fit the data best in all three age groups, and the authors stated that their results suggest that DSM-IV ADHD is best conceptualized as existing on a severity continuum rather than as discrete diagnostic categories.

When it comes to intellectual functioning, the continuum framework is already in place within some parts of the current diagnostic structure. The intelligence quotient (IQ) is widely accepted as a dimensional quality, and individuals with an IQ below 70 are diagnosed with mental retardation or intellectual disability. Further designations of mild, moderate, severe, and profound mental retardation correspond to specific IQ ranges. These IQ thresholds may not hold as much scientific meaning as we might like, but they work as a compromise between the true quantitative nature of the variable and the practical need to work within categories. One analogy that has been used by many temperament researchers is bottled salsa, which is marketed as mild, medium, or hot, despite the fact that everyone knows the degree of spiciness exists along a continuum.

How well does the continuum model hold up in other arenas? We examined this issue in child anxiety, with a focus on the condition of childhood generalized anxiety disorder, or GAD (Rettew, Doyle, et al., 2006). According to the DSM-IV, children and adults who worry excessively about everyday things are candidates for GAD. The distinguishing feature of the disorder is not the content of the worry but rather the extent of it. In GAD, the worries can't be turned off and can lead to associated features such as poor sleep, irritability, and somatic symptoms such as muscle aches.

On the surface, GAD sounds a lot like very high levels of negative emotionality or harm avoidance and thus may be an excellent place to investigate how well the continuum model holds for both temperament and diagnosis. If GAD is really just harm avoidance turned way up, then beyond some threshold score for harm avoidance, the vast majority of subjects should also meet DSM criteria for GAD. In the study, we used a statistical procedure called receiver operating characteristic analysis to quantify this relation and help us establish a threshold score based on prediction sensitivity (how often subjects with a sufficiently high harm avoidance score meet criteria for GAD) and specificity (how often subjects with harm avoidance scores lower than the threshold don't meet criteria for GAD). Our results indicated a very high degree of overlap between harm avoidance and GAD, although perhaps not to the degree that would support a pure continuum model between the two entities (see Figure 6.1).

There are many more individuals who meet criteria for GAD on the right-hand side of the graph, indicating higher harm avoidance scores, than on the left, but the difference is not straightforward. For example, there were several children who manifested high levels of harm avoidance but didn't meet criteria for GAD, and many individuals who met GAD criteria but had only moderate harm avoidance levels. These cases could reflect measurement inaccuracies, or they could also indicate that even when a disorder seems like an extreme level of a temperament trait, there may be more to the story.

Looking at this simple graph became a turning point in my way of thinking. Coming into this area of research, my hunch was that temperament and psychopathology were really a unitary concept that had been kept apart by tradition and history rather than science. I expected that a few key studies would be enough to convince the world to build a system

FIGURE 6.1

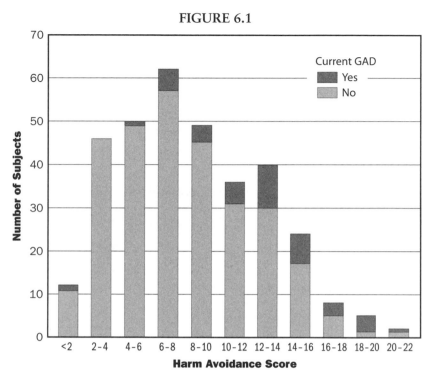

Harm avoidance scores in children and adolescents follow a distribution similar to other quantitative traits such as height or IQ. The lighter shading indicates subjects who have DSM-IV diagnosed generalized anxiety disorder (GAD). A continuum model would predict that after some cutoff point for harm avoidance, the vast majority of subjects would also meet criteria for GAD. The actual pattern reveals substantial but not complete overlap between harm avoidance and GAD, suggesting that other models may also need to be considered (adapted and used with permission from Rettew et al., 2006).

that blends temperament and psychopathology along a single borderless scale. While I can't say that I have completely given up on that aspiration, the data are telling us that the story just isn't that simple.

Today, not many people in the field endorse a straightforward continuum model, especially between a single temperament dimension and a single disorder. For a number of psychiatric conditions, there is simply not enough content similarity between the disorder and the traits as they are defined. Certain conditions such as substance use or psychosis seem to lack a corresponding temperament trait to latch onto. Other disorders, such as depression, seem to be connected to more than one associated trait (more on this idea later), which definitely complicates a continuum perspective. However, even disorders that appear to be prime candidates for a spectrum model, such as GAD or ADHD, can't quite put it together convincingly. This fact does not deny the quantitative nature of psychiatric symptoms across the range of disorders, but clearly other types of models need to be considered.

Many such ideas have now come forward. Table 6.1 displays some of the major hypotheses for describing how temperament and psychopathology may be related to each other. Aside from the continuum model, the following mechanisms have also been proposed and have some degree of empirical support.

TABLE 6.1. Mechanisms of Association between Temperament and Psychiatric Disorders		
Mechanism	Description	Possible Example
Continuum	Psychopathology and temperamental traits are the same thing with psychopathology representing the extreme end of the continuum	Activity level and ADHD
Risk	Psychopathology and temperamental traits are different entities with temperament an important risk factor for psychopathology	Novelty seeking and drug abuse
Scar	Psychopathology causes differences in temperamental traits	Autism and sociability
Bidirectional	Psychopathology and temperamental traits are different but mutually interact and influence each other	Extraversion and major depression
Common Pathway	Psychopathology and temperamental traits originate from common factors but diverge with other influences	Negative emotionality and anxiety disorders

The Risk Model

Under a risk or vulnerability model, temperament and psychopathology are inherently different entities, but temperament is a risk factor that influences the development of future psychiatric disorders. This model has been strongly advocated in the case of behavioral inhibition (BI) leading to later anxiety disorders, most specifically social anxiety disorder. Kagan and his colleagues have maintained that BI itself may predispose a child to later anxiety disorders but is clearly distinct from them. The first manifestations of BI can be seen as early as a few months of age or perhaps even earlier (Kagan, 1994). How could an observable psycho-pathology be present at that age?

I was involved in a study that piloted an intervention for preschool children with BI, which illustrates some of the difficulty with this model as it relates to behavioral inhibition (Hirshfeld-Becker et al., 2008). This study was designed to help prevent future psychiatric disorders: one of the Holy Grails of our field. The intervention was called Being Brave, and the researchers worked with both parents and children using techniques similar to cognitive-behavioral programs that are used for older children with full-fledged anxiety diagnoses. Recruitment focused on the children of parents who were being treated for anxiety at the clinic. Both temperament and psychiatric disorders were assessed before and after the 20-session intervention. The idea was to find a group of young children with BI who did not already have a diagnosable anxiety disorder, but it turned out that most of the young children with BI did in fact qualify for an anxiety disorder diagnosis at baseline. The study proceeded with the BI sample, many of whom also had an anxiety disorder. The Being Brave sessions did result in a significant decrease in the number of anxiety disorders and anxiety symptoms. Temperament measures of observer-rated BI and parent-reported shyness, however, were not significantly different after the intervention, indicating that inhibited temperament or shyness did not change over the treatment or follow-up intervals. The results were interpreted as evidence that the intervention does not change temperament but rather prevents a child's temperamental inhibition from causing symptomatic and functional impairment (marked by DSM-IV disorders) that interferes with developmental tasks such as meeting and socializing with new children. Notably, however, the parent-rated inhibition (but not clinician ratings) did significantly drop after the intervention and probably would have become statistically significant with a larger sample.

For DSM disorders that do not bear descriptive similarities to the temperament dimensions themselves, the risk model can be used more easily. Eating disorders such as anorexia or bulimia, for example, don't square up with particular temperament dimensions—"body shape preoccupation" isn't considered a temperament trait. Consequently, temperament dimensions such as negative emotionality and regulatory ability, which do show associations with eating disorders, are interpreted as risk factors rather than low-grade manifestations of the disorder itself.

The Scar Model

Turn the risk model upside-down, and you get the scar model. Once again, temperament and psychopathology are considered to be separate concepts, but here the disorder leads to temperament change rather than the other way around. From this perspective, the pathological processes that cause psychiatric symptoms hijack the brain's temperament and personality pathways, leading to changes in traits like impulsivity, extraversion, and negative emotionality. Scar, in this instance, does not necessarily refer to actual scar tissue but rather to pathological processes of the psychiatric disorder that alter the brain circuitry involved in temperament and personality.

In geriatric psychiatry, personality changes often precede, by years, the development of Alzheimer's disease—a classic example of the scar model. Specifically, the amyloid plaques and neurofibrillary tangles that develop in the brain, which eventually lead to profound memory disturbance and confusion, first cause more subtle personality changes such as increased passivity and irritability (Copeland et al., 2003). Another arena where the scar model is invoked is traumatic brain injury (TBI). The story of Phineas Gage, the railroad construction foreman who suffered a tremendous head injury in 1848, appears in many psychology and neurology texts. An explosion drove an iron rod through his head, damaging much of his left frontal lobe. While he survived the accident, the once hard-working and responsible man became extremely disinhibited and impulsive. It is now well known that head injury from any source, including work accidents, sports collisions, and combat, can result in profound and irreversible changes in an individual's personality.

Unlike TBI or Alzheimer's disease, where the pathology is visible and defined, core illnesses such as schizophrenia or depression are still not described in terms of the underlying brain pathology. Nonetheless, it seems plausible that a scar mechanism may be at work in some cases, particularly in disorders that lead to severe disability. Schizophrenia, for example, often strikes in adolescence and then begins a slow but progressive decline over time. The earliest part of the illness, often referred to as the prodromal phase, is marked by a number of changes (Cornblatt et al., 2003) that certainly fall in the temperament or personality realm and would be picked up on instruments designed to measure traits. Increased irritability, declining sociability and spontaneity, heightened fear that can progress to paranoia—all of these traits are subsumed under the domain of temperament and personality and seem to be part of the tragic progression toward hallucinations and delusions.

The scar model is not commonly discussed in children's mental health. Autism, however, is a disorder that may drag temperamental traits into its operations. Unlike schizophrenia or Alzheimer's disease, in which observable personality change marks the beginning of the illness process, the symptoms and associated temperament traits of autism tend to be present from the start. While there is quite a lot of heterogeneity in autistic symptoms, high negative affectivity, low extraversion, and very low sociability are frequently the traits that tip parents off to a potential problem, as these traits are typically present before language deficits appear. Although the central pathological process of autism remains unknown, many experts believe it involves aberrant development of the different layers of the brain and abnormalities in how brain regions are organized and interconnected (Wegiel et al., 2010). In contrast to localized brain damage, the global pathology present in autism would be expected to involve a wide range of neurological functioning, including temperament.

Cyclical disorders may be important in our efforts to understand how brain "disease" processes can impact temperament. A person with bipolar disorder, for example, can be doing just fine one week and then rapidly develop symptoms of mania the next week. Manic symptoms can include grandiosity and racing thoughts, as well as temperamental aspects such as elevated mood, increased impulsivity and distractibility, and disinhibition. Furthermore, the same individual may then suffer a depressive episode characterized by the exact opposite features, before returning to the usual baseline. Researchers have found a number of baseline temperamental differences among individuals with mood disorders compared to control groups (Akiskal et al., 2006). The scar model may not be appropriate here due to the fact that, although disease processes are the engine behind the dramatic temperament change, the "scar" may not be present as the person returns to the usual state after the manic or depressive episode is over.

Once again, however, the scar model would be much easier to support if we were able to characterize the specific brain changes involved in manic or depressive episodes. In the 1990s, the emergence of pediatric autoimmune neuropsychiatric disorders associated with streptococcus (PANDAS) offered a glimmer of such hope. The startling hypothesis that some childhood psychiatric disorders (OCD in particular) may be due to an autoimmune process emerged from the National Institute of Mental Health in the early 1990s. I happened to be working there as a research assistant in my first "real job" after college. I wish I could say that I chose that research position due to the extraordinary science being done, but the truth is that I stumbled into the job with little appreciation of the magnitude of work that was taking place there.

The story begins with Sydenham's chorea, a movement disorder that results from a bacterial (streptococcal) infection (Swedo, 1994). In genetically susceptible individuals, the antibodies that the body produces to fight off the infection cross-react with certain neurons in a region of the brain called the basal ganglia, which is involved in the successful execution of motor function (among other functions). The cross-reaction results in local inflammation and abnormal functioning of that brain region, which in turn causes abnormal movements that are usually temporary.

After the infection but usually before the movement disturbances, many of these children would manifest rather sudden behavioral changes, becoming much more anxious and obsessive. In contrast to children with anxiety disorders or those whose history indicated a fairly anxious baseline temperament, some of these children literally seemed to wake up one day with a different personality. Furthermore, these changes seemed to be attributable to specific autoimmune processes in specific brain regions—processes that were occasionally visible on MRI scans. Like the movement disturbances, the obsessive-compulsive features typically faded out over weeks to months, but occasionally they persisted. In these cases, some children improved not with typical psychiatric treatment but with autoimmune disorder interventions such as plasmapharesis, a process that removes large proteins, including antibodies, from the bloodstream.

The existence and precise mechanisms underlying PANDAS remain debatable to this day, as many aspects of Swedo's findings have not been consistently replicated. The PANDAS story, as well as that of PANS (pediatric acute-onset neuropsychiatric syndrome; Swedo, Leckman, & Rose, 2012), are good ones, but the primary purpose of this chapter is to illustrate the potential mechanisms through which psychiatric illness and temperament are intertwined. Suffice it to say that many examples within psychiatry suggest that changes in temperament and personality often seem to go along for the ride when pathological brain processes develop.

The Pathoplastic or Bidirectional Model

A hybrid of the scar and risk models, the pathoplastic or bidirectional model holds that temperament and psychopathology are inherently different entities, but the direction of causality can work in either direction, depending on the disorder, the trait, or even the individual. These arrows of influence can even work cyclically within the same person. For example, a temperament trait such as high negative emotionality puts a person at risk for a major depressive episode when he or she experiences a major stressor or loss. The depressive episode involves abnormal brain functioning that takes on a neurobiological life of its own, in turn altering the brain circuitry involved in certain temperament traits, such as extraversion. For another individual, high levels of novelty seeking might increase the likelihood that he or she will experiment with drugs such as cannabis, which can lead to psychotic symptoms in genetically susceptible people (Caspi et al., 2005). Those psychotic symptoms might affect the brain circuitry involved in social functioning, leading to decreased sociability as measured by a temperament or personality scale.

These bidirectional mechanisms of association logically apply to disorders that are episodic or have a clearly defined onset. While the model makes sense in many instances, it has yet to be mapped out in a specific temperament-psychopathology interaction pattern. Additional knowledge of the precise brain pathways of both psychiatric disorders and temperamental traits would certainly support the wider use of this model.

The Common Pathway Model

The common pathway model approaches the relationship between temperament and psychopathology from a developmental point of view. According to this hypothesis, temperament and psychopathology start out as the same entity, but then, as unique experiences and developmental influences accumulate, they diverge, sometimes leading to full-fledged illness involving features not shared by the corresponding temperamental trait.

Consider, for example, the association between shyness and generalized social anxiety disorder. Imagine two very shy little girls, both with a predisposition for social anxiety disorder. One of the two girls sadly experiences intense humiliation from classmates, while the other is much better supported. Over time, the first girl becomes progressively more anxious and develops such a deep fear of negative evaluation from others that she begins to withdraw from all social encounters. The withdrawal stifles her exposure to other people and her social skills to the point that, when her family brings her in for an evaluation, she is diagnosed with a social anxiety disorder. The second girl, by contrast, receives support and encouragement to confront her shyness and develop strategies to manage her social anxiety. While it remains with her, the level stays within a functional range. These qualitatively different experiences have now resulted in the two girls having different phenotypes, despite starting from a very similar place.

Many readers may recognize this proposed mechanism as sounding very similar to the classic diathesis-stress model of mental illness, in which the combination of a constitutional propensity (diathesis) becomes pathological when some form of environmental adversity (stress) serves as a trigger. Here, temperament serves as the diathesis, which is necessary but not sufficient for the development of psychiatric illness.

Like all models, these mechanistic frameworks oversimplify reality. They do, however, offer a road map and in many cases provide a testable hypothesis regarding the relations between temperament and psychopathology. With these mechanisms in mind, researchers have moved beyond traditional studies of association to more novel explorations of these intricate relations. In the next section, some of these studies are outlined to illustrate how the field is moving forward.

Beyond Associations: New Studies in Temperament-Psychopathology Interplay

More Than Means

When researchers examine temperament dimensions within the context of psychiatric disorders, the focus is usually on the mean or average level of that dimension. In most cases, the mean is the only aspect of a temperament dimension that is examined. A recent study from Ghent University in Belgium, however, shows that including more properties in the analyses can broaden our understanding of how temperament and psychopathology are associated (De Pauw & Mervielde, 2011). In the study, children with and without ADHD were assessed both for psychopathology, using the Child Behavior Checklist, and for temperament, using two different scales. The expected mean differences between ADHD and non-ADHD children were found on a number of temperament dimensions, but other parameters of these dimensions such as the variance, internal consistency, and degree of association between trait and psychopathology scales were quite similar between the two groups. The authors interpreted these data as supporting a continuum model for ADHD (although not with a single trait), stating that "differences between children with and without ADHD can be conceived as quantitative rather than qualitative, because they are mainly confined to mean level differences" (p. 286).

Profiles Instead of Pairs

For many trait-disorder pairs, the relations do not appear as straightforward, and traditional studies that examine the relations between a single disorder and a single trait may fail to capture the full scope of association between these two domains (Krueger & Tackett, 2003). Recall that when we tested the continuum model using the trait of harm avoidance and its link to general anxiety disorder (Rettew, Doyle, et al., 2006), many subjects showed unexpected profiles: either high harm avoidance with no GAD, or only moderate harm avoidance with GAD. These data showed us that we needed to look further, possibly by looking at other traits beyond harm avoidance. As described in Chapter 2, traits don't operate in a vacuum or combine randomly to create an infinite number of combinations at equal frequencies. Rather, naturally occurring profiles can be found at various frequencies in populations using person-centered techniques such as latent class and latent profiles analyses. Thus, in order to understand temperament-psychopathology relations on a deeper level, it may be necessary to consider that the association between one trait and its corresponding disorder might depend on the presence of other traits.

We saw this concept in the discussion of depression, which is thought to be associated with the temperament combination of high negative affectivity and low extraversion. One prominent personality theorist, Robert Cloninger, has extended this concept to all types of psychiatric disorders. To illustrate the concept, he depicts a three-dimensional cube with the axes representing different levels of different traits and each disorder occupying a specific point in that three-dimensional space (Cloninger, 1999).

This idea that multiple traits are important in underlying psychiatric disorders was the focus of a previously cited article about naturally occurring profiles of child temperament traits (Rettew, Althoff, et al., 2008). To recap, latent profiles analysis was used to show how particular combinations of traits manifested at different frequencies in specific psychiatric disorders. We identified three main profiles: the moderate profile (average levels of all traits), the steady profile (low novelty seeking and high persistence), and, least common, the disengaged profile (high novelty seeking and harm avoidance, low reward dependence and persistence). In addition to identifying these groups, a secondary aim of the study was to look at relations between these groups and both psychopathology and adaptive functioning. From both a quantitative (problem scale scores from the Child Behavior Checklist) and a binary (the presence or absence of specific DSM-IV disorders) perspective, there were dramatic differences in psychopathology between the groups. The rate of oppositional defiant disorder (at 68% in the disengaged group) was almost four times the rate found in the steady group, with the moderate group distinctly between the two other groups. A similar pattern was found for other types of emotional-behavioral disturbances such as mood and anxiety problems.

Looking at measures of competency and wellness, the reverse pattern appeared, with the steady group having significantly higher social and school success and more activities compared with the moderate group. The moderate and disengaged groups varied significantly with regard to social competence, but not for activity level or school achievement, as shown in Figure 6.2.

The use of person-centered analyses revealed some interesting clues that might have been missed using traditional variable-based approaches. The disengaged group, for example, was found to have a somewhat unique profile that combined high levels of novelty seeking and high levels of harm avoidance. In variable-centered studies, these two dimensions are usually inversely related, with high novelty seeking related to low harm avoidance and vice versa (Kuo et al., 2004). For these children, however, a temperamental pull to explore new environments was coupled with high levels of fear and anxiety in doing so. In other words, they seemed primed to want to explore situations that they couldn't easily handle in a sort of push-pull phenomenon. We wondered whether these relatively unique temperamental conflicts might be responsible for some of their behavioral difficulties.

A similar study was done in collaboration with our colleagues from Ghent University, led by psychologist Barbara De Clercq (De Clercq et

FIGURE 6.2

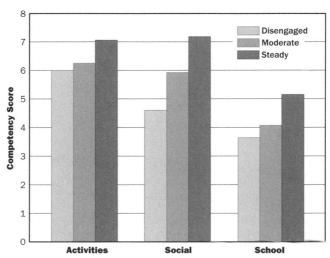

When temperament profiles take into account multiple dimensions, robust associations may be found in measures of child wellness and competence that are missed using analyses that examine only one temperament dimension at a time (adapted from Rettew, Althoff, et al., 2008, and used with permission)

al., 2011), albeit from a personality rather than a temperament framework. This study examined a community-based Flemish sample of 10–11-year-olds. Personality was assessed using the Hierarchical Personality Inventory for Children (Mervielde & De Fruyt, 1999). The instrument adapts the Big Five structure of personality to children using five broad dimensions: emotional stability, extraversion, imagination, benevolence, and conscientiousness. Using the same type of latent profiles analysis, we found four different personality profiles: moderate, protected, undercontrolled, and vulnerable. Subjects were assessed at baseline and then two years later. At follow-up, children who had been classified in the moderate and protected groups had no significant associations with later behavioral problems. The vulnerable group, by contrast, showed a diverse array of behavior problems (both internalizing and externalizing), whereas the undercontrolled group showed significant associations with externalizing problems such as aggression and rule breaking.

Using a different type of methodology, Albertine Oldehinkel and her colleagues at the University of Groningen and Erasmus University in the Netherlands examined the possibility that certain temperament traits are related to psychopathology severity (regardless of type), while others are more strongly associated with the type of psychopathology (Oldehinkel et al., 2004). The authors used a more variable-centered approach called discriminant analysis and found that the tendency to become easily frustrated was associated with the severity of behavioral problems globally, whereas traits such as shyness and high-intensity pleasure (related to novelty seeking) loaded more strongly onto the types of emotional behavioral problems that were experienced.

Another study reported that children with high levels of activity manifested clinically significant behavioral problems only if they also showed high levels of emotionality (Janson & Mathiesen, 2008). Indeed, some of the most active children were in a cluster called the confident group, which tended to show low levels of psychopathology, although the diagnosis of ADHD was not specifically assessed. These results make intuitive sense and shed light on why continuum models, at least those that pair one temperament dimension with one disorder, tend to be inadequate.

Both variable-based studies that use statistical techniques such as multiple regression and person-based studies that use techniques such as latent profile analysis contribute to our understanding of temperament and psychiatric disorders. Indeed, similar studies using emotional-behavioral problems, rather than temperament traits, have been done to discover how symptoms also cluster together naturally and quantitatively (Markon & Krueger, 2005). A frequent conclusion from many investigations is that a single temperament trait does not suddenly become problematic by itself; outcomes usually depend on the intensity of other traits as well.

Goodness of Fit

The importance of considering how traits work together can extend to the interpersonal realm as well. Just as high activity levels can be related to good outcomes when paired with some traits and poor outcomes when paired with others, the same principle can be applied when thinking about how well a trait "gets along with others." Certain qualities, especially at extremely high or low levels, are maladaptive under most circumstances. However, the degree to which a particular temperament escalates into a full-blown behavioral disorder depends to a large degree on the particular environment that surrounds that trait. This idea is not new, even in the world of temperament research. Chess and Thomas introduced the notion of "goodness of fit," postulating that in many instances, what matters most is not the level of a particular temperament dimension, but rather how well or poorly the trait works within a specific environment (Thomas & Chess, 1977).

Thinking in more modern terms, the idea of goodness of fit sounds similar in many ways to an evocative gene–environment correlation in which a child's behavior pulls out or evokes particular aspects of that child's environment, which in turn might reinforce the behavior in question. The difference, theoretically, is that gene–environment correlations may actually modify or accentuate a trait (sometimes masking the importance of the original genetic influence), whereas a greater or lesser goodness of fit simply indicates that a given trait works or doesn't work under different conditions. In the real world, it is probably naive to think that a very good fit or a very poor fit has no effect on the stability of that trait, but academically it may be useful to distinguish between these concepts.

Consider a temperamentally active 6-year-old boy being raised by two quiet, mellow parents. One can easily imagine how the fit between child and parents may quickly become problematic. The child's high activity level is frequently unwelcome and becomes a source of conflict and criticism, possibly leading the boy to feel badly about himself. Because the parents don't enjoy rough and tumble play, the family struggles to find activities to do together, thereby weakening the bond between them. Over time, the boy's activity level becomes a source of tension that wedges ever more space between parent and child (in the upcoming chapters on parenting, I will address how the fit might be improved if the family decides on intervention).

Despite its importance in developmental psychology, the goodness of fit concept has not been extensively tested, especially from a temperament standpoint. Using data from the Vermont Family Study, we investigated how much temperament fit mattered in behavior problems, beyond the independent contributions of the child's or parent's temperament traits (Rettew, Doyle, et al., 2006). We measured temperament in both parents and children using the Temperament and Character Inventory (Cloninger et al., 1994) and its child version, the Junior Temperament and Character Inventory (Luby et al., 1999). Behavioral problems were assessed through reports from informants (parents, self-report, teachers) using instruments such as the Child Behavior Checklist and the Teacher Report Form (Achenbach, 1991a, 1991b). Our main outcome measures were global scores related to internalizing and externalizing behavior problems, in addition to attention problems (which are considered nei-ther internalizing nor externalizing).

Using multiple regression analyses, we looked at the association between child and parent temperament operating both alone and in com-bination (i.e., as an interaction term) and found moderate evidence for the importance of fit. There were many examples in which child tempera-ment alone was related to psychopathology and a few examples in which parental temperament alone was related to child psychopathology. But there were also particular parent-child temperament combinations that predicted behavior problems when the traits individually did not. One example was in the association between novelty seeking and attention problems, as shown in Figure 6.3.

FIGURE 6.3

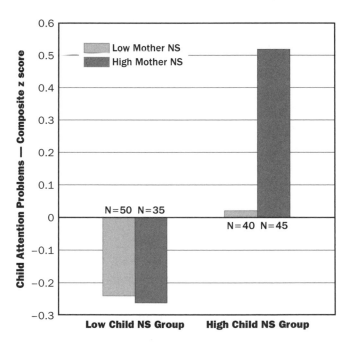

An example of the importance of poor goodness of fit with regard to novelty seeking (NS) and attention problems. Children with low NS showed lower levels of attention problems regardless of maternal NS. In high-NS children, however, greater attention problems are found in families that include a high-NS mother, but not in families that include low-NS mothers (adapted and used with permission from Rettew et al., 2006).

While neither child nor parent novelty seeking alone was related to the child's attention problems, the specific combination of a high novelty-seeking child with a high novelty-seeking mother did correlate with attention problems that were about half of a standard deviation higher than what was seen for a high novelty-seeking child with a low novelty-seeking mother. Other combinations, such as high harm avoidance in both children and fathers, were related to internalizing problems, although child harm avoidance by itself was also significant in this case. Sometimes combinations of different dimensions were found to be related to increased child behavioral problems, such as the combination of child novelty seeking and maternal persistence.

These examples illustrate the mechanism of temperamental fit in what is considered childhood psychopathology. The traits alone do not result in a degree of distress and impairment that meets the criteria for a full behavioral disorder, but they might do so in the presence of a suboptimal fit with certain environmental factors, including traits in others. Interestingly, this perspective makes it difficult to assign "blame" to the child or the parents for behavioral difficulties. As we will see in Part II, this fact can be utilized productively in a clinical setting, both as a way to describe problems accurately without pointing fingers and as a road map for interventions directed toward the entire family.

The Role of Culture

We have progressively expanded the focus of this discussion from individual temperament traits, to temperament combinations within individuals, to temperament combinations within families. Going further still, we might as well examine how traits match up with particular cultures and subcultures.

It is certainly tricky territory to consider temperamental predispositions of people on the basis of socioeconomic, regional, national, or ethnic divisions. Such an undertaking can quickly lead to stereotypes and misrepresentations that do not accurately account for the full diversity of most societies. A major multinational study examined differences between countries in the level of behavioral problems and concluded that the variability within a country far outstripped the variability found between countries (Rescorla et al., 2007).

Potential pitfalls aside, it is probably fair to say that subgroups within a society, on average, tend to value temperament traits differently. One stereotype about nonnative Americans, for example, is that our history of leaving home and creating a new and expanding country put a premium on the trait of extraversion and novelty seeking. People with higher levels of those traits might have been attracted to the idea of coming to America in the first place, and then the same traits would have drawn them to explore the new land even further. Novelty seeking may have been reinforced through the demands of living at that time. And while most of us are no longer crossing dangerous lands in covered wagons and scouring the wilderness for gold and silver, these esteemed qualities of industriousness or having an "entrepreneurial spirit" have endured. Consequently, the trait of extraversion might be valued more in Americans than in people of other cultures, and the threshold at which it is seen as problematic is probably relatively high in the United States. On the flip side, a trait like shyness may be seen as suboptimal, and the link between it and psychopathology may be somewhat stronger in the United States than in other countries, either because of a relatively low threshold for diagnosing social anxiety disorder (according to a continuum model) or because children who are shy are made to feel inferior, which in turn leads to disorders such as depression (according to a risk model).

These theories are intriguing but largely untested, perhaps because of the political delicacy involved and the potential for misinterpretation of the results. Nonetheless, it is reasonable to speculate that the idea of goodness of fit can extend beyond the dyadic relations between a child and parents and into the larger context of society as a whole.

The Shared Biology Between Traits and Disorders

Ultimately, studies that focus only on phenotypes, or the outward behavioral manifestations that are measured through questionnaires or observer ratings, can only take us so far. The shared language used to describe both traits and disorders, the measurement error inherent in having even skilled raters judge another person's temperament, and the somewhat proprietary ways in which different traits are labeled and placed together under various structures all point to the need to move beyond outward behavior and into underlying neurobiology. A child's activity level, for example, is a quantitative construct that varies within the population. Ignoring the semantic question of when activity turns into hyperactivity or ADHD, it is still possible to look at brain function in people across the full spectrum of activity levels and ask whether the biological signatures of high activity are amplified versions of lower activity or whether entirely different brain mechanisms underlie different activity levels.

It is tempting to assume from the smooth distribution of traits and psychiatric symptoms on the phenotypic level that such shared neurobiology is present. However, this assumption could easily prove to be wrong. For example, overall red blood cell count looks like a nice bell-shaped distribution when a large number of individuals are measured. Indeed, variation in this trait is typically due to a number of quantitative factors, such as the levels of hormones that trigger red blood cell production. At the low end of the range, however, there may be people who have a hole somewhere in their body and are losing blood. While we can't immediately know this by looking at the overall distribution, it is very important to have a way to identify that group as the management of a hemorrhage is quite different than that of other types of blood disorders.

Using another example from Kagan and Snidman (2004), the distribution of intelligence scores in a large sample might show a nearly perfect bell-shaped curve, suggesting a common mechanism that underlies the entire range. Such a conclusion, however, would miss those with Down syndrome who have a specific genetic anomaly: an extra copy of chromosome 21.

Thus, scientists are beginning to look more closely at the degree to which disorders and their corresponding traits share similar underlying features such as genetic and environmental causes, or patterns of brain function. As reviewed in Chapter 4, quite a bit of neurobiological research has been done on temperament, and the genes, neurotransmitters, and brain regions that come up are frequently the same old friends that arise in studies of psychopathology. Stronger evidence from studies that assess directly both temperament and psychopathology has been surprisingly slow to emerge, however.

Twin studies allow for this opportunity, even in the absence of DNA analyses, to examine the question of whether or not the genes that are involved in a particular temperament trait are the same as or overlap with the genes underlying a particular disorder. What is required is a sufficiently large sample of different types of twins and a good way to measure both the trait and the disorder. In adults, this issue was examined in two reports from John Hettema and his colleagues from Virginia

Commonwealth University. In the first study, the trait of neuroticism was measured using the Eysenck Personality Questionnaire while GAD was assessed using a structured interview. Using a statistical procedure called a bivariate Cholesky model, the researchers were able to measure the extent to which the genetic and environmental influences on neuroticism were shared with those for GAD (Hettema, Prescott, & Kendler, 2004). One way to get a sense of this analysis is to examine the cross-twin cross-measure correlations; in other words, how strongly is the neuroticism in Twin 1 related to GAD in Twin 2, and how do those correlation patterns differ between monozygotic and dizygotic twin pairs? The results of these analyses showed that the "genetic factors underlying neuroticism are nearly indistinguishable from those that influence liability to generalized anxiety disorder" (p. 1585). Environmental overlap, however, was much more modest, suggesting that the paths that lead one person to have trait levels of neuroticism while another person suffers with full GAD differ more in environmental components than in genetic ones. A second study from this group, led by renowned genetic researcher Ken Kendler, looked at the relations between neuroticism and a broader array of anxiety and depressive disorders and found similar results, although the genetic overlap in this study was less dramatic (Hettema et al., 2006). In children, a longitudinal study found that the genetic influence for early effortful control was held in common with the genetic liability to later develop ADHD symptoms (Goldsmith, Lemery, & Essex, 2004).

A relatively recent study out of King's College in London by Marco Picchioni and colleagues used a twin design to assess whether or not the social and behavioral abnormalities observed in childhood among individuals who later develop schizophrenia are best conceptualized as a risk factor for the illness or an early manifestation of it (Picchioni et al., 2010). One limitation of the study was that the childhood histories of the adult patients were assessed retrospectively. Nevertheless, they found that as children, these individuals had detectable personality differences; specifically, they had more schizoid and schizotypal traits compared to controls. Moreover, the genetic analyses revealed that there were common genetic effects underlying both the childhood traits and the later psychotic disorders.

Our group approached the same question from a molecular genetic perspective, asking the question of whether or not the particular genes that are associated with a psychiatric disorder are also associated with a corresponding temperament trait. As discussed earlier, we will never find "the gene" for most disorders; more likely, relatively common alleles (those held by a significant minority or even a majority of a population) each contribute a very small amount toward a particular disorder. While this is likely an oversimplification, some psychiatric disorders result from a number of risk alleles adding up (hence the finding of additive genetic effects in twin studies) to a full-blown disorder, especially in conjunction with specific environmental factors. Under this hypothesis, then, we may find that the rate of a particular risk allele for an important gene is high among those with clinical levels of a problem (inattention, anxiety, depressed mood), low among those with little or no levels of that problem, and intermediate among those with trait or subthreshold levels. Such a pattern, if found, would certainly suggest that there is a common mechanism underlying both the trait and the disorder, and the difference is more a matter of degree.

We investigated this hypothesis in a group of around 350 children whose mean age was 11 years old, and our findings were presented at the 2011 conference of the American Academy of Child and Adolescent Psychiatry (AACAP; Rettew, Althoff, et al., 2011). In an attempt to circumvent some of the methodological issues of using both a temperament and a psychopathology scale, we used a single scale, the Child Behavior Checklist, and compared genotypes between groups with high, low, and intermediate scores. Our main focus was to determine whether or not the intermediate or what we called the "trait group" would show genotypic frequencies of certain risk alleles that were in between those with clinical levels of a certain behavior and those without that problem at all. We chose three symptom areas: anxious/depressed, withdrawn/depressed, and inattention, as previous work had suggested a continuum model for these symptoms and because each of these traits has been associated with specific genetic risk factors.

What we found was a mixed bag. The trait group had rates squarely in between the none and clinical groups for the risk allele in a single-nucleotide polymorphism (SNP, relating to genetic variation regarding a single base pair at a particular locus on a gene) region for two gene-disorder combinations, the serotonin 2A receptor (HTR2A) in its association with attention problems and the alpha-adrenergic 2A receptor (ADRA2A) in its association with withdrawn/depressed problems. For these two SNPs, the frequency of the risk allele was lower than it was for the clinical group, but higher than that found with the none group. For the same HTR2A gene and its association with withdrawn/depressed problems, however, the risk allele rate for the trait group was statistically equivalent to that of the none group, suggesting some genetic discontinuities between temperament traits and disorders.

Taken together, these molecular genetic studies support the conclusion that while there certainly may be some qualitative biological differences between children with moderate amounts of a trait and those with disorder-level amounts of that trait, substantial overlap also exists. The links between temperament traits and psychopathology, then, extend beyond surface similarities and into shared neurobiological underpinnings. Indeed, there is accumulating evidence that when it comes to many psychiatric disorders, we inherit temperament and personality traits that are linked to that disorder, rather than inheriting genes for the disorder itself (Martel et al., 2010).

Our One Brain

A lot of ground has been covered in this chapter. While there is conclusive evidence that temperament is related to psychopathology, there remains much to learn about how the two domains are linked. Straightforward distinctions using markers of impairment or "change from the usual state" don't hold up under scrutiny, and simple continuum or spectrum models of the relations between a single trait and a single disorder, although appealing, are ultimately not sufficient. My attempt to pull several of these conclusions together graphically to create an overall model is shown in Figure 6.4.

This schematic summarizes both the continuities and discontinuities that underlie the mechanisms of temperament as it relates to psychopathology. While incorporating some additional complexity compared to earlier models, this depiction itself certainly leaves out several layers of sophistication, such as the fact that different types of genetic mutations, even within the same gene, will have different effects.

Although it would be nice to find universal mechanisms through which temperament traits are linked to psychiatric disorders, it seems likely that it just doesn't work that way. The media may struggle getting the full length of the truth to fit in their sound bites, but in the end, even the most refined models will need to take into account the following realities:

FIGURE 6.4

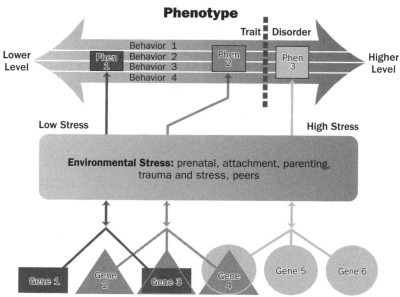

A graphical depiction of how temperament is linked with psychopathology. Genetic variations interact with environmental factors to determine levels of quantitative behaviors that can combine to form different phenotypes (phen). Beyond a certain point, these phenotypes are considered to cross a diagnostic threshold that is often subject to interpretation.

1. The way temperament relates to psychopathology differs for different disorders. For example, the link between temperament and inattentive ADHD may be closer to a continuum model than, say, the link between temperament and autism, where other mechanisms also play a prominent role.

2. The way temperament relates to psychopathology differs between people with the same psychiatric disorder. Given two people with major depression, for example, one person's illness may be strongly connected to a long history of high levels of negative emotionality and low levels of surgency, while another person's illness may be due to cyclic processes in the brain that result in dramatic shifts in how that person thinks, acts, and feels.

3. The way temperament relates to psychopathology changes within the same person. Consider an adolescent who is showing signs of developing schizophrenia. He has always seemed withdrawn, irritable, and prone to interpret others' actions as hostile. These

behaviors are common to both temperament and psychotic disorders. After experimenting with cannabis, however, he begins to experience auditory hallucinations that don't abate, even when he stops smoking. The mechanism operating to maintain these new behaviors may be the result of a subtle brain injury that is independent from mechanisms underlying temperament or personality.

As clinicians and scientists continue to try to parse out distinct territory for temperament, personality, psychiatric disorders, and personality disorders, one point that is absolutely crucial to remember is that we each have one brain that does not obey labels or boxes that we create for it. Dysregulated behavior may, for example, reflect particular brain mechanisms that are present regardless of whether that dysregulation is described as bipolar disorder or borderline personality disorder or with temperament labels such as effortful control. Like a bird whose migratory route crosses multiple national boundaries without regard for those borders, the brain operates without concern for conventions and constructs. Perhaps more important than labeling these developing tendencies will be our efforts to work with them in different settings to help children make the most of their unique potential.

Part II
Applications

Chapter 7

Clinical Settings

The previous chapters have presented a lot of information about the new science of child temperament and its role in clinical psychiatry and psychology. Now, we turn to the question of how to put these principles into practice. Advances in our understanding of child temperament over the past few decades are not solely academic; the clinical implications are profound and could represent a major departure from how clinicians approach children and families with emotional-behavioral challenges. Although this discussion is aimed at mental health professionals, most of this chapter should be relevant for other medical professionals or parents as well.

Ryan and Lisa

Consider two clinical examples of children that might easily present to a child psychiatrist under the very typical circumstances of an ADHD evaluation.

> **RYAN.** *Presentation*: Ryan is an 8-year-old boy who presents with his mother to a child psychiatrist on recommendation from his pediatrician. They would like an evaluation regarding whether or not he should be diagnosed and treated for ADHD. His parents have struggled with Ryan's behavior for a long time. At home, he has a hard time sitting still (except when playing video games—his favorite activity) and he often doesn't listen or follow directions. These behaviors lead to frequent arguments and disciplinary actions. His mother notes that Ryan's father also has some of

Ryan's characteristics, which can lead to "pushing each other's buttons" and intense but nonabusive arguments. His mother, in trying to minimize the amount of family conflict, admits that she sometimes gives in to Ryan's demands when he is upset. At school, he is considered to be quite bright and his behavior seems to be better than it is at home. His grades are average, and there have been increasing problems with getting homework completed to the point that teachers have now voiced concerns.

Assessment and Plan: The psychiatrist performs a typical initial evaluation. He reviews the DSM criteria for ADHD with the mother and finds that Ryan meets 6 of the 9 inattentive criteria and 7 of the 9 hyperactive-impulsive criteria. He therefore makes a diagnosis of ADHD, combined type. Noting both the family history and the number of ADHD criteria that Ryan meets, the psychiatrist tells the family that Ryan has ADHD and prescribes a stimulant medication to treat his symptoms. On the basis of Ryan's improved behavior at school, he confronts the parents about their parenting skills, stating that their giving in to his demands is "teaching" him to act poorly through principles of reinforcement. Six months later, the school has noticed some improvement, but the medication wears off later in the day, resulting in continued clashes at home. The pediatrician urges the family to return to the psychiatrist for a dosage adjustment, but the mother is resistant, stating that she felt blamed for Ryan's behavior during the evaluation.

LISA. *Presentation:* Lisa is a 10-year-old girl who comes for an evaluation at the request of her family physician, who is concerned that she may have ADHD. Lisa is not doing well at school. Although not known to be disruptive in class, she is easily distracted and frequently gets lost in daydreams. Previous IQ testing has shown that she is in the low average range in intelligence. Her parents have tried a number of things to help her, including a quiet, distraction-free place to do her homework and incentives to help her stay on task. Her teacher has placed her in the front of the classroom so she can concentrate as well as she can. Despite these efforts, Lisa continues to lag behind and is growing more and more frustrated with school.

Assessment and Plan: On review of the ADHD criteria, she meets 5 of the 9 inattentive criteria for ADHD and only 2 of the 9 hyperactive-impulsive items. She and her parents are told that she does not have ADHD and Lisa is sent back to the care of her pediatrician with reassurance. Six months later, little has changed other than the fact that Lisa now tells her parents frequently that she hates school and wishes she could stop going entirely.

These two scenarios do not describe actual patients, but they certainly could. Their presentations and the actions of the hypothetical psychiatrist are typical of the way that emotional-behavioral problems are assessed and managed in mental health clinics. Three elements in these vignettes are in particular need of updating according to a temperament-based perspective:

1. The binary nature of diagnosis. The clinician is expected to give a diagnostic opinion about whether or not the child has ADHD. Most psychiatrists, psychologists, and other mental health professionals who perform mental health assessments are aware of the quantitative nature of ADHD symptoms (and other types of emotional-behavioral problems). Yet evaluations are still structured around making a yes or no determination for each diagnosis. This continuing practice may be due to a number of factors. First, psychiatrists are trained as medical doctors and in medicine, illnesses are typically present or not present. Diseases from pneumonia to myocardial infarction to cancer generally are binary in nature. Physicians are taught the process of starting with a broad list of symptoms and then narrowing or ruling out possibilities, eventually reaching a diagnosis. Second, this all-or-none approach is reinforced by the DSM, which maintains its categorical framework of mental illness. The DSM-5 includes some adjustments toward a more dimensional structure, but these adjustments are relatively minor and they are restricted to a few specific areas. Finally, many clinicians maintain that a binary diagnostic structure is necessary because treatment decisions are binary, such as starting a medication (or not) or beginning psychotherapy (or not).

2. The disease model. In the two examples above, the mental health professional got involved after a problem had developed, and he

or she was expected to treat the illness in order to stop it from progressing. The treatment plan reflects this disease model approach, emphasizing treatment with medication, which, in ADHD, certainly has the backing of a large body of scientific evidence (MTA Cooperative Group, 1999). Psychiatrists in particular are seen in our society primarily as doctors of mental disease rather than promoters of behavioral wellness.

3. Exclusive focus on the child. Largely disregarding the intricate mechanisms between children and their environment (as reviewed in Part 1 of this book), standard clinical evaluations continue to focus on the child's symptoms alone. The official recommendations from the American Academy of Child and Adolescent Psychiatry (AACAP) regarding the psychiatric assessment of children and adolescents, for example, give little guidance about examining psychopathology in the parents (King, 1997). According to the guidelines, "where any such (psychiatric) disorders have been present in family members, inquiry should be made about their severity, treatment, outcome, and impact on the child" (p. 10S). In practice, however, a full inquiry is unusual, especially in this era of diminished time for evaluations. In the example with Ryan, the physician does learn that Ryan's father has some of the same difficulties as his son, but the information along with the knowledge that ADHD symptoms have a strong genetic influence is used solely to support the diagnostic conclusions for Ryan. The idea that the father's symptoms might have an impact on his son and their relationship is not brought into treatment plan. This omission is sometimes due to the belief that the father's behavioral difficulties are entirely in reaction to the son's symptoms. While we have reviewed the possibility that a child's behavior can evoke suboptimal responses in parents (Perlick et al., 2004), it is important not to take such evidence to the extreme by expecting that successful treatment of a child's symptoms, pharmacologically or otherwise, will result in the resolution of the parent's own behavioral difficulties.

These three core features of the traditional psychiatric approach are all challenged by a comprehensive view of temperament and the way it is associated with child psychopathology. There is now ample scientific evidence showing that domains of child behavior exist quantitatively with very blurry boundaries between what is considered a trait and what is considered a disorder. It is also clear that a large number of genetic and environmental factors (many involving parents and the family) play important roles in reinforcing or altering a child's developmental trajectory. For clinicians, incorporating these new data and the temperament perspective can lead to substantial alterations in both the way we understand and explain child behavioral problems to families and how we develop intervention strategies to relieve them.

Clinical Adjustments Using a Temperament-Based Perspective

For a clinician, a shift in thinking from the binary disease model focused on the individual child to a quantitative temperament-based model encompassing the environment has significant practical implications. Following these principles means changing how we structure evaluations, how we give feedback to children and families about what we see happening and what it means, and perhaps most important, how and where we devote our clinical energy in the hopes of making things better for our patients and their families. While these changes may sound drastic, we have found in our clinic that they can be incorporated reasonably easily within a standard practice. To many clinicians and families, most of the concepts are neither new nor especially controversial; the innovation lies in how the various elements are combined and emphasized.

The rest of this chapter describes in more detail how a temperament-based perspective can inform clinical approaches in a child mental health setting. It includes specific recommendations and examples regarding how these changes can be integrated into a busy practice setting and additional scientific evidence that supports such an approach. From our own experience of teaching this approach to medical students, residents, and child psychiatry fellows, we have found that at first it can be challenging. Compared to a more straightforward medical model, more people and variables have to be directly assessed, and the clinical formulation takes time and skill to present to families. This approach also asks more of the family members themselves, which may surprise those expecting their role to be confined to ensuring the child takes his or her medicine every day. Ultimately, however, we are finding that this approach is both a more scientifically valid way to understand child behavior and a more rewarding method of practicing our craft.

A Clinical Model: The Vermont Family-Based Approach

Over roughly the past 15 years, our outpatient child psychiatry clinic at the Vermont Center for Children, Youth and Families, under the leadership and vision of director Jim Hudziak, has incrementally applied the notion that child psychopathology is best understood in quantitative, developmental terms as the product of complex genetic and environmental interplay. The model has been called the Vermont Family-Based Approach (Hudziak, 2008). It serves as both the framework of our clinical methodology and as the backbone of the way we teach clinical psychiatry to our medical students, psychiatry residents, and child psychiatry fellows (Rettew, DiRuocco, et al., 2011). A manual is currently being developed for those interested in learning the details of the technique, but an overview is presented in Table 7.1.

TABLE 7.1.
The Vermont Family-Based Approach

Evaluation Components

1. Child psychopathology: assessed by multiple informants using quantitative, standardized, developmentally sensitive instruments, and DSM criteria.

2. Family environment: broad review of the child and family environment including parenting practices, stress and trauma, media habits, music, sleep, nutrition and dieting, family cohesion and structure, sports, and structured activities.

3. Parent/caretaker psychopathology: self and spouse report using quantitative instruments.

4. Standard psychiatric evaluation: typical medical evaluation (history of present illness, past psychiatric and medical history, review of systems, substance use, medication, allergies, social and developmental history, and mental status exam).

Treatment Focus

1. Individual psychotherapy: with emphasis on evidence-based treatments such as cognitive-behavioral therapy.

2. Medications: with informed consent.

3. Parental assessment and treatment: if parent/caretaker shows evidence of possibly having a psychiatric disorder.

4. Parental guidance: using evidence-based recommendations and incorporating temperament principles.

5. School interventions: formal programs such as Individualized Education Programs or 504 plans or less formal strategies designed with teachers and parents.

6. Environmental changes: improving health-promoting aspects of the child's environment such as sleep routines, nutrition, limits in the type and quantity of screen time, music lessons, and sports and structured activities.

When a family calls our clinic, we send them a series of rating scales and instruments for completion before the evaluation is scheduled. We assess the child's behavior from as many vantage points as we can, using an integrated family of instruments called the Achenbach System of Empirically Based Assessment (ASEBA; www.aseba.org). Parents rate children using the Child Behavior Checklist and children 11 years and older rate their own symptoms using the Youth Self Report (Achenbach & Rescorla, 2001). We also try to get at least one teacher to rate the child using the Teacher Report Form. All of these instruments have been standardized in studies of large groups of children with and without behavior problems, so that developmentally appropriate norms exist. There are eight subscales that assess levels of problems in the following areas: anxious/depressed, withdrawn/depressed, somatic complaints, thought problems, social problems, attention problems, rule-breaking behavior, and aggression. These eight domains were determined using a statistical technique called factor analysis, which groups problems together in a way that reflects their groupings in the real world. This bottom-up approach stands in contrast, somewhat, to the DSM's top-down approach in which experts decide by committee consensus on the disorders and their diagnostic criteria. In addition to the eight core subscales, more global ratings of internalizing problems, externalizing problems, and total problems are also provided. For each problem area, a child receives a particular raw score from an individual informant, which is then converted into a standardized T-score. This T-score allows a clinician to see the score relative to other children of the same age and sex. For example, a 6-year-old boy might receive a raw score from his teacher that indicates attention problems, but the T-score shows the clinician how this score compares (by percentile) to how other teachers rate other 6-year-old boys. The scores about the child from all informants can then be compared side by side to get an idea of the degree to which different informants agree.

Although these instruments don't officially diagnose anyone, cutoff scores aid clinicians in determining whether or not the problem is in a clinical range. Essentially, a score in the 97th percentile or above receives a clinical designation, and scores between the 93rd and 97th percentiles receive a borderline–clinical designation, on any of the eight subscales. These designations are somewhat arbitrary, but provide important guidelines for clinicians and families. Often, parents observe a particular behavior but aren't sure whether the level is beyond developmental expectations; this is when mental health professionals are asked to judge, and they need guidelines to do so effectively.

The Achenbach scales are some of the most widely used child behavioral instruments in the world and have been translated into at least 80 different languages. There are other instruments, however, that also provide standardized scores of a broad array of child behavior problems from multiple informants. The purpose here is not to promote a particular set of instruments but to illustrate the utility of having scales that deliver a numerical score for a particular problem area that is normed by age and sex (and, more recently, by culture).

While many clinics use rating scales to aid in evaluations of the child, a relatively unique element in the Vermont Family-Based Approach is the provision of formalized mental health assessment of the parents of every child that we see. To accomplish this task, we use parallel instruments to the Child Behavior Checklist and the Youth Self Report, namely the Adult Self Report (parents rate themselves) and the Adult Behavior Checklist (parent rates the spouse or partner if there is one). The outputs from these instruments are similar to those of the child rating scales, with T-scores in multiple problem domains that are normed by age and sex.

Some mental health professionals have argued that formalizing a quantitative system into an official assessment procedure is too cumbersome. After all, no such steps are required by our field's governing body. Generally, assessments of children and adolescents are far less structured than the protocol described above; the clinician simply reviews the diagnostic criteria for a particular disorder and determines for each item whether or not it is present. The criteria often contain language such as "often" or "excessive," which requires a certain amount of discernment. The clinician then counts up the number of "yes" responses and compares it to the DSM cutoff for diagnosis.

This system "works" in that diagnoses are clinically based and can be made without needing additional procedures or resources. Some clinicians don't even reference the DSM criteria, but rather use their intuitive impressions to make a diagnosis. Others are less concerned with diagnostic labels than with trying to pick up deeper psychological themes or conflicts. In other areas of medicine, physicians don't expect diagnoses to be made on the spot by taking a history alone. A patient's complexion might look pale to a primary care physician, but before making a specific diagnosis, the physician typically orders blood analyses and other specialized tests. In this light, is it really so far-fetched to think that ADHD diagnoses, for example, should be based upon the results of psychometrically valid rating scales from multiple informants?

The Vermont Family-Based Approach assessments also differ from traditional child psychiatry evaluations in the extent to which environmental variables are systematically investigated. Practice recommendations from AACAP certainly include the examination of developmental, medical, and environmental variables (King, 1997). In practice, however, environmental variables are often treated in a cursory manner. Our clinic, in contrast, gathers detailed information through questionnaires on a wide range of important family environmental factors, including sports and club participation, parental disciplinary practices, sleep and bedtime rules, nutrition and eating habits, quantity and quality of television and video game usage, and religious practices. The answers to these questions serve as more than necessary documentation for our write-ups; rather, they become major focal points in our intervention plans.

Surprising as it may sound, we do not currently require that families complete temperament questionnaires. We have certainly administered temperament and personality scales to families enrolled in our research studies, but they are not part of our standard clinical protocol for families seeking evaluations. We held back from doing this for two practical reasons. First, families are asked to fill out a fairly substantial set of questionnaires prior to getting an appointment, and while we firmly believe that these instruments are necessary for a comprehensive evaluation, there is some concern that too many requirements might cause significant delay or even prevent families from being seen here. This is of particular concern for lower-functioning families who might find the rating scales most onerous to complete. Second, unlike the ASEBA ratings scales, whose output provides a clear indication of where a person falls in comparison with other individuals of the same age and sex, child temperament rating scales have not achieved this level of standardization in large, representative samples. At best, one can purchase, administer, and score a temperament rating scale and compare the mean scores to a reference or other published samples, but the scope and precision of these efforts fall short of what is currently available for scales such as the ASEBA instruments or adult personality measures such as the NEO Five-Factor Inventory (NEO-FFI; Costa & McCrae, 1985, 1992).

The lack of standardized scores for temperament instruments may come as a surprise, after hearing about all the research that is happening in the field. Perhaps it speaks to the fact that child temperament still remains somewhat beyond the purview of mainstream clinical practice. With time, it seems quite likely that new temperament scales will emerge or existing ones will augment their databases with large community samples, but we are not there yet. This gap, however, does not present an impasse. From a research standpoint, one can still administer a temperament scale to a group of subjects and calculate the interrelations between temperament and other variables within the study and without a need for standardized cutoff scores. From a clinical perspective, it is also possible to use clinical instruments such as the ASEBA scales to get a fairly good approximation of temperament. Correlations between Child Behavior Checklist scales and corresponding dimensions of personality and temperament can be as high as 0.8 (De Clercq, De Fruyt, Van Leeuwen, & Mervielde, 2006). As discussed previously, this may be due, in part, to the overlapping language of temperament and psychopathology scales. Thus, if we take to heart one of the main conclusions of Chapters 5 and 6— that temperament and quantitatively assessed psychopathology lie along a single continuum—then the clinician gathers temperament information in the course of using other quantitative instruments of child behavior.

The factors that are or are not assessed in questionnaires or clinical interviews will undoubtedly continue to change in each practice, especially as technology continues to facilitate the rapid administration and scoring of instruments. The Vermont Family-Based Approach will similarly continue to evolve with further experience and research. Its core principle, however, of viewing child emotional-behavioral functioning as quantitative dimensions determined by multiple genetic and environmental factors is here to stay. Flowing from this conceptualization is the idea that such multiply determined problems therefore require multimodal interventions that incorporate health promotion strategies. In the next section, we will explore three core features of this new clinical approach and look at some implications of working within this model.

Diagnosing by Degrees

With these assessment tools and models in mind, we can move toward a fresh way of conceptualizing child emotional-behavioral problems and treatment plans that incorporates the new science of temperament and psychopathology. As described in detail in Chapter 5, researchers have found over and over again that childhood emotional-behavioral problems of most every type exist along a continuum that overlaps substantially with temperament traits. Thus, at least on a behavioral level, there is very little on which to hang your hat that will help a clinician decide whether or not a presenting problem should be classified as a typically occurring trait or a psychiatric disorder. In some cases, of course, the level and nature of a set of behaviors is so extreme that a specific diagnosis is warranted. In others, parents might mislabel quite expected levels of behavior as pathological. Frequently, however, mental health professionals encounter children with clinical presentations that don't fit the circumscribed set of DSM criteria for diagnosis or exist at intermediate levels given the child's age and sex. Indeed, these children are most commonly those whom we are asked to evaluate, knowing that our official "call" will lead to important actions (or lack thereof) from that point forward. Concerned parents often bring a mix of hope and trepidation that the clinician will be able to apply a specific name to their child's behaviors, thereby supplying some degree of order in a chaotic situation and a plan for how to manage it.

As clinicians, we shouldn't underestimate the comfort that many families feel when a particular set of challenging and perplexing behaviors can be named. With a label comes the knowledge that other people are in the same boat, that professionals have seen this before, and that someone knows what to do. A diagnosis can signal a shift in a family's status from "What is going on?" to "How do we make this better?" A diagnosis also opens doors to services and communities working on similar issues.

At the same time, many families respond negatively to a diagnosis, especially a psychiatric one. Parents may worry that the child will feel like damaged property and that others might treat the child unkindly or unfairly. For some, any psychiatric diagnosis can feel very global and all-encompassing, whether the label is schizophrenia or ADHD. And families that have been hoping to avoid treatment with medications might be wary of a diagnosis, which often further justifies the need for treatment.

A clinician needs to explore the assumptions behind the family's urgency to receive or avoid diagnoses. Very often, those assumptions are based on beliefs that are untrue or only partially true, such as the idea that a diagnosis will automatically bring an effective treatment plan. Parents may also be under the false impression that not getting a diagnosis means they will be turned loose with no support or suggestions, or that they will be blamed for a child who is just bad or lazy. Taking the time to understand the underlying belief system can lead to opportunities to educate families about what a diagnosis actually means, and what it doesn't.

The presentation of diagnostic information to a family or child can sound different when coming from a temperament-based perspective versus a traditional disease model. For example, a 14-year-old adolescent girl with a long history of shyness is evaluated to see if she might have "something more," namely, social anxiety disorder. The discussion with the family might sound something like this:

> Putting everything together that you and your daughter have told me in addition to the rating scales that you all completed, I see that your daughter is very much at the high end of the range in feeling uncomfortable and nervous in social situations. Almost all of us feel shy in some situations and there are no clear boundaries for when that trait crosses the line of being considered a disorder. In your daughter's case, she does meet criteria for social anxiety disorder based on her history of being so anxious in many social situations that she has trouble making friends and doing things that she otherwise would enjoy. While it is likely that she will always tend to be more socially anxious than many of her peers, there are a number of things we can consider doing that could bring the intensity level of her discomfort down and allow her to engage more fully with other people.

An introduction like this one might be followed by some explanation of how genetic and environmental forces may have conspired to reinforce her temperamental predisposition toward shyness. A tendency to feel more comfortable when alone, for example, might lead her to avoid interacting with peers, thereby decreasing her opportunities to develop social skills. This, in turn, might make her feel inferior or lacking in confidence when she is forced to be social. By including the idea that there is no solid boundary between traits and disorders, I help the family understand that with help she might be able to move down this spectrum to a point where she no longer meets criteria for social anxiety disorder. She may very well continue to be more shy than others, but not to a degree that interferes with leading a happy and productive life.

Further exploration into other temperament traits might reveal the degree to which she really wants to have social interaction. Many people assume that shy people and those meeting criteria for social anxiety disorder would choose to spend more time with others if it weren't so difficult, that their avoidance and solitude is a choice of lesser evils. Sociability and extraversion, however, appear to be somewhat independent dimensions, and a better understanding of her status with regard to these dimensions should inform the clinician's decisions about treatment goals. This young woman might not want to be a social butterfly; her main goal might be to simply feel more relaxed during the times that she chooses to spend with others.

In speaking directly to this patient, I might touch on many of the same themes as I did with her parents, but perhaps in a slightly different way:

> I've heard a lot about you today and one of the things that I hear from you and your parents is that you are a very kind person who can really tune in to other people. That is a wonderful quality that will serve you very well in the future. At the same time, I also hear that you can get so concerned about what others think about you that you avoid things you like doing just so there is no chance that you will feel embarrassed. These feelings are strong enough that they disrupt your life and hold you back. Doctors sometimes use the term social anxiety disorder to describe this situation, and if you are willing there are things we can do to help you feel more at ease in social situations.

Remembering the "yet" problem discussed in Chapter 3, I make a point of highlighting not only the negative aspects of a trait but also some of the positive components. I want her to realize that being shy has both drawbacks and some potential benefits. I also don't want to go overboard in promising that we will be able to completely eliminate the unwanted parts of a broad trait like shyness. I do include the name of the disorder while putting a little distance between her and the term by saying that it is a convention that doctors use to communicate with one another.

When a patient seems to be right on the boundary of meeting criteria for a disorder, I often say so. Many mental health clinicians have this funny tendency to gather clinical information and then wrestle with it privately in order to come to a tidy conclusion that can be presented to patients and their families. I have found, however, that if I share some of my own indecision openly, patients and families can appreciate more fully the complexity of the situation and at times they are prompted to offer additional information that helps me get off that diagnostic fence. It can be important, however, to tell families that your ambivalence comes not from a lack of experience or clinical information but rather from the fact that the child's behavior puts him or her right around the diagnostic threshold. Being able to convey this situation confidently, however, requires an ability to distinguish clearly between the limits of the field's knowledge on a particular topic and one's own limits.

One criticism that has been voiced against applying a dimensional temperament-based perspective is the idea that clinical decisions are binary and therefore diagnostic decisions should be as well. While it is indeed true that a pill is either taken or not, models such as the Vermont Family-Based Approach reveal the many ways in which treatment decisions can also be dimensional. Consider the dimensional understanding of a nonpsychiatric condition such as hypertension. At first glance, it seems that an internist needs that 140/90 cutoff to convert the dimensional construct of blood pressure into the binary diagnosis of hypertension (or not), which in turn determines whether or not the patient should take antihypertensive medication. In practice, however, it doesn't quite work that way. One patient with blood pressure around 148/96 might have few other risk factors for cardiovascular disease. Therefore, the doctor might first recommend dietary modifications and salt restriction rather than medication. A second patient with a blood pressure of 170/100 and several other cardiovascular risk factors, such as obesity or diabetes, is more likely to quickly receive a prescription to lower the risk for complications. They both qualify for an official diagnosis of hypertension, but the understood dimensional component shapes the clinical decision, even when it comes to the binary choice about medicating.

Parallel situations are common in child mental health, especially when using a perspective like that contained in the Vermont Family-Based Approach. To the clinician who fully embraces the variety within diagnoses and who sees treatment recommendations that extend beyond the prescription pad, the landscape of choices begins to look increasingly dimensional. Milder cases might be addressed with environmental modifications at school or at home, which can vary in intensity. Even the choice of medications and dosages might reflect dimensional assessments. The risk/reward profile of various drugs may be considered with this quantitative framework in mind.

Many if not most child mental health experts already do this sort of thinking when making clinical judgments. The shift stemming from a temperament-based perspective, therefore, may have less to do with how clinicians think about various diagnoses and more to do with how these thoughts are put into practice and presented to families. From our experience, the output from the ASEBA questionnaires provides a wonderful tool for showing families the degree to which various behaviors are outside of developmental expectations. Comparing data from different informants side by side also helps illustrate the variability of child behavior from place to place, prompting important discussions about how the temperament of the child and characteristics of the environment might be interacting in positive or negative ways. Finally, direct conversations with the children that utilize quantitative language (e.g., "You tend to behave more like this and less like that") instead of binary language ("You are like this or you have this diagnosis") tend to promote that all-important but sometimes elusive therapeutic alliance.

Wellness in Illness

Despite the politically correct description of our field as mental health, we psychiatrists have been trained to think of ourselves as doctors of mental illness. The American Academy of Child and Adolescent Psychiatry defines me as "a physician who specializes in the diagnosis and the treatment of disorders of thinking, feeling, and/or behavior affecting children, adolescents, and their families" (AACAP, 2012). There is nothing in that statement about preventing children from becoming ill, let alone helping well children lead happier, fuller, more productive lives. If you want to know about adolescent depression, ask a child psychiatrist. If you want to know about adolescent happiness, ask . . . well, whom exactly? A pediatrician? An academic psychologist? Why are psychiatrists, who claim to understand the behavioral centers of the brain and the pathways that can lead to trouble, usually left out of the discussion on wellness?

One answer is that we have excused ourselves from the table. In psychiatry residencies and child psychiatry fellowships, little if any time is spent on wellness training. In the clinic, we rarely see people who are healthy and looking to become healthier; we tend to see those struggling with severe and persistent mental illness. In seminars, trainees learn about the epidemiology, course, neurobiology, and features of every known psychopathology—from schizophrenia to bipolar disorder to ADHD. We also learn how to treat these conditions using two primary types of intervention: psychotherapy and medication. Little mention is made of other factors that can help to enhance the lives of those who are thriving or to prevent those who are at risk from sliding onto a negative trajectory.

As psychiatry has become increasingly medicalized, its orientation toward illness and away from wellness has intensified. When depression is portrayed as a thing that comes out of nowhere and disables a person just like pneumonia or an attack of gout, how could we justify focusing our energy on lofty ideas like happiness or fulfillment? Better, instead, to memorize the potential drug interactions that might occur when we combine different classes of medications in our aggressive chemotherapy of this disease.

Ironically, other medical specialties have moved to incorporate wellness more extensively into their purview. One example, often cited by Hudziak when he explains the rationale for the Vermont Family-Based Approach, is the field of cardiology. Yes, cardiologists are called in when someone is having a heart attack or a dangerous cardiac arrhythmia, but they also appear on the covers of cookbooks for heart-healthy diets. Similarly, orthopedists may treat broken legs, but they are also working with elite athletes, trying to help them become even stronger and faster.

Child psychiatry training fares a bit better than adult psychiatry in this regard, due to its emphasis on development. In seminars for child psychiatry trainees, we learn about Piaget's cognitive stages of development (Inhelder & Piaget, 1958) and Erikson's eight stages of man that span from infancy through old age (Erikson, 1950). The emphasis, however, tends to be on what happens when things go wrong rather than how to maximize positive momentum going forward. Are these not the same thing? Very often, the answer is no. Understanding the toxic effects of trauma and abuse on early childhood development and the later manifestation of PTSD does not necessarily teach parents how to be optimally responsive and nurturing. Learning how prenatal exposure to nicotine, alcohol, or drugs affects the brain does not inform a pregnant mother about prenatal nutrition.

Many child and adolescent psychiatrists have limited exposure to typically developing children. In my training program at Massachusetts

General and McLean Hospital in Boston, we spent some time during our first few months observing and interacting with regular kids. We would go to a day care center to interact with preschool children. Our instructor also took us to playgrounds where we would watch and discuss the kids until their mothers, nervous about a clump of well-dressed adults observing their children, herded them away.

Now, as a training director of a new child and adolescent psychiatry fellowship program at the University of Vermont, I see many opportunities to include health promotion and wellness in the curriculum. Before starting our seminar on psychopathology, we cover the elements of happiness and well-being, and we are planning to add an entire new course on the subject. In our approach to children with attention problems, our fellows are trained to be facile not only in discussing the potential benefits of medications but also the potential benefits of reading and physical activity. These efforts tend to be welcomed by professionals in other areas. The multispecialty entity called the Vermont Child Health Improvement Program (VCHIP), for example, supported us in creating a blog run by child psychiatrists (Rettew, 2013). The blog includes topics related to diagnostic assessment and treatment as well as parenting, education, and family life.

The field of mental health in general and child and adolescent psychiatry in particular does not have to be defined so narrowly in terms of illness. Our experience and training can be used and expanded to incorporate principles of health and wellness more fully into our province. We are already taking steps in this direction. When Hudziak took the chair of the AACAP Prevention Committee, he renamed it the Health Promotion and Prevention Committee. The AACAP's peer-reviewed journal, which is seen as an important public interface for our field, has begun to include articles about wellness in addition to illness (Hudziak, Copeland, et al., 2003; Rettew, 2008), bolstered by scientific evidence that health promotion activities not only help the fit stay fit, but also help people who are at risk of or struggling with the burden of psychiatric illness (Gapin, Labban, & Etnier, 2011; Hudziak, 2008).

We now know that the boundaries between what is considered a trait and what is considered a disorder are not carved in stone, that the underlying biology and causative agents of temperament have much in common with those in psychiatric disorders, and that the factors that can make children well are frequently the same ones that help make children not sick. It is time to reinvent ourselves as true mental health profession-als, armed with this new knowledge and prepared to embrace the full potential of the developing brain.

Focusing on the Family

In adult psychiatry, a physician typically works directly and, in most cases, exclusively with the individual patient. Certainly there are excep-tions, especially in acute situations or with severely impaired patients, but by and large, we perform assessments by asking the patient a lot of questions, and we engineer treatment plans in one-on-one discussion with that person alone. We usually hear about other people—the malevo-lent boss, the criticizing spouse—but it is rare for a clinician to contact other figures in a patient's life directly. Instead, we try to strike a balance between empathizing with the patient's perspective and observing areas of daylight between this perspective and certain realities that may be hard for the patient to see. The clinician who can successfully accomplish both tasks can then be in that unique position of knowing both where the patient is and where the patient needs to be. If the clinician can only see the patient's view of things, then it is difficult to know what he or she needs to change. If the clinician doesn't spend enough time understand-ing the patient's perspective, there is a risk that the clinician's sugges-tions will be resisted because he or she just doesn't get it. If a balance is achieved, however, conditions are right to help the patient begin the arduous task of behavioral growth.

Child psychiatrists, in contrast, are taught to get clinical information from many different sources. Due to developmental limitations, most children are unable to provide an accurate history of their thoughts, feel-ings, and behavior without input from parents or guardians. Often, our evaluations have a "musical chairs" quality with various people being included and excluded from the office at different times within the same extended session. And since school performance is often a primary rea-son for seeking a child mental health consultation, teachers' reports are frequently included in the evaluation as well. Some clinicians strongly encourage older children and adolescents to talk first, without the par-ents present, in order to give the child first say. Others spend little time alone with the child, preferring a more efficient process of getting infor-mation mainly from the adults in a child's life.

A family history is taken either by simply asking questions (often without the child present) or through the use of questionnaires. Most mental health professionals ask about the presence of psychiatric disorders among immediate family members and close relatives. Family history inquiries are performed primarily in the service of accurately diagnosing the child. As the genetic influence of most psychiatric disorders is further appreciated, clinicians start to use diagnostic information in family members to make diagnoses in the presenting patient. If a parent has been diagnosed and treated for bipolar disorder, for example, and the diagnosis in the child is uncertain or hinging between bipolar disorder and something else, then the clinician may be more inclined to go with bipolar disorder based on the known family risk. The merits of such a practice can be debated but are not the focus here. Rather, the change in emphasis that is suggested comes from the idea of using family mental health information not just as a child diagnostic aid but as a potential target for further investigation and treatment.

Scientific evidence from both inside and outside the realm of temperament supports this shift. As described earlier, Thomas and Chess's goodness-of-fit theory postulated that behavioral problems result from combinations of child temperament and environmental characteristics (Rettew, Stanger, et al., 2006; Thomas & Chess, 1977). It follows, then, that positive change can develop not only from adjusting the child's behavior but also by modifying the environment, which often means working directly with parents and the family milieu. Parental psychopathology, such as depression or PTSD, can affect children quite dramatically, even apart from the shared genetic risk between offspring and parents (Beardslee, Versage, & Gladstone, 1998). And research has shown that successful treatment of parental psychiatric disorders can improve child behavior, even when the child is not treated directly. In a landmark study by Myrna Weissman and coworkers, the children of depressed mothers were followed over time (Weissman et al., 2006). Whereas behavioral problems significantly decreased among children whose mothers' depression was treated to remission, they remained constant in children whose mothers remained symptomatic. Of the children with a psychiatric diagnosis at baseline, one-third were in remission themselves if their parent was also not depressed at the time of follow-up. A study at the University of Vermont demonstrated that family-based cognitive-behavioral therapy in families with a depressed mother led to significantly reduced levels of anxiety and depressive problems in children at follow-up (Compas et al., 2009). Overall, the data show that a family-based approach benefits children who already are ill and is also an effective prevention for children who are at risk.

These findings are distinct from the vast literature on the importance of parenting and the efficacy of parenting-based interventions on a range of emotional-behavioral problems (Barkley & Benton, 1998). As appreciation for the role of genetics in child behavior increases, the idea that parenting is the exclusive or even primary influence on child outcomes is becoming outdated (Collins et al., 2000; Mekertichian & Bowes, 1996). Evocative gene–environment correlations, for example, suggest that poor parenting practices are sometimes an effect rather than a cause of negative child behavior. Although some studies have surely overemphasized the role of parenting by not controlling for genetic effects on child behavior, there is little doubt concerning the efficacy of parental guidance and environmental modifications in improving long-term outcomes.

All assessments in our clinic involve mental health assessment of the parents using rating scales completed prior to the appointment, and we discuss the results with the parents during the appointment. If a parent meets diagnostic criteria for a disorder, then the clinician schedules a more in-depth evaluation of the parent, refers the issue to the parent's primary care physician, or helps the parent find a mental health professional. Even if a parent does not meet diagnostic criteria, the instruments we use sometimes reveal "temperamental" levels of different traits that are still worth discussing, according to a goodness-of-fit model. Anxious parents may be prone to overprotecting their anxiety-prone children. Impulsive or aggressive parents may have trouble responding calmly to their impulsive or aggressive kids. This topic is covered in more detail in the next two chapters.

Furthermore, specifics about dietary habits, bedtime routines, video game usage, exercise and sports team participation, music and arts opportunities, religious ideas and practices, charitable activities, and so on may reveal important areas in a child's life where changes could have a significant impact. If a psychiatrist asks only about symptoms, then these important subjects will be missed, especially with parents who are hesitant or embarrassed to bring them up spontaneously.

The most common response I receive after describing the Vermont Family-Based Approach, and its parent-focused aspects in particular, is "that makes a lot of sense," followed by "doesn't everyone do this already?" Surprisingly, the answer is no. Psychiatrists are prone to get hung up on the individual symptoms of a child and the medications that might best match up to those symptoms. Child therapists can get very focused on the inner thoughts and feelings of the child, perhaps excluding direct work with the parents for fear of losing the child's trust. Even someone very skilled in psychotherapy, however, is often no match for the tide of a maladaptive family environment.

Another question that is frequently asked about the Vermont Family-Based Approach is how parents feel about having the spotlight turned on them. It is a great question, and the answer is that the vast majority of time the process goes smoothly. Occasionally parental rating scales are mailed back to us empty, and once in a great while a family will walk out of an appointment when we talk about this aspect of our care. But that isn't a bad record given the number of evaluations that we have done.

Our relative success likely has to do with a couple key provisions. First, we let families know how we think in our introductory letter and in a video on our website. That way, few people are surprised when they come for the first visit. Perhaps more important, we make an effort to frame the topic of parental responsibility in a positive light. As mentioned previously, psychiatry had its phase of blaming all child problems on the parents, before the pendulum swung the other way and child behavior was thought to be mostly due to genes operating more or less automatically. Science has taught us that both impressions were faulty and that child traits and emotional-behavioral problems are the result of complex and mutually influencing genetic and environmental variables. Armed with this understanding, it makes little sense to blame parents or exclude the family environment altogether.

For example, if frequent outbursts occur because a temperamentally irritable child struggles with a temperamentally irritable parent in the context of a chaotic home environment, then who is really our patient anyway? To us, that whole pattern of interaction is the true "client"—cocreated by the child, the parents, and other aspects of the family surroundings. As we heard in Chapter 4, genetic influences on child temperament traits evoke particular responses from parents (who themselves tend to have some of the same traits), which in turn reinforces and magnifies those traits. If we embrace this mechanism in clinical practice, then our work must include the parents not as the origin of the child's problems but as a critical treatment element that needs to be fully empowered. As Hudziak often likes to say, "It is tough to be a parent, tougher to be a parent of a child with emotional-behavioral problems, and tougher still to be a parent of a child with emotional-behavioral problems when you yourself are struggling with many of the same challenges."

It can take time to explain this perspective, but when framed well, conveying the importance of parenting and parental psychopathology does not sound blameful, but rather supportive and squarely on the mark. One surprise I have encountered in the course of discussions with parents is that many people don't personally identify with their own genes. As someone who has done genetic research, genes seem to me something very personal, but I seem to be in the minority with this position. Instead, many parents are quite comfortable blaming "those genes" that cause them to be impulsive when dealing with their impulsive child, for example. As long as the parent understands that genetic influence is malleable, focusing on genetic tendencies can help some parents take ownership of their contribution without feeling criticized or humiliated.

In summary, an appreciation of the multiple environmental forces shaping both temperament and psychiatric disorders compel us as clinicians to widen the net beyond our identified patient and to examine the entirety of his or her environment. If parents are suffering under the burden of psychiatric illness, or even if they find themselves locked into responding to their child in suboptimal ways because of their own temperamental predilections, much can be gained by trying to incorporate all of these elements into a comprehensive treatment plan. Framing this approach through an understanding of science and an appreciation that most parents are doing their best and are not deliberately trying to damage their children can go a long way toward creating a collaborative atmosphere between clinicians and parents.

It is worth mentioning that the Vermont Family-Based Approach and other models like it are beginning to generate momentum not only in child psychiatry (Reiss, 2011) but also among some of our adult mental health colleagues. All psychiatry residents at the University of Vermont in their third of four years, including those with no interest in child psychiatry, are required to spend one day per week in a pediatric psychiatry clinic, where they learn and implement the Vermont Family-Based Approach. Many residents, after returning to their adult psychiatry settings, tell me that they now seek additional input about their patients' behavior before making a final assessment. They are also quicker to spot opportunities to reach out to spouses, parents, and children in instances where further evaluation and treatment might be useful to them.

Ryan and Lisa Revisited

Although replacing a binary yes/no disease model focused on the individual patient with a quantitative health-promoting model focused on the entire family seems relatively logical and simple, the resulting treatment plans might be markedly different from a more traditional model. To illustrate this point, let's return to the hypothetical vignettes of Ryan and Lisa.

Ryan was manifesting some difficulties with attention, hyperactivity, and impulsivity that were especially prominent at home. The family atmosphere was tense due to frequent conflicts with the father, who reported having some of the same behavioral tendencies as his son. The psychiatrist did an evaluation based on DSM criteria, diagnosed the child with ADHD, and began stimulant treatment. This type of scenario happens routinely in medical settings every day.

Incorporating the principles of quantifying behaviors, promoting wellness and health, and treating the entire family environment, the formulation and outcome might look something like this:

> The psychiatrist performs an evaluation not only of the child but of the whole family. While Ryan indeed meets DSM criteria for ADHD, a quantitative scale indicates that his ADHD symptoms are relatively mild. Ryan's father also demonstrates clinical levels of inattention and aggression, although he is not abusive. The psychiatrist explains, with Ryan in the room, that activity level and attention span exist on a continuum just like height or blood pressure and that everyone falls somewhere along this continuum. Ryan simply falls toward the higher end compared with most other children. The clinician encourages Ryan's father to speak about his own struggles in these areas both now and as a child, which seems to make Ryan feel less "defective." While not ruling out a medication for Ryan at some point, the psychiatrist proposes a series of nonpharmacological interventions to try first, including participation on a sports team to get regular exercise, a firm bedtime, a

good breakfast every morning, and some parental coaching to help Ryan's parents come up with additional options for responding to these very challenging behaviors. After showing the father the outcome of his own behavioral screening, the psychiatrist helps the father make an appointment with his physician for further assessment and possible treatment. Six months later, the father is now taking a medication for ADHD and reports that this has helped increase his resilience, resulting in a noticeable drop in hostility at home. Ryan himself has responded to the behavioral interventions and, while he is still "on the active side," there does not seem to be a compelling need to begin pharmacological treatment.

By taking a broader view of Ryan's behavior, bringing in wellness components of diet and exercise, and dealing directly with the father's own difficulties, the overall system has been decompressed from multiple vantage points. Ryan's behavior has not "remitted" according to a disease model, but it has shifted down the continuum to a point that lies below most clinical thresholds. The fact that medication was not prescribed is a positive development, but not the primary indication of success.

Turning to Lisa, our new approach could result in a number of changes to her overall treatment plan as well.

The psychiatrist performs an evaluation and commends the family for their efforts to make changes in Lisa's environment. They discuss some additional steps that might be taken, including a more formal plan of modifications and accommodations at school (often called a 504 plan) and possibly having a tutor provide additional academic help at home. The psychiatrist suggests that the parents investigate books that Lisa might really like to help her build her skills and bring some pleasure back to the process of reading. In reviewing the quantitative rating scales for ADHD, he shows the parents that while Lisa does not have the requisite number of symptoms to qualify formally for the diagnosis of ADHD, the severity of the difficulties she does have puts her in the 97th percentile for attention problems compared to other girls her age. He thus recommends a trial of a medication to help with these problems and to increase the likelihood that the nonpharmacological interventions will take hold. Before recommending medication, the psychiatrist had weighed the results of IQ testing, which indicated that Lisa may not have the degree of compensatory cognitive skills that many other children have in order to overcome her attentional deficits. Six months later, the combination of treatments has helped Lisa catch up academically and enjoy her time at school.

Here, the psychiatrist did not see his role as a gatekeeper of psychopharmacological treatment but rather as someone who can evaluate the big picture and make recommendations with a goal of improving Lisa's attention and reducing her frustration with school. He also was not beholden to a binary and somewhat inflexible DSM system; instead, he took into account the severity of the attention problems along with her overall intellectual profile. The presumptive diagnosis in this case might be something like disruptive behavior disorder not otherwise specified, an unsatisfying term that in many ways seems off the mark in Lisa's case, but it does help Lisa qualify for the additional academic help that she certainly needs.

In summary, a temperament-based viewpoint on psychopathology, especially one that appreciates the many interacting influences that cause traits to magnify or diminish, opens the door to a new clinical model that stresses health promotion and appropriate treatment for a child's entire family. Like a tropical plant growing in a terrarium, a child's health depends on the proper functioning of the entire ecosystem. The best plant food or even full sunlight will not be enough to help the plant thrive if the environment is otherwise not conducive to growth. Mental health models like the Vermont Family-Based Approach push us to define ourselves beyond traditional labels (pharmacologist, therapist, psychiatrist) and oblige us to look at the larger landscape, even if we are not the one who is directly working on each aspect. Using a model that pushes us out of our comfort zone can be challenging, especially at first: The boundaries aren't so clear, the causal pathways are not so straightforward, the number of moving parts is much greater. The end result, however, is a clinical model that most closely reflects current scientific knowledge and provides a flexible toolkit for making a real and sustainable difference.

Chapter 8

Temperament and Parenting, Part I

Chapter 7 contended that a temperament-informed view of development compels family members to be very actively involved in any efforts to increase wellness and deal effectively with child behavioral challenges. The logical question that stems from those supportive of such a position, then, is how exactly that goal is accomplished. Here, we try to put some meat onto those bones with more specific principles and strategies that family members can adopt both in general and in response to children with specific temperament profiles. This chapter outlines a number of general parenting topics as they relate to child temperament, while Chapter 9 goes into more specifics about strategies that work with specific temperament profiles. Once again, the section is written from the perspective of a clinician who is working with a family, but it can be readily adapted to more direct recommendations for parents reading the book themselves.

I would love to be able to claim exclusive rights to a specific "temperament program" designed to accentuate the positive and diminish the negative aspects of every trait. If we accept the amalgamation of temperament and psychopathology, however, the truth is that the many approaches and programs that have demonstrated efficacy in particular psychiatric conditions will likely also be worthwhile in temperament. Indeed, many of these packaged remedies often share critical elements with each other, even if the particular slogans or acronyms sound quite distinct. Such is also the case here, with the caveat that the emphasis for the following recommendations is on adapting effective principles learned from scientific study rather than a "shoot first and ask questions later" framework of making a shiny and highly marketable program whose efficacy is never tested.

These two chapters are not meant to be a firm clinical manual with specific topics addressed within strict time frames, but rather a basic framework that might guide clinicians who are interested in a temperament-informed treatment paradigm. For clinicians working with new families, this outline could be put into practice as a time-limited intervention. For those already working with children and their families, such as a therapist using a more supportive approach or a psychiatrist looking to go beyond a "med check," the guide could be used to provide additional structure to an existing treatment, although many of these activities would likely best be conducted without the child present. A concise outline of the topics covered in this chapter can be found in Table 8.1.

First, a word of caution and, hopefully, reassurance related to learning about optimal parenting behavior. Very often, such exercises can leave people feeling criticized and defensive about their abilities as parents, a stance that is not particularly conducive to change. Others can be left feeling as though their children would be better off adopted by somebody else—perhaps the clinician, author, or speaker, who seems to be in total command of this stuff. In my own practice, it is not uncommon for me to be asked whether I have children of my own. The subcontext of a question like that often seems to be related to the issue of whether or not I really understand that parenting is difficult, imperfect, and, at times, exasperating. Believe me, I do. From this perspective, I often approach the topic using language such as this: "I want to start the conversation about parenting from the radical position that I bet there are certain things you are doing as parents that are truly awesome and other things that are a struggle. I'm also going to disclose from the start that I make no claims to have the right answer every time or to be perfect in my own execution of these principles with my own family."

The good news is that parenting can also be some of the most joyful and rewarding work we ever do, and that perfection, apart from not being possible, may not even be ideal. In our slip-ups and mistakes in the course of "good enough" parenting (Winnicott, 1953), there are ample opportunities both to take a step toward real self-improvement and also to demonstrate to similarly imperfect children that parents too are humans who have the ability to use our lapses productively. While the

TABLE 8.1.
An Outline for a Temperament-Based Parental Guidance Program

Topics	Major Tasks
Education around temperament and major dimensions or types	1. Explain principal dimensions and profiles of temperament 2. Describe mixed genetic and environmental causes of temperament
Assessment of child (and sibling) temperament	1. Measure temperament using rating scales or accompanying table
Measurement of parental personality or temperament	1. Measure personality using rating scales or accompanying table
Labeling in pencil	1. Engage family in discussion about what labels may apply and what they do and do not mean 2. Present specific family temperament data according to these principles
Acceptance	1. Explain positive and negative aspects that are part of all traits 2. Engage parents in honest discussion of their "ideal" child 3. Discuss positive aspects of child's temperament
Education of parental types—general and specific to family	1. Outline the four major parenting types 2. Help family identify their type and areas of improvement regarding warmth and limits
Coaching up and coaching around	1. Contrast interventions that are designed to change child with those designed to change environment 2. Determine areas where additional modifications would be helpful 3. Assign changes and check back on progress
The override button	1. Explain how child's behavior can evoke suboptimal responses in parent, which then reinforce original behavior 2. Identify examples in family 3. Discuss alternative responses 4. Assign homework and report on progress

continued on next page

TABLE 8.1 *continued*	
Modeling	1. Explain importance of modeling
	2. Identify areas (particularly around shared parent-child traits) of suboptimal modeling
	3. Challenge a change in parental behavior and monitor progress
Shielding and exposing	1. Help parents understand dual needs of shielding children and letting them overcome things on their own
	2. Identify area where balance is not ideal
	3. Discuss specific areas for modification
	4. Assign homework and monitor progress
United stance	1. Help parents assess own level of agreement when it comes to parenting
	2. Identify different parental roles and comfort level with those roles
	3. If needed, challenge and reassign roles and monitor progress
	4. Help parents compromise on key areas of disagreement

parent-blaming era has passed, its remnants linger in our culture, and it is rare to encounter a family in a child mental health clinic that does not harbor at least some guilt and shame related to their child's struggles.

More and more, science has been reminding us that some sort of balance is required between the idea that parenting is the sole determinant of child behavior and the idea that parenting is merely a by-product of child behavior. The previous section on genetic and environmental interplay described many examples of the intricate mechanisms through which genetic factors can increase the likelihood that certain environments will be present and how, in turn, environmental factors can have a strong biological effect on gene expression. There were also many examples of how particular environmental factors can have smaller or larger effects based on a person's genetically influenced vulnerabilities.

These studies and findings are not only fascinating in their own right but immensely practical in helping us conceptualize child behavior and consequently, how we deal with it. In many ways, they prevent parents, doctors, and child mental professionals alike from ignoring convenient aspects of development that we might prefer not to address. Now we have to understand and work with the whole picture and not just a single piece of the puzzle. Parenting, in this new light, may get neither the credit nor the blame it used to have, but at the same time it is once again a centerpiece of child development and a critical target of intervention. The trick is to help the parents we work with see themselves as intensely relevant in shaping developmental outcomes without believing that they are the only important factor.

One metaphor of this balance might be winter driving. Up where I come from in New England, we see ourselves as pretty capable drivers when it comes to snow and ice, and we base this confidence on our general ability to get around reasonably well when the weather is poor. Sure, there are accidents from time to time, but mostly traffic copes with the conditions quite well, with minimal injury or disruption. In contrast, we watch the evening news and notice how seemingly much less intense winter weather can cripple metropolitan areas that are not accustomed to it. The screen shows motorists spinning in circles, banging into trash cans, and careening out of control. These images instill a bit of smugness in drivers up north, while making many from the south doubt themselves even further at the first falling snowflake.

What we forget in these appraisals is that while there may be some real differences in our experience and skill in winter driving conditions, much of our success or failure when we venture out in the snow has to do with the condition of the road. In New England, there are large workforces and budgets to stack the odds of an uneventful road trip in our favor. The salt, sand, and plowing often make the roads actually not that difficult to drive on. In contrast, the lack of those same things causes roads in other parts of the country to become treacherous even with relatively minor amounts of snow and ice. The truth is that if I drove on those roads, things might not go as smoothly as they do up north.

Assessing Family Temperament

The first steps in the process involve identifying the temperamental tendencies of all family members and how they can play out in a parenting context. To achieve this goal, it can be useful to obtain standardized ratings of behavior of both the child or children and the parents. Our clinic,

as previously mentioned, uses the ASEBA scales, which are not temperament scales per se but are strongly associated with them. They further
have the advantage of being well normed for both children and adults,
so the clinician can easily see where someone's behavior falls along the
continuum based on sex and age. You can also choose to use one of the
many actual temperament scales described in Chapter 2 but may need to
do more work in terms of interpreting the results since they don't come
with handy reference ranges. In our research studies, we have utilized the
temperament scales of Rothbart and colleagues (2001), which do have
published studies on representative samples that can be applied to the
scores of your patient or client. We have also had success with the Temperament and Character Inventory (Cloninger et al., 1994) and its Junior
version, which is adapted for children (Luby et al., 1999). Easier to use
but less scientifically validated temperament assessment tools are also
available (Harkey & Jourgensen, 2009). In the personality realm, parents
can complete instruments such as the NEO-FFI (Costa & McCrae, 1992)
that are relatively user friendly and come with established norms. Finally,
it is also possible to have a more informal discussion with the family
about the major dimensions of temperament that family members possess at higher or lower levels. Table 8.2 offers an easy way to document
the temperament of family members using either a dimensional approach
or by categories, according to the structure outlined in Chapter 2. Clinicians can utilize and modify the table as appropriate.

   In the process, it can be very illuminating to have individuals try to
rate not only themselves but also other family members. For lower-con-
flict families where there is not a great concern over labeling, this part of
the process can often be done with the children present. In doing so, families may find a big difference between the way a person describes him- or
herself and the way someone else describes that person. The factors
behind such a discrepancy are varied but can be explored in a productive
discussion under the right circumstances. Someone might see himself as
very shy, much to the surprise of everyone else. Conversely, someone who
labels herself as very calm and rational might be rated as quite agitated
by other members of a family. Giving everyone the space to voice their
impressions safely and constructively can, in many cases, be more beneficial than arriving at "the truth" for each person. Sometimes, the source
of these differences of opinion says a lot about how temperamentally
based outward behavior is modified over time. Children who may be

	TABLE 8.2. Documenting a Family's Temperament by Dimensions			
	Child (Identified Patient)	Sibling	Mother	Father
Negative emotionality	High	High	High	High
	Medium	Medium	Medium	Medium
	Low	Low	Low	Low
Extraversion/surgency	High	High	High	High
	Medium	Medium	Medium	Medium
	Low	Low	Low	Low
Activity level	High	High	High	High
	Medium	Medium	Medium	Medium
	Low	Low	Low	Low
Sociability	High	High	High	High
	Medium	Medium	Medium	Medium
	Low	Low	Low	Low
Regulation	High	High	High	High
	Medium	Medium	Medium	Medium
	Low	Low	Low	Low

prone to be more impulsive, shy, or aggressive, but who also possess good regulatory abilities to resist those emotions, may find, as adolescents or adults, that the self-appraisal of their temperament continues to reflect those internal states while the judgment of others follows the observable actions that come under the control of those increased regulation skills. Which is the real temperament—the anxious feelings or the composed presentation—is probably less important than understanding and appreciating the process.

To avoid individuals feeling overly judged or criticized, it is important for the clinician to frame the discussion, keeping in mind both the potential benefits and drawbacks of a particular trait. It is here that the idea of the "yet" phenomenon can be brought up (see Chapter 3). Most parents would idealize the child who is, for example, high exuberant yet highly self-controlled, but that combination is rather unusual. The idea is that the task for families is to work to overcome the negative aspects of a trait but also to draw upon and accentuate the positive ones.

The Four Parenting Styles

Before plunging into general parenting principles, it can be useful to introduce more general concepts of parenting to the family. Parenting styles have been classified into different types, just like temperament dimensions. While parents would love to believe that they have fully chosen their particular style, there are likely many influences upon our choices of how to parent. Indeed, parental temperament is likely a major contributor to the development of a particular style, in addition to a number of other factors such as the parenting style one experienced as a child (or perhaps wanted to experience but didn't), and the values and traditions of one's culture.

Over the years, a number of parenting scholars have tried to classify parenting styles into discrete categories. Probably the most widely known is a four-category model that crosses two major dimensions of parenting behavior, namely the level of warmth and the level of control (Baumrind, 1991; Maccoby & Martin, 1983). The framework divides parents into possessing either high or low levels of warmth and control with an acknowledgment that, just like temperament categories, the characteristics exist in more quantitative form. With high or low levels of warmth on one axis and high or low levels of control on the other, we form four different parenting styles (Table 8.3).

TABLE 8.3

Supervision and Control

		High	Low
Affection and Warmth	High	Authoritative	Permissive
	Low	Authoritarian	Uninvolved

Authoritative (High Control, High Warmth)

Authoritative parenting is characterized by parents maintaining firm limits on their children but doing so in an atmosphere that is loving, compassionate, and sometimes flexible. Mothers and fathers in this category try to offer choices when possible and provide explanations. They listen to their children carefully and use punishment sparingly. At the same time, however, this parenting style tends to be rather active and deliberate, with parents establishing clear expectations for their child's behavior and then monitoring that the expectations are being met.

Authoritarian (High Control, Low Warmth)

In the authoritarian category are parents who, like the authoritative ones, set limits and expect them to be followed. Here, however, the rules tend to be more strict and rigid, with decisive action following any transgressions. The reasons given for following rules may be phrases like "because I said so" rather than deeper explanations. In contrast to that of authoritative parents, the government structure in these families tends to be much more of a dictatorship than a democracy (although many advocates of authoritative parenting would likely say that the democracy includes a strong president). Further, families with a more authoritarian structure often feature quite a bit of criticism, with praise being in short supply.

Permissive (Low Control, High Warmth)

Families with permissive parents have fewer rules and rarely use punishment. The children often have much more autonomy, and confrontation between parents and children is kept at a minimum. There can remain a great deal of love and affection for children in these families, but less in the way of firm expectations. When children from permissive families grow up, they often describe their parents more as friends than any kind of authority figures. Permissive parents generally want their children to develop good values and habits but tend to let their children arrive at them through their own means and timetable. Natural consequences rather than consequences imposed by the parents predominate in the developmental process.

Uninvolved (Low Control, Low Warmth)

In the uninvolved group are families who spend considerably less time with their children and leave them to their own devices out of a general lack of regard. When uninvolved parents do engage with their kids, the tone is often harsh and critical. One pattern that is often observed with uninvolved parents is not to deal with a child's negative behavior at first and then to yell at the child when the behavior exceeds a threshold beyond which it can no longer be ignored. At its extreme, uninvolvement can progress to frank neglect, although more commonly a child's basic needs are attended to but the parents are simply more preoccupied with their own independent lives or are overwhelmed with life struggles.

With the exception of the uninvolved group, the idea is that there is no universally correct style for every child, although the authoritative position is generally viewed as the one most conducive to positive development for the greatest number of children. This broad conclusion, however, does not mean that more authoritarian or permissive styles are necessarily wrong for specific combinations of parents and children or at certain times during a child's life. The setting of clear limits for children may be critical when the child is in elementary school, for example, but then needs to be relaxed later in adolescence to allow for those principles to be internalized and fully embraced. The presence of particular temperamental traits, especially at more extreme levels, can create a need to modify a parent's usual mode of parenting. Indeed, Chapter 9 is devoted to some parenting behaviors that deserve particular attention among the major temperament types. Before proceeding to these specifics, however, it is probably worth first going over more global principles relevant to temperament and parenting.

Labeling in Pencil

Sometimes during this assessment process, parents ask about the pros and cons of attaching labels, diagnostic or temperamental, to a developing child. Parents can feel motivated to promote self-understanding in their children while at the same time trying to avoid stigmatizing labels. These two goals may seem quite reasonable and attainable at first blush; after all, self-understanding relates to the mind's ability to reflect upon itself and build perspective, while labeling tends to denote a more dismissive, negative, and overly simplistic characterization. Many parents might be happy to find out that their child is able to "use his words" and recognize a feeling of worry when meeting new people. Most parents would similarly resist a child seeing herself as a "scaredy cat." In the first instance what is being labeled is fleeting emotion, while in the second example it is a broad description that might constrain a child in the future. The boundaries between the two poles, however, can begin to get muddled, especially when it comes to many of the terms used to describe temperament traits. How should parents react to their child's announcement that, after some self-reflection, she realizes that she is "a shy person"?

The concern about even benign-sounding terms such as shyness is that they are confining and can be used not only as a framework to understand past behavior but also as a boundary that limits options going forward. We have learned from scientists of social cognition that people often use their self-descriptions as a crutch or shortcut to guide them in how they act in new situations or think about new information. We like to think that our self-identity is the result of our ability to recognize how we have felt or acted in the past, but such terms can also become lenses through which we make future decisions. If you have first defined yourself, for example, as a Democrat or Republican, then the task of staking out a political position on the hot-button issue of the day becomes a bit simpler than having to slog through the details, trying to shape a new attitude from scratch.

Would the little girl who identifies herself as shy begin to raise her hand in class and then stop because such behavior doesn't compute with being a shy child? Would the boy who sees himself as the class clown be more likely to restrain his antics if he didn't carry that internal stamp? Finding that balance between helping your children know themselves temperamentally while not imprisoning them with labels can be made easier through applying the new knowledge reviewed earlier: Far from being immovable destiny, temperamental traits often change quite a bit over time. Thus, it is not the term itself that is limiting but its conventional definition. In response to the girl who sees herself as shy, one quite reasonable and potentially beneficial response might be, "What does that word 'shy' mean to you?" The answer might provide an opportunity to explain that shyness is a tendency to feel a bit nervous around new people but that many things can be done to increase someone's comfort in social situations.

The language parents use can also be important. Our culture has now embraced the idea of labeling behavior rather than individuals in everyday situations. For example, a boy is *behaving badly* rather than *being a bad boy*. I believe the differences, while seeming subtle and simply politically correct to some, do have importance in how children begin to construct themselves internally. Temperamental terms can be used the same way. Instead of saying, "That a girl isn't a very social person," one could say, "She does not feel like playing with a lot of people today." In this way, a behavior is recognized and understood while not introducing parameters that don't belong there: a label written in pencil that can be erased and changed over time.

Acceptance

This statement may be preaching to the choir, but it is important for parents to be able to accept and to cherish their children for who they are. Most kids crave approval and validation from their parents. Withholding that validation, especially for things beyond children's full control like temperamental traits, can be quite harmful. Optimal growth is often achieved by helping children work best with what they have rather than waging a continuous battle to turn an apple into an orange. Recalling Chapter 3's discussion of temperament stability, the finding emerged that although there certainly can be quite a bit of change over time in the levels of temperamental traits, it is unusual for a child to move completely across the spectrum and change from being, for example, a shy and sensitive toddler to a dominant and gregarious adolescent.

As I have observed in my clinical practice, it is not uncommon for this struggle of accepting children for who they are to play out among some of my more high-functioning families, albeit in somewhat subtle ways. Parents in these families are usually very invested in their child's development and welfare and often have clear ideas about what is optimal for their child's well-being. These attitudes come largely from feelings of genuine love for the kids, but often can be mixed with the hope that through their children, the parents' own status and self-worth will be elevated. Bringing up a "good kid" with high achievement will reflect well on parents and their abilities. In some cases, often voiced through the very generous-sounding hope that a child will do better than the parents, the pressure to complete the unfulfilled dreams of the parent can push children in directions that aren't right for them. Sometimes this drive is more obvious, for example, in the case of the injured athlete who transfers his or her own sports ambitions onto a child. In other instances, the process can be more insidious. Since these parents are often quite competent and loving, the pull on a child to be who the parents want him or her to be can be quite strong (Miller, 1981). Winnicott described this progression as leading to the development of a "false self," but I believe a conversation with parents about such pressures can be held without invoking a lot of psychodynamic theory or lingo. Indeed, some exploration with parents about a child's ideal versus actual temperament can invoke many of the same themes.

All that said, parental acceptance of a child's temperament is not the same as resignation. Rather, it is the idea of working within a system rather than trying to force a new one and striving toward goals that are authentically in the service of the child as opposed to the parent. When an ocean swimmer begins to be dragged into deeper waters by an undertow, what gets him back safely is not to swim directly into the current but rather to move parallel to the shore to find less turbulent water. When a sailboat's course is impeded by a stiff headwind, the captain doesn't point the boat directly at the wind, but rather tacks back and forth to reach the destination in smaller segments.

There's no doubt that it can be difficult to balance the necessity of acceptance and the imperative of shaping behavior in directions that ultimately benefit the child. Stumbles off this fine line are bound to occur, and it is important for clinicians to anticipate them and to help parents recognize that such lapses are unlikely to undermine the overall momentum. The ability of parents to encourage target behavior more than criticizing less desirable behavior, to remain warm and positive, and to be able to listen and to incorporate their child's input to the fullest extent possible can all go a long way toward pulling off this delicate but important equilibrium.

Coaching Up and Coaching Around

Once a family has a sense of everyone's temperamental predispositions and an understanding of what such tendencies do and do not mean, parents can begin the process of balancing an acceptance, even a treasuring, of those traits while at the same time embarking on a very conscious course of modifications that can diminish certain features that are problematic or less adaptive. One of the fundamental principles for this and the next two chapters is that the pathway to maximizing temperamental predispositions involves striking a balance between efforts to change the environment to best suit the child and efforts to change the child to thrive in a particular environment. In sports parlance, it is the blending of coaching up and coaching around.

The notion stems from a particular trait's goodness of fit with the environment. Here, the environment can refer to a number of elements including characteristics of the neighborhood, socioeconomic status, culturally bound customs, the educational system and practices, and of course the specific home milieu and personality of the parents. For many families, characteristics of the environment, especially related to the physical surroundings and the stressors associated with a particular country or neighborhood, are not easy to change directly. Other aspects, such as specific parenting practices, are more amenable to adjustments and are the focus of this section. Traditionally, these adjustments, under the older notion that temperament traits are fixed, have emphasized steps one can take to alter the environment so that an existing trait fits better and is less problematic (i.e., coaching around). While such actions continue to be important, our more contemporary view of temperament supported by the emerging research tells us that temperament traits can also be coached up to improve their fit with the environment. Thus, it is not the job of the parent simply to take a figurative machete to the environment and clear an easy path for the child's temperament as it currently exists. Such a strategy, without striving for any concomitant change in the child, can stunt emotional growth and ill prepare the child for many of the realities of the modern world. At the same time, focusing only on changing child behavior often results in high levels of conflict and frustration by trying to push someone further than he or she realistically can go. It also can send a very clear message to the child that he or she is fundamentally not okay and needs to be altered.

Fortunately, parents don't have to go on record and declare particular interventions as either child changing or environment changing because the boundaries between these types are frequently unclear. Many things parents can do to improve temperamental fit would qualify as changing both the child and the environment. Consider, for example, the extra preparation that a father might do with an anxious 6-year-old boy before the first day of first grade. The father might take the child to the school a few days before classes begin to make sure he knows where the classroom is and perhaps to meet the teacher early for some one-on-one time. After that, the boy may feel more prepared and confident when the day comes and may get through it without any major problems. Such an intervention could be seen as changing the environment or coaching around, as the father created his own "get to know your new classroom" day that otherwise may not have happened, but at the same time the boy was coached up to become less anxious while still doing exactly what every other child was expected to do, namely, to show up on the first day of school and begin learning with his new class. In the end, what matters is not what category each type of action falls into but promoting methods that foster positive growth and adaptation.

One common misinterpretation of the goodness-of-fit principle is that a good fit equates with similarity between characteristics of the child and characteristics of the environment. What elements make a fit good or bad are not always obvious. In some cases, such similarity can indeed lead to good fit, such as when an active girl who tends to need higher levels of stimulation learns well from a teacher who herself is dynamic and lively. In other instances, however, analogous qualities between the child and environment can produce a poor fit, which leads to an exacerbation of difficulties. When this energetic child has a birthday party, for example, a better fit may be created by having fewer guests and more low-key activities, as the opposite could well lead to complete over-stimulation and an eventual meltdown that could spoil the fun of the day. Chapter 4 showed examples of child temperament traits that were amplified by an environment that had the same characteristics as the child, such as a similar trait in the parent, leading to more overt behavioral problems and sometimes even a diagnosable psychiatric disorder (Rettew, Stanger, et al., 2006).

When talking to families, I often use the term *inertia*: the idea that a body at rest or in motion will stay that way unless a force acts upon it. The presence of high levels of a particular trait can generate a significant amount of momentum that, in the absence of concerted effort, will often cause that trait to snowball. At that point, the trait can become less flexible and more maladaptive. For example, a school-age boy who tends to be low in the trait of surgency often will not take the initiative to get involved with his world and may seem quite content to sit at home and watch TV or play video games. If this trait is paired with similar features in the parents, who may let the weekends pass watching sports in the next room, inertia is building toward an outcome of disengagement, isolation, and perhaps depression. What is required here is for the parents to be the force that can change that momentum (or in this case the lack thereof) and begin to set a new course. The clinician can help the parents identify this tendency in themselves, recognize the impact that it may have on their child, and support (without blaming) them in overriding that tendency for the sake of the entire family's health. Since parents generally have more control over their behavior than children, it is important to help parents remember that the onus falls on them to adjust elements of the environment (including themselves), which can result in an improved fit.

The Override Button

The critical skill of a parent being able to engage with a child in a way that is not dictated by either the parent's or child's temperament deserves some additional discussion. It comes directly from the science of evocative gene–environment correlation, described earlier, and the way that certain environmental factors are more likely to occur because they are literally being pulled out of us, based upon the genetically influenced temperament of the child. This richer context for understanding how behavior develops can go a long way toward describing such interactions as more than just poor parenting choices. A father of a temperamentally irritable boy who is prone to shout at the boy for relatively minor infractions is certainly not relieved of responsibility for his behavior, but it can be understood from a perspective that some of his suboptimal responses are evoked by the child's behavior, partially influenced by shared genes that cause both of them to escalate in negative ways.

Models such as the Vermont Family-Based Approach and others incorporate this emerging science and move past mere documenting of symptoms by addressing the entire family environment. Once these important aspects are assessed, they then become a principle focus of intervention. People joke that families leave our clinic with medications, but it is parents rather than the child who are taking them. At the same time, scripts are written not just for methylphenidate and fluoxetine but also for exercise, book reading, or violin lessons.

In this model that views child behavior as changing fluidly along a continuum from the level of a temperamental trait to the level of psychiatric disorder, parents are actively encouraged and supported to change some of their own behavior, not because they are inherently deficient but, as our director Jim Hudziak often comments, because they need to learn how to be super parents in order to respond to the intense challenges posed to them by their children. Parenting youngsters with strong temperamental tendencies or full-blown psychiatric disorders is "twice as hard, and twice as important." In my own work with families, we often say that parents need to learn how to hit the override button when it comes to mustering alternative and often more constructive parental reactions than they would have under typical circumstances. The task requires a degree of self-understanding on the part of the parents as to their own behavioral tendencies, in addition to strong knowledge of the child. The arena for change, consequently, is not the "bad" child or the "bad" parent, but rather the behaviors and interactions themselves, generated by a multitude of genetic and environmental influences.

After introducing the topic, clinicians can probe for specific examples with the family by asking in what way the child is a master of "pushing their buttons" or "bringing out the worst in them." Highly driven parents, for example, might become quickly exasperated with a child who is more lackadaisical and distracted, leading parents toward two suboptimal responses: (a) doing everything for the child for the sake of efficiency, or (b) becoming outwardly frustrated and critical. If parents can identify this trend in themselves and learn to navigate through a different response such as calmly holding the line and helping the child finish what he or she is supposed to do, they will slowly recognize the rewards of their new strategy.

Thinking about the earlier example of the low-intensity child paired with low-intensity parents, the clinician working with this family might counsel the family with language like this:

> In our work together we have determined that, temperamentally, your child often tends not to have a lot of initiative and drive on his own. While it may not be productive to try and mold him to run for president, I do have concern that this trait might snowball over time to the point that it becomes more and more difficult to achieve whatever goals he has for the future. By not participating in many of the things kids do, he is losing opportunities to develop skills and interests. This could eventually develop into his feeling isolated and depressed. Dad, you rate yourself much the same way

in this trait and told me earlier that as a child, you felt as though your peers were passing you by. It is possible that both you and your son have some of the same genetic influence on this trait, but we know that many things can be done to change our trajectories. What I want to try to do today, then, is to supportively push you to push him. Let's make a plan today that you will discuss with your child the requirement that he will participate in a new activity or sport for the season. We will give him a choice of exactly what it is and try to find one that doesn't push him too far or set him up for failure, but he will commit to doing something and you will commit to getting him through it. Why don't we talk now about some possible choices that might work? Then at the next visit you can tell me how it went.

The intervention involves both aspects of changing the environment to fit the child and changing the child to fit the environment. If things work successfully, the child might come to enjoy his new activity, thereby reinforcing the behavior and increasing the likelihood that he might try additional activities in the future. By not overshooting the goal and allowing the child to pick among a number of possible choices, the environment will conform to his temperamental style so that he won't be pressed to be the proverbial square peg in a round hole. The strategy actively involves the father by recognizing that he is one of the driving forces shaping this child's environment that, up until now, has been conspiring to magnify the child's low surgency to diminishing and counterproductive levels. Pushing the father, however, is done with the explicit appreciation that he will have to swim against the current of his own temperament and override his own tendency to disengage. Indeed, the comment about reporting on their progress at the next visit is designed to add some external motivation, similar to a homework assignment, to overcome a relative lack of intrinsic drive to accomplish the task.

In discussing parental overrides, I realize that the advice sounds like it may go against the suggestions of legendary parenting authors such as Dr. Spock to parent in a way that feels natural and intuitive. However, these two directives don't need to be contradictory. Indeed, a blending of both recommendations can serve to keep temperamental tendencies in balance so that they don't expand into full-blown behavioral syndromes and psychiatric disorders. In working with families, it is important to acknowledge how difficult it can be for parents to work against their own temperamental currents and natural reactions evoked by the child's behavior. To help parents be good swimmers, their own behavioral predispositions need to be recognized and their efforts to work through them celebrated.

Modeling

In Chapter 1, we briefly reviewed the two main types of learning that are responsible for shaping behavior. Associative learning occurs when an unconditioned stimulus that provokes a certain response is paired with a conditioned stimulus. In certain stressful or traumatic situations, for example, nondangerous elements of a scene can become associated with dangerous ones so that even the neutral cues evoke a feeling of fear. If a child is physically bullied in a bathroom, for example, he may refuse to use any bathroom in the future. Overcoming these associations can involve demonstrating to the child that such fears are not valid and that bathrooms, for example, can be quite safe. To do this task, however, requires that the child take the risk and expose himself to the feared stimulus so that the process of extinction can take place.

The other major type of learning is operant conditioning. Here, behavior is shaped through the process of rewards and punishments. A certain behavior will be more likely to occur again either if it is rewarded or if a punishment is removed. This type of learning is the cornerstone of many parenting guides and recommendations. A parent who can actively ignore low levels of negative behavior teaches the child that such behavior is not rewarded with parental attention. Likewise, a parent who gives in to a temper tantrum demonstrates to the child that a tantrum gets results.

Although both types of learning are absolutely vital in understanding behavior and how it changes over time, scientists realized that these two important principles weren't enough as they began to look further. Certainly, some of the missing pieces came from genetics, but it was also evident that young animals and humans would do what their parents did even in the absence of any reward or association. Imitation seemed to occur even in the absence of other stimuli or specific rewards.

Through the work of scientists such as Albert Bandura and others, it became increasingly clear that people also learned by modeling the behavior of others. Since then, the importance of modeling and social learning theory has been recognized as another key mechanism through which parents influence a child's behavior. Even without being explicitly taught, a boy will learn how to interact with girls and women by modeling how his father does so. Likewise, a girl begins to learn how to handle frustration partly by following the blueprint put in front of her by her mother. In one offshoot of modeling, called social referencing, children in an ambiguous situation look to others for cues on how to respond. The most widely used example involves the toddler who falls down and then looks at his mother's face to "decide" whether or not to get upset about it. If the mother looks afraid, he starts crying; if the mother looks calm and reassuring, he picks himself up, dusts himself off, and moves on.

These different types of learning play huge roles in how temperament-based behavior is molded over time. What can make processes like modeling even more important is the likelihood that often parents have traits similar to those of their children, due to shared genes. This similarity allows parents many opportunities to show their children how to develop most productively the traits that they have.

In my opinion, one area of modeling that doesn't get the attention and credit it deserves is the modeling of failures rather than success. There is a natural tendency for parents to want to inspire a child by featuring their own achievements and demonstrating that the child too can have similar triumphs. Certainly, letting children see their parents shine is important and can provide them with a road map for success. At the same time, however, it may be even more valuable for children to observe their parents struggling against some of the negative pulls of temperament as they try to hit their own override buttons. In the masterful movie *A League of Their Own*, the fiery manager of a women's baseball team, played by Tom Hanks, at first screams at one of his players for making a mistake in the famous "There's no crying in baseball!" scene. Later in the movie, after the same player makes a similar mistake, you see Hanks straining against every impulse in his body in an effort to respond to the player in a calmer and more productive manner. Similarly, children can learn volumes from their parents as they watch their often clumsy and not always entirely successful attempts to work against their temperamental currents (as the sweat streams down their faces).

Parents sometimes contend that modeling is not that important and that their kids just tune them out rather than paying attention to the parents' behavior. In my experience, that belief should often be challenged. As the owner of the Bellagio hotel and casino in the movie *Ocean's Eleven* says, "In my hotel, there's always someone watching." Indeed, it can be precisely those moments when a parent is interacting with other people that kids pay attention most to what is going on. These off-duty moments can be viewed by children as important windows into the real behavior of Mom and Dad.

In summary, a "do as I say, not as I do" approach to parenting often comes up short. Children learn a great deal by watching and imitating others. Even during times when kids aren't listening, both literally and figuratively, the effects of modeling are often preserved. Parents would do well to seize these many opportunities, not only during examples of great success but also in those stumbling moments when we try to reach past our temperamental limitations and make attempts to, as Thoreau would say, "live deliberately."

Shielding and Exposing

Most parents will freely acknowledge that it can be almost unbearable to see their child in real distress. It is totally natural that such instances provoke a visceral emotional reaction in parents and an intense urge to rush in and fix the problem, thereby relieving the child's suffering. As parents, one of our primary responsibilities is to protect our kids from danger and shield them from the parts of our world that are unsafe or that they are just not ready to see. Early traumatic experiences can have long-lasting consequences, particularly among those who are more temperamentally vulnerable from the start. Repeated failures can lead to frustration, developing into outright dejection.

At the same time, however, it is very difficult to teach our children the critical attributes of hard work, perseverance, and the ability to overcome obstacles if they never experience setbacks or are immediately rescued every time they are in trouble. Moving forward developmentally involves taking risks at the right time: the first step as a toddler, the first shot at the hoop in a basketball game, the first call (maybe now a text) to ask someone out on a date. In all of these moments there is the possibility of failure and the opportunity to try again. As much as we might want to stack the deck and soften the blow to ensure our children's success every time, we know that such a stance robs them of chances to practice some of the most essential skills in life and ill equips them for the challenges that they will eventually have to face.

Research has pointed out the hazards of both under- and overprotecting children based on their temperamental momentum. The child with high novelty seeking may be at increased risk to experiment with alcohol and drugs, especially in the absence of strong limit setting on the part of the parents. At the other end of the spectrum, the development of adolescent anxiety disorder can be exacerbated by overprotection by parents who often struggle with anxiety themselves (Lieb et al., 2000).

Thus, once again, parents are faced with trying to achieve a difficult but important balance, this time between shielding children from harm and too much failure while still exposing them to challenging and at times difficult situations in which they need to succeed on their own. While there is no simple recipe that can achieve this balance for all kids, clinicians can help parents find that middle ground that is custom made for each child. Parents can be helped to feel when it is working, much like that perfect point in a wave that pushes a rider forward without crashing into a giant wet mess. During these times, the child often delights in the small steps that are being made and feels energized to tackle the next challenge. At that point, he is surfing.

Having a Unified Stance

It is neither ideal nor realistic to expect that all parents and caregivers will parent the same child in exactly the same way. In part based on a parent's own temperament, one may tend more toward shielding while the other tends to push toward exposure. One parent may do better with active play while the other shines in calmer activities. Such diversity and specialization can be very positive for child development, and certainly fits into an overall "play to your strengths" model that is becoming increasingly popular in many circles.

However, these differences do not preclude the need for parents and caretakers to be consistent when it comes to goals, rules, and disciplinary strategies. As in any hierarchical organization, mixed messages from the top can be confusing and may be less effective than a unified position. When it comes to children, as most parents will readily acknowledge, small cracks in the parental armor can easily be wedged wide open as kids try to play these differences to their advantage. In more high-conflict families or those divided by divorce and separation, disagreements about parenting can provide an easy way for one parent to influence children to prefer that parent, thereby putting children in the destructive middle position. In these cases, it is far better for parents to reach some kind of fair compromise than to play out these struggles with the children as the proverbial pawns.

A more subtle process that is worth exploring under this general theme comes out of the structural family therapy literature, namely the idea that temperament-based parental roles can become cemented and exaggerated over time. Just as minor child temperament traits can snowball to more extreme levels due to characteristics of the environment, so can family roles become polarized. How this process happens isn't always clear, but it may have something to do with an attempt to maintain some sort of equilibrium when one parent begins to veer in a particular direction. As an example outside of the parenting realm, consider a couple stuck driving in traffic and facing the prospect of being late for an important appointment. Both of them are annoyed, but then one of them (we'll say the husband, who is temperamentally more prone to getting irritable) starts to become visibly upset and slaps the steering wheel. His wife, in response, shifts out of her own annoyance and begins offering some soothing comments about it not being a big deal if they are a few minutes late. If the wife's threshold had been exceeded first and she began to get upset, the roles very well could have been reversed; the point being that some sort of compensatory response was needed in that situation to keep an overall balance.

Parenting roles can similarly become polarized. For example, a father who temperamentally is a bit more anxious may find himself taking on the role of worrier when the child is sick, taking a risk, and so on, thereby freeing up the other parent to be one who encourages risk and minimizes danger. Similar scenarios can unfold when it comes to being the disciplinarian, the fun parent, or the one who nags the child to finish his homework. At first blush, this scenario may seem fine in a kind of yin-yang way. If this role becomes inflexibly maintained over time, however, a parent can begin to resent having to play the same part every time.

Thus, it may be worthwhile for the clinician and parents to examine these often temperamentally based parental roles and the extent to which they may have become exaggerated as the children develop. The parent can be challenged to try to consciously diminish a role that looks like it has become maladaptive. Some parents can even experiment with the idea of switching roles altogether, at least temporarily. The trick, overall, is for parents to be able to present a united front to their children without losing the richness of parent temperamental differences on one side or falling into rigid and polarized roles on the other.

In summary, there are a number of key general principles of parenting that clinicians may want to discuss with parents in the course of treatment. After child and parent temperament has been assessed, and general parenting behavior explained, further conversations about labeling, acceptance, changing the environment versus changing the child, overriding one's typical reaction, the importance of modeling, the balance between shielding and exposing, and the benefits of having a consistent approach between parents can follow in subsequent appointments, moving along at a natural pace. While it is likely that parents have considered many of the topics previously, their discussion in the context of temperament can provide new and more complex material to be considered. Following these topics, the work can extend into more specific parenting guidance based upon the specific temperamental profile of the individual child.

Chapter 9

Temperament and Parenting, Part II

The principles described in Chapter 8 are widely applicable to most child-parent combinations. In addition, however, it is important to consider specific strategies that apply more selectively to children with particular traits or profiles. To organize this chapter, we use the profiles described in Chapter 2 of the five main temperamental types. Such an approach offers some advantages over the more typical structure of making recommendations at the single-trait level. First, we can cover specific temperament combinations (such as children with both high extraversion and high negative emotionality) that research has shown do exist together and can present with unique challenges and recommendations that may be different from the consideration of high or low levels of each trait considered separately. Second, we can examine the question of moderate levels of traits and the issue of what steps (if any) should be taken in these commonly encountered circumstances. Each profile is summarized briefly and the suboptimal responses that can easily be pulled out of a parent, based upon these temperamental tendencies, are discussed prior to the presentation of specific strategies that can help override these natural reactions and minimize the negative aspects of each type.

After making an assessment to determine the specific temperamental profile to which a child belongs, clinicians can engage the parents in some education about the profile and the types of parental reactions that such a profile often evokes. For more negative interactions, the topic can then turn to how to recognize and override that response in an attempt to find alternatives that may serve to moderate those behaviors. Clinicians can explore these possibilities within a particular family and work to practice and customize each recommendation that seems applicable. Parents working without a therapist or counselor may want to consider implementing suggestions for their children gradually for a smoother transition and in order to test the relevance of each suggestion. It should be stated that while the following recommendations are based on research findings on temperament as well as particular behavioral disorders, some of the elements reflect recommendations based on clinical judgment and experience. More empirical work is needed to validate the efficacy of temperament-based interventions, especially as they apply to specific temperament profiles.

The Mellow Profile

We will start by considering a group of children who may not be considered particularly "temperamental" at all, namely, those who fall into what we label the mellow profile. To recap, these children tend not to become easily afraid or angry but at the same time also tend to be less extraverted and driven. Their regulatory abilities often look pretty good, but this feature may result from not being challenged that often. As infants and toddlers, many of these kids are considered quite easy as they don't get rattled too quickly and can be content to follow the parent's plan most of the time. If the trait continues, however, more energetic parents may become concerned that they lack some industriousness or ambition. These kids seem to need prodding and reminders all the time to finish (or start) their homework, contact their friends, join and follow through with sports or structured activities, and generally just to get out there and do something. Children who are stable in this profile can frequently start out with the more positive term easy, which over time can morph into the much more negative description of lazy.

What This Profile Can Evoke in Parents

While it's true that children with the mellow profile often avoid the turbulent explosions with parents that can characterize other temperament types, many hazards can still develop based upon the parents' personalities. When these children are paired with parents who share the mellow profile, a significant amount of inertia can develop to keep these children at rest. The child often does not cause huge amounts of trouble or insist on doing a hundred different things each day, and that suits these parents just fine, as they would just as soon not be particularly active themselves. The problem, however, is that without anyone pushing the child to engage the world more fully, important opportunities can be lost to develop new interests or learn skills that would prepare the child for the future. The child can develop a reputation for being lazy, which in turn can reduce expectations further. Eventually, some of these children can wind up as adolescents feeling as though they are on the outside looking in, with little to do other than hang out with similarly minded friends.

Kids with more driven parents, in contrast, may grow up to feel judged, criticized, and harassed. The parents themselves can feel as though their job is to be the full-time nag who constantly is riding their child. Out of frustration and more desperate efforts to motivate their child, parents may find themselves making direct comparisons to other children or even to their childhood selves as in, "When I was a kid, I just got my homework done without anyone having to ask!" These criticisms can be internalized by the child and erode self-esteem. It is also extremely tempting for these parents to do things for their children, thereby improving efficiency and avoiding negative interactions. Such tactics, however, can lead the child to become even less skilled and self-motivated.

Override Strategies

The general strategy for children whose temperament most fits the mellow profile is a lot of active, positive encouragement. Especially when these children are young, the parents are the ones who will need to provide the wind to get the child's boat moving, with the hope that in time the child will find a breeze of her own. Parents may do well to take the initiative and make the child participate in a reasonable number of activities. These kids are not likely clamoring to join a sports team, take music lessons, or wake up early to start a project. However, since they are also relatively compliant, often there is only token resistance to the plan once they realize that the parents are going to hold firm. More industrious parents also need to learn to resist the urge to perform tasks for their children and instead take the time to teach and show them how to get things done, and then step back and let them complete the task, often in their own meandering way. Some additional recommendations for parents are as follows.

*Maximize the use of incentives and consequences rather than
nagging and scolding.*

For example, if a child is expected to take out the trash by the morning
of trash day in order to get an allowance, let the child fail and not receive
the allowance a couple of times rather than reminding him every 5 minutes to get it done.

*Show flexibility in allowing your child to choose activities,
but make the child do something.*

The football-playing father, for example, may be highly invested in seeing his son play football too, but this sport may not be ideally suited for
the child's temperament. Rather than forcing it, explain that there is an
expectation to join some sport or club and then help the child find something that he or she can really enjoy.

Do things together.

This one may sound easy, but many busy parents find themselves saying
something like, "Turn off the TV and go outside!" much more frequently
than, "How about I hit you some ground balls to get ready for your
softball game Saturday?" The prospect of doing activities with a parent
can make those things much more reinforcing and increase the likelihood
that the child will continue them in the future.

Teach and then back off and let children learn at their own pace.

The first-grade mellow profile boy may feel no urgency to learn how to
tie his shoes. Parents should teach him how nonetheless, and be encouraged to risk getting to school 3 minutes late while he methodically labors
through the process.

Create strict limits on television and video game time.

For these kids, restricting overall quantity of screen time may be a higher
priority than limiting the content.

The Agitated Profile

Children with an agitated profile tend to be fairly active, but they are
stuck in a difficult double bind of having both high levels of novelty seek-

ing and high levels of negative emotionality. This combination means that these kids want to engage the world but can have trouble handling those interactions. With low activity they can get bored, but with high activity they can get overstimulated. Furthermore, small frustrations can lead to large meltdowns, shutdowns, and giving up. In more extreme forms, the behaviors can be sufficiently intense to qualify for various psychiatric diagnoses, including oppositional defiant disorder, ADHD, and, perhaps most famously and not without controversy, bipolar disorder. The new DSM-5 diagnosis of disruptive mood disorder with dysphoria may also capture many of these kids with the agitated profile at more extreme levels. Some of these children may be taking medications to help with their behavior, with families often finding out that pills alone are insufficient to bring the frequency and intensity of negative outbursts down to where the family would like them to be.

On the positive side, these children are often passionate and enthusiastic. Metaphorically speaking, they are eager to plunge in, even at the risk of drowning. Some of these children have histories of very difficult or chaotic early environments and even trauma, which may have contributed to delayed development of important emotional regulatory skills.

What This Profile Can Evoke in Parents

In the clinic, parents of agitated children often use expressions like "walking on eggshells" to describe the home environment. Everyone lives in fear of setting such children off, especially in public places. Under these circumstances, it is easy to see why these parents often go to extremes to avoid provoking outbursts. When no demands or limits are placed on them, there can be moments of precious peace in the household. As a result, parents can easily be swayed to give in to the child's demands for candy at a vending machine, or extra time at a video game to "finish the level" before bed. There can be increased avoidance of activities that involve other children, such as teams or religious groups, so that everyone is spared the embarrassment of a public meltdown. Effective as these modifications may seem initially, in the long run the children suffer the consequences of both the indulgence itself and the lack of training in how to manage the everyday frustrations of life.

In addition to the very understandable desire to give in to the child's demands and avoid potentially triggering situations, many parents also struggle with keeping cool themselves, particularly if they share similar temperamental predispositions. It can often seem like yelling and scream-ing are the only ways to get through to these kids and the only things that work. The problem, however, is that it significantly raises the volume of the entire household and does not equip these children with the tools they need to regulate themselves.

Override Strategies

Many books have been written specifically about how parents can most effectively raise these fervent but very challenging youths. While they share common ground, at times the recommendations can directly con-tradict each other. For example, it is fairly standard in parent guidance circles to advocate for a "no negotiation" policy. Parents set reasonable limits and rules and if those are violated, consequences must be applied consistently and firmly. To do otherwise is to risk teaching the child that tantrums and defiance work, thereby encouraging more of them in the future. More recently, however, some child experts have sug-gested that such an approach may be ineffective for these kids and may result in higher amounts of conflict than is necessary or desired. In *The Explosive Child*, Ross Greene (1998) argued that traditional reward and punishment strategies designed to maximize motivation often don't work because the root problem isn't motivation. Instead, these kids lack essential skills that need to be developed in a context that is some-what more flexible and allows for some degree of negotiation. These techniques, called Collaborative Problem Solving, have been tested and found to be effective in clinical research trials (Greene et al., 2004; Greene & Ablon, 2005).

Consequently, some parents who read books and search the Internet are going to be confused as to how best to approach their kids. I believe the literature is not at a point where an official winner can be declared between the two approaches. Even if there were one, the same approach might not be optimal for every child. Thus, clinicians may want to con-sider recommending the "no negotiation" approach at first with the idea that alternative techniques may need to be considered if the first strategy, when fully applied, fails. Such a recommendation is based on my general assumption that children are more capable of controlling their behavior than they think. Under these conditions, the true limit of a child's capac-ity can be seen and subsequent modifications can be made if I end up being proved too optimistic.

As mentioned, the specific parenting techniques for children who tend to be highly oppositional and dysregulated have been well documented in the work of many researchers, including Patterson, Forehand, Barkley, Greene, and others (Barkley & Benton, 1998; Forehand & Long, 2010; Greene, 1998; Patterson & Forgatch, 1987). It is, however, worth describing some additional points for parents, specifically as they relate to children with an agitated temperament style in perhaps a less extreme form.

Don't take it personally.
This is particularly tough for the mother standing in the supermarket with all eyes upon her while her 8-year-old boy (who really ought to be past this by now) is lying down in the middle of the aisle screaming because he has been told he can't have a cereal that is full of sugar. The thoughts that run through such a parent's mind, other than "Just get me out of here," relate to being exposed as the horrible parent who can't manage her kids. As understandable as these automatic thoughts can be, they tend to fuel the fire of the parent's own frustration, and it is crucial that she hit the override button and remind herself that if she were raising a child with a mellow or moderate profile, they would already be in the dairy section by now, checking the eggs for cracks and getting ready to find the shortest checkout line. As embarrassing as a tantrum may be, parents need to be supported in viewing it as a teaching moment that can be used either to perpetuate or to diminish the likelihood of future episodes just like it.

See it coming.
The situations that trigger major outbursts in these children are often predictable, if not fully avoidable. Reviewing these triggers with parents can help them organize their thoughts and develop strategies. At first, a parent may view the outburst as coming out of nowhere. However, a careful play-by-play analysis may reveal triggers that, if recognized earlier, might have helped avoid the outburst.

Reexamine the "overreaction" perception.
Sometimes the trigger to a meltdown is identified but seems way out of proportion to the response. In these instances, it can be very useful to investigate whether a small provocation actually taps into a much

larger issue. If so, the child's reaction may be not excusable but more understandable. For example, an outburst by a 10-year-old boy triggered by a parent simply letting a sibling do something first may look quite excessive, but in the child's mind confirms his belief that he is loved and valued less than the sibling. If work is directed at finding and correcting the core belief, these huge reactions to what otherwise appear like small transgressions may be reduced.

Build regulatory skills.

Certainly, to some degree, regulatory skills can be taught and cultivated through specific activities. Cognitive-behavioral therapists often explicitly teach deep breathing and relaxation skills to their patients and clients who struggle with emotional regulation. Mindfulness and martial arts programs can also help hone these skills and are often tailored to children and youth. Even activities such as reading may help quiet the mind. Mary Fristad and her colleagues at Ohio State University have developed a group therapy for children and their parents that has been shown to reduce behavior problems and teach these essential skills (Fristad, Goldberg-Arnold, & Leffler, 2011).

Be a model.

Remember that children learn by watching and imitating. While it may not appear so, they are paying attention to how you handle being upset. The teaching process here can be augmented by making your response more explicit to your children. It can be very useful for parents to explain how they worked though frustration that they just experienced, and which the children witnessed. For one, it helps to show children that they are not alone in these struggles. Further, it can provide them with a bluprint of potential strategies for self-regulation that they may not be able to pick up on their own simply through observation. If parents do not handle their own frustration well, their apology and stated commitment to do better also can serve as an excellent model.

Create regular positive experiences.

Most recommendations for interacting with dysregulated kids center on preventing and managing the negative aspects that inevitably arise. However, it can be just as critical to make extra efforts to have happy and positive experiences with these children. One of the most insidiously difficult recommendations for parents is to carve out time each day to engage in an activity that the child enjoys and just participate without directives or a flood of questions. During this period of time, the child is in control and the parent follows the child's lead, commenting in a more descriptive way as opposed to guiding the play or activity. This skill has been called a number of things, including attending, the term used by Rex Forehand, child parenting expert and author of *Parenting the Strong-Willed Child* (Forehand & Long, 2010). For younger children, attending often can occur at home while playing in a way that the child chooses. It sounds easy but can be extremely difficult, especially the part about holding back one's questions and subtle directives. With older children and teenagers, it can be more challenging to find something to do together, and parents may need to take the plunge and try to participate in anything from video games to skateboarding. The rewards, however, can be well worth the trouble, as the experience builds invaluable positive interactions and gives the child a turn to be in charge.

Act before exploding.

Children with the agitated profile are masters at setting off what child parenting researchers call a coercive parenting cycle. This pattern develops when a temperamentally irritable child does not comply with a parental directive, putting pressure on the parent to either give in or explode. Neither outcome is particularly beneficial, as giving in essentially teaches the child that defiance works, while exploding creates a hostile environment in which the child learns that the parent only "means it" when she is very upset. These pressures are prime examples of why an override button is needed. When parents are able to keep their wits about them, often the best approach is to invoke the predetermined consequence before everyone's temperature rises too high. If it is time to turn off the video game and the first command has been given, for example, the next step can be literally to pull the plug and put the video game away. This course is a good alternative to successive commands while the parent becomes increasingly enraged. For children who are temperamentally more responsive to rewards, it can be remarkably effective as they learn quickly that a parent means business. For children whose agitated profile is in the more extreme range, however, such actions may invoke a major meltdown that may not necessarily diminish with successive trials. In these circumstances, other methods such as collaborative problem solving might be required. The next two strategies may also be particularly useful for such children.

Take space.

In the families of some children who possess the agitated profile, the level of hostility and irritability can reach outright toxic levels. Nerves are stretched so thin that virtually anything can set someone flying off the handle. Whether in a particular moment of tension or in a more global atmosphere of irritability and anger, it is important for parents to recognize that the environment is reaching a boiling point and to consider getting some distance from it for a minute, an hour, or for several days if necessary. Doing so not only allows the parent to recharge his or her batteries doing something healthy or enjoyable but may also bring the child's irritability level down as he or she resets the clock with a different caretaker. In some families, it may not be that difficult to tag team with another parent or enlist the help of friends or relatives who live nearby. In other cases, however, it may be quite difficult for a parent to disengage even for short periods of time. Clinicians may need to get more creative in looking at community supports such as respite care or after-school programs or finding groups, clubs, or teams that might provide both a positive experience for the child and some welcome relief to an overwhelmed parent.

Parental health.

Parents challenged by temperamentally extreme kids are often under tremendous pressure and need to take extra care of themselves. During our assessment process, the parents themselves often screen positive for possible psychiatric conditions. When this happens, it is very important to discuss a parent's own evaluation and possible treatment as an enormous step toward helping the children, which frequently is a greater motivation than getting help for one's own sake. While this recommendation is listed last, in many ways it may be advantageous for the clinician to bring up this point first, as parents who are able to get their own symptoms under better control are more likely to be able to use the other suggestions.

Families with children whose temperament fits the agitated profile are often most obviously struggling and thus may be most willing to try anything to make things better. While for some of these children the techniques and suggestions outlined above will be enough to cause substantive improvement, for others a more comprehensive approach will be required that may include consideration of medications, school modifications, and individual child therapy.

The Confident Profile

In contrast to youth with the agitated profile, children whose temperament matches the confident profile are much less likely to wind up in the offices of a mental health professional. To recap, the confident profile is characterized by fairly high levels of both extraversion and sociability while being fairly low in negative affectivity. They tend to have good regulatory skills. Thus, many of the children can be quite popular, especially when this profile is paired with particular talents, high intelligence, and good looks. Since temperament does not imply a particular morality, however, confident-profile youths with lower moral standards can also be manipulative and sometimes antagonistic toward others. They can be the ones who parents and teachers universally adore but who are recognized by many peers as being bullies or con artists. Their positive qualities can also sometimes go to their heads, leading some to be arrogant and condescending to others. In some ways, this is a high-reward, high-risk profile with a very wide range of potential with regard to developmental outcomes. These can be the children whose parents can't stop talking about their wonderful nature and astounding accomplishments as well as the ones who can suffer spectacular falls from grace.

What This Profile Can Evoke in Parents

Parents of children with the confident profile often feel like quite excellent parents, thank you very much. As these children's extraversion and sociability help them make friends and their regulatory skills and enthusiasm propel them to achieve at school, the parents generally feel like they are doing a lot of things right. In many cases, they are correct, as this temperament evokes warmth, engagement, and trust within the family that can reinforce those initial tendencies.

That is not to say, however, that parents can't get off track once in a while. The lavish praise that can be heaped onto these kids can turn confidence into conceit, especially if that praise comes in the form of comparisons (e.g., "You must be the smartest kid in your whole class!"). The combination of success and praise can build an insatiable ego at the expense of thinking and caring for others. A more subtle process can also develop in which the child becomes so attached and the family becomes so in need of the child's role as the stable confident one that he or she begins to feel as though it is not allowed to struggle or fail even once in a while. This phenomenon is more likely in families in which some members are thriving and others are struggling.

Override Strategies

There may be many instances in raising kids with the confident profile when overriding isn't a priority. By contrast, it is often best to let the child ride the wave of the positive inertia that often develops from this particular temperament combination. At the same time, the same general principles that apply to most other kids still apply here. Further, when some intentional modifications do become necessary, the general principle behind them relates to preventing these children (or the parents) from getting an overinflated ego. The following are some more specific recommendations that follow along that general principle.

Instill compassion.

It is easy for children with this profile to get swept up in their own success. Such accomplishments can feel very good and be quite reinforcing. As this cycle develops, it is important to remind these children about the rough road that many other individuals face and the importance of using their time and talents to the benefit of others. Participation in religious, civic, or charity organizations and modeling the act of thinking and caring for more immediate friends, families, and neighbors can all help instill a more global perspective that helps children see beyond their own day-to-day ambitions and develop kindness and compassion for others.

Don't overdo benign neglect.

This one may not apply in all families, but some of these kids can seem to function so well on virtual autopilot that parents don't supervise enough, especially in families with other children who tend to be the squeaky wheels and require the bulk of attention. The risk here is threefold. First, some of these kids might start to feel outright ignored, sending them on a quest to be even more high achieving and successful motivated by stronger efforts to gain the favor of parents rather than internally driven self-efficacy. Second, many children with the confident profile may not have the experience and judgment to make good decisions as consistently as it might appear. Third, they can come to resent the belief that they have to be the "perfect child" all the time. To avoid these hazards, parents can do well to keep many of their rules and monitoring procedures in place. While some measure of conditional increased independence may certainly be in order, it is important to remember that children and adolescents with the confident profile are still kids who need, and may even desire, limit setting and active monitoring.

Keep their feet on the ground.
Whether due to a multitude of activities and engagements or from a heightened sense of importance and self-worth that these children often have, there can be pressure among these kids to avoid the mundane aspects of life such as chores, family dinners, or visits to a grandmother suffering from Alzheimer's disease in a nursing home. As tempting as it may be to exempt some kids from more basic duties in order to focus on loftier pursuits, however, such special treatment can often have negative effects on both the child and the entire family. Siblings, in particular, will often use their exquisite sense of fairness (at least when things are tilted against them) to perceive favoritism, which over time can undermine family cohesion. In contrast, a family system in which nobody is above the law and everyone needs to contribute can be beneficial, not only to the overall family unit but to the sense of humility and belonging for the individual child.

In conclusion, these principles for confident profile children can help them fully realize their often considerable potential. Clinicians may not be forced to think clinically about children with the confident profile that frequently, but their consideration in the context of working with other members of a family can be a welcome addition to the overall treatment plan.

The Anxious Profile
Children with the anxious profile, as the name would suggest, often tend to be nervous and manifest high levels of negative emotionality that can come out not only as fear but also as irritability and anger. Unlike children with the agitated profile, who also possess high levels of negative emotionality, those with the anxious profile tend to have low levels of extraversion, so they are not drawn to situations that can be too much

for them. Instead, they are often quite content to avoid such situations altogether. Such a combination presents its own set of challenges and rewards and can necessitate a different set of strategies.

Work by Forehand and his colleagues examining the role of parental guidance components when children present with different types of behavioral problems has revealed some interesting findings (Forehand, Jones, & Parent, 2013). In contrast to children with more disruptive and oppositional behavior, for whom working on the parental responses has been shown to be a critical and central focus of treatment, the role of parents with more anxious children is less as direct shapers of behavior than as facilitators of small steps the child may be trying to enact already. With a defiant child, the parent often needs to be taught to be that immovable object that confronts the seemingly unstoppable force. With an anxious child, parents are important in more subtle ways, such as being cognitive reframers, opportunity creators, and cheerleaders.

To overcome anxiety, the key ingredient is exposure, which leads eventually to mastery. A critical component of exposure is that it must occur before the anxiety is gone. Such a plan can be counterintuitive to many parents. After all, when something is broken, generally you fix it first and then it functions properly in the expected situation. For a broken car, for example, nobody would suggest that the act of driving up a hill while the car still isn't working properly will increase the chance that it will function better on the next hill. Unfortunately, this strategy hardly ever works when it comes to anxiety. Although steps can be taken to increase the chances for success prior to exposure to the feared situation, from relaxation exercises to cognitive restructuring to medications, it is rare that these steps remove the anxiety so that the child no longer feels it. Rather, anxiety is conquered in small steps, with the still-anxious child confronting the anxiety in a graduated fashion, building momentum and confidence with each little success. In working with families, it is vital that clinicians present this process and how it works up front in order to help parents overcome their understandable reluctance to push their children before, in their minds, they are fully ready.

What This Profile Can Evoke in Parents
Studies of parent-child interactions with anxious children have revealed that parents interpret higher degrees of threat in ambiguous situations and present solutions to problems that tend to feature more avoidance

than prosocial responses (Barrett et al., 1996; Dadds et al., 1996). Obviously, few parents are intentionally trying to frighten their children, and it is likely that some of this parental behavior is a response to the child's worries. Parents may also be somewhat anxious themselves and are conveying the thoughts and solutions that they have learned and experienced over time. Frequently a cycle may develop that ends up reinforcing the early anxious predisposition (Figure 9.1).

FIGURE 9.1

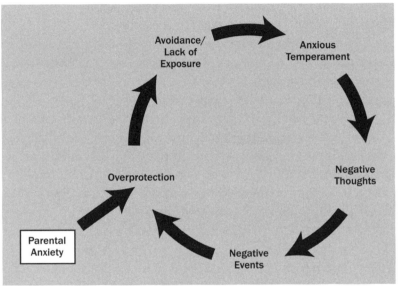

The cycle of increasing anxiety. Child's predispositions to the anxious profile trigger anxiety-provoking thoughts, which in turn can lead to negative events. To protect the child, parents might be tempted to be overprotective, thereby restricting opportunities to overcome the anxiety.

As an example, consider the temperamentally anxious 6-year-old boy who signs up for Little League baseball. During a close game in which he is playing first base, he begins to experience negative thoughts such as, "I am going to lose the game for the whole team," or "Please don't hit the ball to me." When a ball is thrown to him, his anxiety interferes with his skills, and he drops the ball and becomes very upset. His father, who is watching the game, is heartbroken for his son and can hardly bear to see him suffering so much. The boy no longer wants to play and his father agrees to this decision in order to protect him from further pain. The boy's skills fall further behind those of his peers, and now he dreads playing even casually with his friends or at school.

In a word, the trap for parents of children who manifest the anxious profile, particularly those with some anxious tendencies themselves, is overprotection. This overprotection reduces the child's opportunities for exposure and, eventually, mastery. And while parental overprotection may not be difficult to spot, it can be quite difficult to correct, in part because the opposite approach, namely forcing children into situations in which they are going to fail repeatedly, is also likely to make anxiety worse. Striking the right balance between these two extremes requires coordinated efforts directed at both the child and the parent, and may be best accomplished through the help of a counselor or therapist who can implement these override strategies in a way that optimally fits the individual child and parent.

Override Strategies

One positive aspect of the anxiety cycle shown in Figure 9.1 is that it has a number of entry points at which positive changes can develop and the cycle can be broken or reversed. The overall goal here is to help parents adjust their current practice of either over- or underprotection in such a way that the child begins to take small risks to confront his or her anxiety in situations that have a good probability of success. Along the way, a number of other components can also help to turn fear and avoidance into an appropriate level of caution and forbearance.

Identify a small number of arenas in which anxieties play out.
Coping with heights, sleeping alone in one's room, talking in front of people, playing a new sport, and approaching a potential new friend are just a few specific goals that could be set. Often a good place to start is to pick one that is not too difficult and that the child is motivated to achieve. In most cases, it is beneficial to be very explicit to the child about what will be happening and why, for example, "We see that you are very worried about bugs and that this worry keeps you from going outside and playing with your friends. We are going to work together to help you with that so that soon your fears won't be so strong."

Set up gradual exposures that are primed for success.
If, for example, an 8-year-old girl is afraid to sleep in her own bed overnight, an intermediate goal might be that she can spend some time in her own bed before moving to her parents' room or perhaps will stay in bed with her parent as she falls asleep. Each step should optimally be

something that the child has to exert some effort to accomplish while not being too strenuous. In popular culture, it is not uncommon to hear some people advocating a "flooding" approach in which the child is pushed to confront the fear at full force (e.g., sending this girl to an overnight camp). While these strategies can be effective, I generally do not advocate them as they often can breed distrust and resentment later.

Use more rewards and fewer punishments to achieve these goals.
It is generally not recommended to use discipline techniques such as time-outs to motivate children to overcome anxiety. However, parents should also ensure that they are not unwittingly reinforcing anxiety. A child who is fearful of going to school, for example, should not be granted a day at home full of video games and one-on-one play time with a parent, for example. Incentives can often be helpful, especially when the child has no strong intrinsic motivation for change. Ideally, incentives will be related to the anxiety that is being targeted. For the child afraid to go outside because of insects, for example, a good incentive might be new toys or activities that the child could play with or engage in on the lawn.

Monitor and gently challenge language that may reinforce anxiety.
This recommendation applies to both parents and child. Parents who believe and communicate that the world is a dangerous and cruel place will often find that their children pick up on this worldview and demonstrate behavior that corresponds to these thoughts. Similarly, children will also reveal thoughts related to their anxieties that tend to fuel the fire. One very common misperception of children who see other kids doing things they are afraid of is that those things came easily to others. Being able to explain, for example, that a child who swims with ease had to work hard to overcome his own worries about water can help reset the child's expectations to a more realistic level. Emphasizing positive aspects of the environment and the need for effort to achieve one's goals can help replace anxiety-reinforcing thoughts with anxiety-reducing ones.

Limit frightening media.
Related to the previous idea is that it is important to instruct parents that children respond differently to television and movies and that those children who already are more anxious are often the most vulnerable to the negative effects of frightening content. Even if a sibling seems to

be unfazed by a particular show, it may be much better if an anxious child learning to swim, for example, misses Shark Week on the Discovery Channel for now. Some people may be confused by this suggestion and find it contradictory to the suggestion to increase exposure on the path toward anxiety extinction. There are some noticeable distinctions between the graduated exposure advocated above and what can happen when anxious children are bombarded by violent and horrific images on television or at the movies. In some instances, there may indeed be a role for media as part of an overall treatment plan, but often what is shown is simply too much, too soon.

Teach relaxation skills.

Deep breathing and other meditative techniques can be wonderful tools for children to have and can be taught on their own or as part of other activities such as martial arts. Children often enjoy them and learn them easily, although the trick with more anxious kids is being able to access them when worries are starting to build. The specific ability to use the techniques under pressure needs to be incorporated into the training. After learning relaxation breathing exercises in a calm and secure setting, for example, the insect-phobic child might be able to use those skills more effectively while practicing them with a picture of a bee or, even better, while standing near a bee with a parent or counselor.

What about medications?

Even among children anxious enough to meet criteria for some kind of anxiety disorder, the first-line treatment recommended by groups such as the American Academy of Child and Adolescent Psychiatry is cognitive-behavioral therapy (the techniques of which are part of the approach described above) rather than medications (Connolly & Bernstein, 2007). When medications are used, they are most effective when combined with psychotherapy, and many of the recommendations previously listed are best thought of as measures that can help children get into a position to confront and overcome their fears rather than remedies or cures that work in isolation. They also can be used to treat parents with anxiety disorders in order to help them help their children to the fullest extent possible.

Children whose temperaments correspond to the anxious profile can suffer a great deal of impairment as their fears build through vicious cycles of reinforcement. With different types of interventions targeted at each step of the process, however, children can learn to face and gain mastery over their fears. As they grow, many such children will never completely shake the nervous feelings that their feared situations elicit, but they can gain enough confidence that the feelings no longer present major obstacles along their way.

The Moderate Profile

In many ways, this profile, characterized by average levels of the major temperament dimensions, presents the biggest challenge for describing parenting intervention strategies. Indeed, it is probably fair to say that the vast majority of parents may not be looking for change at all, and certainly not from a mental health professional. Like children with the confident and mellow profiles, those with the moderate profile are not usually beating down the doors to the offices of mental health clinicians. Nevertheless, the moderate profile is probably the most common of all the types, and these children and adolescents can affect and be affected by all the same developmental influences that have been described up to this point. Their average temperament status certainly does not mandate an average outcome, and they are capable of the same positive and negative trajectories as everyone else.

What This Profile Can Evoke in Parents

The lack of strong temperamental tides in any particular dimension often means that, compared to the profiles that include more extreme levels of certain traits, there is likely to be less provocation of the child's temperament by particular environments or reactions. In contrast to one with the anxious profile, for example, a child with the moderate profile will have lower levels of negative emotionality and thus will be less likely to stimulate overprotective responses in parents and other adults. This lack of momentum is inherently neither good nor bad: A warm health-promoting environment may be able to exert its positive effect with less temperamental resistance, while the moderate-profile child growing up in a more hostile and chaotic household may not possess the temperamental resilience to overcome those harmful influences. As previously discussed, some research suggests that less extreme levels of temperament traits are more likely to change over time (Kagan, 1994), although more work is needed to demonstrate the tempting and intuitive hypothesis that more moderate levels of traits are actually more responsive to environmental factors. If this does indeed turn out to be the case, it could be argued that it is these moderate-profile children for whom parental choices and behaviors have their most profound effect.

Override Strategies

For the moderate profile, the idea of override strategies may not be the most precise term, although it would certainly be true that the temperament traits in these children are subject to the same principles that promote their increase or decrease in others. These kids still get agitated, anxious, and unmotivated at times, and the absence of deliberate intervention strategies or parental characteristics can generate momentum to accentuate those traits. In this way, the strategies recommended for children with the moderate profile don't lend themselves to a specific list. Rather, the general principles outlined in Chapter 8 and the more specific techniques aimed at more extreme levels of particular traits can be applied to help parents develop these temperament dimensions into character that will serve these children adaptively for the future.

In summary, Chapters 8 and 9 have outlined a means through which clinicians and parents can take our modern understanding of temperament and apply it at home to the benefit of kids. After some education about temperament and its role in development, temperament assessment of the child and family members can illuminate the particular profiles and interaction patterns within an individual family. General parenting principles can then be reviewed that are customized to harness the potential within the child's unique temperament profile. Because most children spend a large amount of their week at school, Chapter 10 extends some of the same applications to the school setting with the hope of creating a global environment that promotes growth and wellness.

Chapter 10

Temperament in Educational Settings

School has aptly been called the vocation of children: their "job." Without a doubt, the ability to navigate successfully at school both academically and socially has tremendous impact on our youth for the rest of their lives. Children's level of preparedness for the global workforce, their sense of accomplishment and self-esteem, and their skills at working collaboratively with others are just a few of the important competencies that are significantly developed in the educational setting, whether it be a typical public school, an alternative placement, or a home school environment. Intelligence and academic aptitude are, of course, critical factors in school achievement and have received their fair share of attention. Temperament traits, however, are also decisive characteristics that form the foundation of many of the skills and tasks that are required for students to maximize their intellectual potential (Keogh, 2003). Yet while detailed cognitive and educational profiles are frequently performed to assess a child's intellectual ability and to create an educational system that works best with particular strengths and weaknesses, formal temperament assessments and intervention strategies are rare. This lack of specific attention often does not present a major problem to skilled teachers and sensitive parents who are able to perceive a child's temperament intuitively and to adapt constructively when the need arises. In other situations, often driven by more extreme levels of traits that fit poorly with the given educational environment, a more explicit and deliberate approach is needed. These folks are fortunate that modern schools have provided more opportunities for individualized learning than in past decades, when a one-size-fits-all attitude was more predominant.

This chapter focuses on aspects of child temperament as it relates to school and educational settings. After a review of some studies that have examined the relations between temperament and school achievement, some practical suggestions are offered for parents, clinicians, and educators motivated to apply some of the new knowledge of temperament and its links with emotional-behavioral problems in the classroom.

Research on Temperament and School Achievement

While the literature on the associations between temperament and academic performance is not vast, a number of studies have come up with consistent and fairly expected conclusions. Overall, temperamental traits have certainly been found to be significantly associated with school achievement. Using the Chess and Thomas temperament dimensions, Michel Maziade and his colleagues examined Quebecois children at ages 7 and 12 years and found significant correlations with all nine dimensions in reading or math ability for at least one of the age groups (Maziade et al., 1986). Another study by Lerner and coworkers from the 1980s also showed some support for the link between academic ability and the temperamental traits of attention and reactivity (Lerner, Lerner, & Zabski, 1985). Subsequent studies since then have confirmed the positive associations between dimensions that fall under the higher-order dimension of effortful control and academic achievement while showing negative associations with activity level and negative emotionality (Guerin et al., 2003; Kristal, 2005). A study called Project Competence followed a group of about 200 third to sixth graders, many of whom were in lower socioeconomic groups, for approximately 10 years (Shiner, 2000). The study leader, Rebecca Shiner, divided personality into four school-related dimensions labeled mastery motivation, academic consciousness, surgent engagement, and agreeableness, based on a factor analytic technique (i.e., she didn't just make up the categories based upon her own ideas). All of the dimensions, with the exception of agreeableness, were found to be related to academic performance even after controlling for the effect of IQ.

In our own previously mentioned study of temperament profiles in Vermont children, we looked not only at parent-rated indicators of emotional-behavioral problems but also had teachers report on the child's behavior and academic progress using an instrument called the Teacher Report Form (Achenbach, 1991b). As you may recall, our statistical clustering program grouped children into groups we labeled moderate, steady, and disengaged (Rettew, Althoff, et al., 2008). We found that children in the steady class, who were distinct in having high levels of persistence and low levels of novelty seeking, were rated as having higher levels of overall school competence than the moderate group, who in turn had significantly higher levels than the disengaged group (distinguished by having high novelty seeking and harm avoidance with low reward dependence and persistence). These significant differences in overall school performance were independent of the significant differences that were found between the groups in teacher-rated behavioral problems, which followed a pattern similar to parents' ratings of child behavior.

Perceived and Actual Intelligence

An important factor that might be contributing to these consistent findings relates not only to the effects generated by the intrinsic qualities of the temperamental dimensions themselves as they bear upon educational tasks but also to the indirect effects of these traits upon teachers, through interactional mechanisms such as those described with gene–environment correlations and interactions. Children with positive moods, enthusiasm for trying and learning new things, and abilities to keep focused and quiet when required are likely to have more positive and encouraging interactions with teachers, which in turn can improve their experience at school even further. Indeed, increased approach and adaptability has been shown to be related to the impression that a child is more intelligent (Gordon & Thomas, 1967). Psychologists have described the "halo effect," meaning that people can have a bias to perceive positive qualities together in others (Thorndike, 1920). Thus, a child who is physically attractive might also be viewed as being intelligent and also having positive temperament traits. Such effects have been demonstrated in teachers rating negative behavior of child actors who were behaving purposely in different ways (Abikoff et al., 1993). These perceptual effects can become quite important as a person's impressions can sometimes become reality through different expectations and response patterns.

What about actual IQ as measured on standardized tests? Temperament differences have been found here as well. On the surface, these findings may seem surprising given the treatment of temperament and intelligence as separate domains. However, digging a little deeper reveals that many aspects of intelligence tests are understandably sensitive to temperament dimensions. The widely used Wechsler Intelligence Scale for Children has many subtests that tap directly into areas that are sensitive to temperament (Wechsler, 1991). In the digit span test, children are asked to recall a series of numbers that gets progressively longer. Performance on this test of working memory is enhanced by better attention skills and an ability to resist distractions, components of the trait of regulatory ability. The general comprehension subscale also requires knowledge of certain facts that a child would learn in school and is thus affected by temperament as it relates to learning in a classroom.

Temperament studies that are comprehensive enough to measure IQ, temperament, and other variables of interest often treat IQ as a potentially confounding variable that can cloud the association between temperament and the variables that the researchers are really interested in. Thus, their analyses often statistically control for IQ in their associations between temperament and behavioral problems, social functioning, school performance, and so on. Upon further examination, the actual correlations between temperament and IQ are often reported and significant (which is why the researchers have to control for this association in the first place). For example, in the Project Competence study described above, the association between IQ and mastery motivation was .37 and for surgent engagement it was an impressive .46 (Shiner, 2000). While it could be argued that these dimensions go a bit beyond the core aspects of temperament, it appears once again that temperament has found its way into areas previously thought to be more separate entities. Getting back to the idea that one brain houses temperament, psychopathology, intelligence, and a whole host of other functions, perhaps such an association is not surprising.

Working With Temperament in the Classroom

Obviously, there can be tremendous variation between and even within schools in their approach to child behavior. One of the major variations involves the degree to which a school is willing to apply different approaches for different students versus a stronger emphasis on getting all children to behave the same way. Certainly over time there has been a gradual shift in many educational settings toward greater accommodation and provisions for children who learn and behave differently. Many educators have welcomed this flexibility, although it is not without its critics, who have disparaged the rising costs of special education, questioned the impact on students who don't require such special treatment, and voiced concern about overall educational standards. Such a debate is beyond the scope of this chapter, but suffice it to say that on the individual level, many children may realize their academic potential best when force is applied in both directions. In other words, improving the fit between an individual and a particular setting ideally involves both (a) efforts to change the child to fit the school, and (b) efforts to change the school to fit the child (see Figure 10.1).

FIGURE 10.1

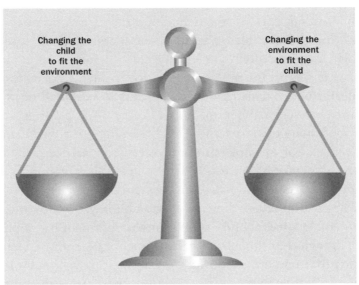

An improved fit between a particular child and a particular setting requires a balance of efforts: Some are designed to change the child and others are designed to change the environment.

The Informal Approach

Many teachers are highly skilled in making adjustments in their classrooms to help children with different temperaments. As a result of this skill (and the intrinsic fit between the child and teacher), some children seem to oscillate considerably between really good and really bad school years. The important changes that make a large difference can often be very subtle. Some happen outside a teacher's conscious awareness while others are quite planned and purposeful. Some are made specifically for only one or two students, or a teacher may decide to make broad changes that affect the entire classroom even though only a minority of pupils require them (similar to the "no nut" policy of many classrooms today that may slightly inconvenience many but help a few quite a bit).

IEPs and 504s

In this country, the two most common mechanisms through which students can formally receive additional instruction or have different types of accommodations and curriculum modifications are the Individualized Education Programs (IEPs) and what are known as 504 plans. These two approaches have many similarities but come from different places. The number 504 comes from Section 504 of the 1973 Rehabilitation Act and the Americans With Disabilities Act. It ensures that children with disabilities are provided with an education that addresses these disabilities so that they receive the same education as others. IEPs developed from the Individuals With Disabilities Education Act and the Department of Education. Their implementation requires that students meet eligibility requirements for special education that can vary from state to state. In practice, IEPs are generally created for a specific learning disability, such as dyslexia, that is determined through testing and documents a significant discrepancy between a student's intelligence and achievement scores in explicit domains such as reading proficiency. For children whose struggles in the classroom involve temperament-based behavioral challenges, especially in the absence of a diagnosable psychiatric disorder, parents are often told that this mechanism does not apply.

That said, when a child is having a lot of behavior difficulties at school, one should consider the possibility that some kind of specific learning disability may be contributing to the problem. Studies have shown that children who are more distractible, less focused, and hyperactive have elevated rates of learning problems (Pliszka, Carlson, & Swanson, 1999). Many of these children meet criteria for a diagnosis of ADHD. In some instances, schools may be reluctant to perform the fairly expensive testing that is required to document a learning problem, especially with a student who is doing pretty well but whose parents are convinced that he or she is not performing up to his or her potential. Parents may then choose to have this testing performed outside of the school by someone like a private psychologist or free-standing learning center. Unfortunately, the cost can be prohibitive to many families. Some of these centers do have scholarships or sliding scales for families with lower incomes.

The mechanism that is perhaps more relevant for children with behvioral challenges is the 504 plan, although these can also be difficult to obtain without a formal diagnosis. Generally, 504 plans are somewhat less rigorous in terms of how they are constructed, who has to be present at meetings about them, specific timelines for follow-up, and other procedural details. While some parents prefer IEPs because of their increased monitoring, detail, and regulatory requirements, 504 plans and even less official-sounding mechanisms can be applied effectively to implement some customized provisions for children needing adjustments to the school.

The often hazy boundaries between traits and a diagnosable disorder can be a source of conflict and confusion at school. Some teachers naturally adapt their style to fit the temperament profile of their students; others are much less inclined to do so, especially in the absence of a compelling medical reason. In these situations, the idea that "it's just laziness and not ADHD" can become a justification to keep the status quo, thus placing the onus of modification exclusively on the child, often with poor outcomes, as in the following example:

> A 12-year-old boy has struggled his entire life with difficulty coping with transition, misreading social cues, and becoming aggressive when feeling uncomfortable. His parents decide to investigate the possibility of an autistic spectrum disorder and pursue a formal evaluation. Testing with instruments such as the Social Responsiveness Scale (Constantino et al., 2003) and the Autism Diagnostic Observation Schedule (Lord et al., 2000) reveals clear elevations in autistic traits compared to other teens his age, but not to the degree that would cross diagnostic thresholds. The parents accept this conclusion but hope to implement some modifications at school similar to those that would be given to adolescents who do meet criteria for an autistic spectrum disorder. The school officials, however, resist, stating that the evaluation results do not indicate the presence of a disorder. One day, the classroom teacher abruptly decides to change the assigned seats of all the students. The student, who has been given no notice of the upcoming change, becomes overwhelmed and responds by overturning his

desk and throwing a chair. The boy is then removed from class and suspended for a day.

This vignette vividly illustrates how people can fall into the trap of all-or-none thinking when it comes to traits and disorders. If the student had been diagnosed with an autistic spectrum disorder, no clinically aware teacher would have dreamed of suddenly changing the seating arrangements without notice. Yet because the student did not cross a fairly arbitrary threshold, no extra consideration whatsoever was given and a wholly predictable but unnecessary scenario played out. The teacher defended herself by saying, "But you said he didn't have autism, so I didn't think it would be an issue." True enough, perhaps, but a more dimensional perspective might have helped staff to realize that many of the same steps that help autistic children would be useful for this student as well. My advice to the school was to think of and treat the student like he had a mild version of autism, although in the absence of a written and formalized plan, this concept can sometimes be difficult to implement consistently.

Many schools, especially for younger children, will solicit input from parents about a child's temperament and learning style and what type of teacher works best for that student. It is often wise to take advantage of these opportunities, keeping in mind that just like child-parent fit, optimal child-teacher fit does not necessarily mean pairing up similar types. A child with the mellow profile, for example, might not get a lot accomplished with a mellow-profile teacher (even though he or she may love the pairing) and instead could respond better with a teacher more temperamentally driven and organized. Teachers and school systems interested in thinking more about their temperament and personality can be encouraged to perform some self-assessment. In addition to more formal instruments described earlier for adults, short surveys are available (Kristal, 2005), such as the Teacher Temperament Survey, that offer some general indications and a place to start a practical discussion about teacher temperament.

Parent-School Conflict Over Classroom Modifications

Unfortunately, it is not uncommon for parents and the school to arrive at different conclusions regarding why a child is struggling and what should be done about it with regard to IEPs, 504s, or even alternative placements such as therapeutic schools. In some instances, the school actively wants to pursue some individualized education but the parents, and very often the child too, do not. This reluctance often stems from two main concerns, namely that (1) the child's academic curriculum level and overall expectations will drop, and (2) the child will be stigmatized and made to feel different with derogatory terms such as "sped" (special education) or "emo" (referring to emotional disability).

These legitimate apprehensions can be addressed through specific actions. Parents and schools can build programs that teach school material differently without compromising its overall volume or level. Increased awareness of the negative effects of bullying has also helped change the climate, at least somewhat, for youths who look, act, or learn differently than others. While more can be done, many states and school systems are required to address complaints of bullying and harassment much more comprehensively than in previous decades.

More commonly in my experience, parents feel strongly that certain accommodations or plans should be implemented but the school does not agree or chooses another, often less intensive, course of redress. Different philosophies and perspectives, concerns about dilution of academic demands and stigmatization as previously mentioned, negative effects on other students, and (frankly) cost all can figure into a school's decision not to pursue psychoeducational testing or to create an IEP. Individual teachers may also resist making even informal modifications with the idea that a child should already "know better" based on chronological age. Conflicts between school and parents can sometimes escalate to the point that legal action is considered. While such measures may be unavoidable, some steps can be taken to minimize the level of antagonism and, importantly, its effects on the child.

First, parents should try not to begin discussions with the school from an adversarial perspective. Parents, of course, never say that they do, but the reality is that all parties involved are often primed for a fight before discussions even get going. It is important to remember that the vast majority of schools are trying to do right by the child using the resources available. Those of us in the medical and mental health fields can be pressured by families to advocate on behalf of the family and against the school's wishes. Under such circumstances, I have found that a more open-minded and collaborative stance with school personnel often works best as there frequently are details about the child of which

I was unaware and areas of consensus that open up. When I have ended up writing letters and making phone calls to push for certain testing or a specific accommodation, I have been amazed both at the times when a note from a doctor seems to trump the opinions of an entire team of educational professionals, and the times when my opinions seem to be dismissed out of hand.

Another useful tip for parents is to keep their child away from the school conflict as much as possible. A good analogy here is the classic and generally sound advice for divorced or separated parents not to attack and criticize each other in front of the child (to say nothing about actively expressing criticism directly to the child). Kids need to respect their school. When a parent openly disparages the school, it opens the door for the child to react negatively in class, sometimes as a show of support for the parent. In my office, I discourage insulting language from parents about the school and try to hold these discussions privately with the child out of the room.

A third useful strategy that can help reduce conflict between parents and teachers about special services involves moving the discussion away from fighting for specific plans or labels and more broadly into advocating for what specifically needs to happen at school for things to get better, regardless of the package it's in. Sometimes a parent is in my office upset that the child has been denied "services" but has little idea what those services actually are. Unpacking what an IEP or 504 plan could entail reveals that many of the components are accessible through other means. A teacher may be able to make changes informally, or a specific type of treatment such as occupational therapy might be available outside of the school (and thus not require the child to miss class). If the rules are more rigid and certain services require a more formal diagnosis for qualification, then the blurry lines between psychopathology and traits may be used to the advantage of a child. If the term "very shy" gets a child nothing at school while a diagnosis of "anxiety disorder not otherwise specified" does, then an honest discussion with the family about the pros and cons of using the diagnosis is appropriate, provided that the child actually would qualify for the term.

These suggestions don't always circumvent the need for other types of conflict resolution but often can go a long way toward facilitating an agreement that provides the adjustments children need to succeed at school. Thinking from the perspective of temperament and its overlap with learning and behavioral disorders can help to overcome needlessly inflexible terms that constrain creativity in helping a child adjust to a school and the school adjust to the child.

Optimizing School for Different Temperament Profiles

The next section takes some of the general principles of this chapter and fills in more specific types of strategies and modifications that can be considered for children who possess the different temperament profiles (Table 10.1).

As each child is different and there is no unquestionable authority on the topic, parents and clinicians should be encouraged to come up with additional ideas that may work best on an individual basis rather than sticking rigidly to things that don't work. In keeping with one of the main themes of this chapter, the suggestions are organized into tips that are designed to change the kid to fit the classroom and those designed to change the classroom to fit the kid.

The Mellow Profile

Teachers dealing with children who display the mellow profile often want to light the proverbial fire under their butts. These kids may not be getting into a lot of trouble but can frequently be distracted, lackadaisical, and seemingly content just to get by with a minimum of effort. Children with more extreme levels of this profile may be diagnosed with ADHD, particularly the inattentive type. One particularly annoying and challenging school-related behavior is repeated "forgetting" of assignments and the materials needed to complete them. It can be tempting for parents, especially now that homework assignments are posted on the Internet, to bypass the child altogether and check assignments for him, especially when the teachers push the child to do more with the idea that he "should be old enough to do this on his own by now." Such a statement might be true enough for most kids, but does little to help the individual child who is struggling to come up with a system that works for him. In these instances, what is often required is some kind of deliberate transition period in which the student is intentionally taught how to assume increased responsibility. Such teaching could take place either at school (where a teacher instructs the child on how to keep track of homework and then checks that the child has written down the assign-

TABLE 10.1.
Summary of Suggestions for Maximizing School Achievement
for Different Temperament Types

	Helping the Child Fit the School	Helping the School Fit the Child
Mellow	1. Improve attentional skills through active measures 2. Teach and reward organizational strategies to remember homework	1. Seat the child up close 2. Give less distracting settings for individual work 3. Use more active and hands-on approaches to learning
Agitated	1. Help children identify early signs of agitation and coach them through preferred coping mechanisms 2. Teach them to challenge and modify thoughts (e.g., perceiving hostile intent in others) that might be fueling outbursts	1. Ensure good opportunities for physical activity each day 2. Give them a nonpunitive quiet space or room that they can use 3. Allow flexibility for options other than sitting in desk seat 4. Use fidget toys 5. Break up quiet time into manageable chunks with breaks 6. Clear schedules with cueing before changes
Confident	1. Purposely pair these children with other temperament styles 2. Encourage extra school and community projects that can develop their traits further	1. Resist the tendency to give these children special treatment for rules and consequences 2. Adjust demands and expectations according to true intellectual ability
Anxious	1. Prepare and practice for new school activities at home 2. If in counseling, include school-related topics in the therapy work	1. Help the teacher understand that what might look like defiance is really anxiety 2. Advance notice of upcoming school activities 3. Provisions to engage more gradually in new school tasks 4. Active check-ins to ensure that material is being understood
Moderate	1. Have the child sit closer to the front if seating is not assigned 2. Encourage more engagement with the teacher	1. Make reasonable contacts with the teacher about the child through e-mail, phone, or conferences 2. Do supplemental learning exercises with children to increase energy and interest

ments correctly each day) or at home if such information is readily available. The idea then is to withdraw this supervision gradually and allow the child to take over this task, even if it means the occasional lapse and natural consequences that ensue.

Additional modifications at school can involve many of the things done for children who meet criteria for inattentive ADHD, regardless of whether the child actually crosses diagnostic thresholds. Seating up front with steps to minimize distractions when working individually (such as a cubicle or earplugs) can help the child stay on task longer during periods of quiet study. More active and hands-on learning can also engage mellow profile kids more readily than the traditional passive method of listening and studying in silence.

In addition to these efforts to shape the environment, there has naturally been interest in the possibility of training improved attentional skills. Biofeedback has been marketed as an effective intervention for children with ADHD, and some research studies have demonstrated moderate success (Drechsler et al., 2007; Fox, Tharp, & Fox, 2005). At this point, however, the publicity has outstripped the evidence and more controlled data is needed. Five- and 10-day attentional training programs administered to 4- to 6-year-old children without ADHD have shown the ability to improve attentional skills somewhat (Rueda, Checa, & Santonja, 2008; Rueda et al., 2005). Ironically, these programs involve using computers and look suspiciously like educational video games, which many experts believe is more of the problem than the solution (Swing et al., 2010). A lower-tech but very effective intervention may be to actively encourage and reward reading. In addition to the obvious advantage of improving a very valuable skill, the idea is that reading and other quiet activities such as meditation help to lower the set point the brain needs to be engaged. If academics are taught using lower levels of arousal (in contrast to things like video games that bombard the senses with sights and sounds), the brain gradually requires less stimulation in order to focus and stay on task.

The Agitated Profile

Children with the agitated profile are prone to meltdowns over what appear to others to be minor problems. Similar to strategies described in *The Explosive Child* (Greene, 1998), some principles of collaborative problem solving have been incorporated into an educational approach called the Responsive Classroom (http://www.responsive-classroom.org). As at home, most of the effort is best directed at teaching the skills and strategies before meltdowns occur. Once they happen, options are much fewer. Individually, a school-based clinician can meet with an agitated profile child to identify common triggers and early signs of an outburst. The knowledge gained from these sessions can be shared with the teacher with the hope that the teacher can anticipate difficult situations and assist the child in accessing coping mechanisms that keep small stressors from becoming major incidents. For example, many children who are prone to intense outbursts are quick to perceive hostile intent in others. A well-prepared teacher might be able to recognize an exchange that the child would perceive as threatening and be ready with a nice cognitive reframe, such as, "Joe, you must feel terrible for accidently disturbing [child with agitated profile's] art project." In terms of helping with coping mechanisms, often a subtle approach works best so that the child is not put in the spotlight in front of peers. A teacher's gentle hand on the shoulder, for example, could be the signal for the child that agitation is beginning to ramp up and it is time to try some relaxation breathing.

Physical activity is often very beneficial for children with the agitated profile. It is a common mistake for schools to withhold recess as a punishment for poor behavior for these children. Research has shown that regular exercise can be an important factor in helping very active children stay calm and focused when the situation calls for it (Gapin, Labban, & Etnier, 2011). Consequences for negative behavior are important, but for very energetic kids who have trouble regulating themselves, it is best to look elsewhere for incentives.

There have been some efforts to use temperament-based programs to help teachers and parents work with behaviorally challenging kids, many of whom would likely be classified in the agitated profile. One effort called the INSIGHTS program was found to be effective in a study based in inner-city New York schools (McClowry, Snow, & Tamis-LeMonda, 2005). The program offered education about temperament and strategies for working with common behavioral problems. Puppets of different temperament types (e.g., Gregory the Grumpy, Hilary the Hard Worker) provided the basis for some sessions with the children themselves (Rothbart, 2011). The program resulted in significant decreases in disruptive or externalizing behavior, particularly for children who were already presenting with clinical levels of behavioral problems. These results are encouraging and speak further to the significant overlap between interventions designed from a temperament versus clinical framework.

Many of the accommodations for children who meet full criteria for ADHD, combined or hyperactive type, can be helpful with this group of kids. They might be allowed to have what many clinicians call "fidget toys" in class: something like a soft ball or other small toy that keeps their hands busy while enabling them to focus. They might also be permitted to use a space or room to cool off when feeling overwhelmed or be allowed to be out of their seats in class as long as their behavior doesn't disturb others.

As many children with the agitated profile struggle with transitions, particularly unexpected ones, it can be quite beneficial to post detailed schedules of upcoming activities with ample cues that one endeavor is ending and another is beginning. The schedule can be modified to minimize long spans of time when the child needs to be quiet and contained, with breaks that punctuate these more difficult stretches.

The Confident Profile

As previously mentioned, children with the confident profile often have energy, social skills, and an ability to pull other kids into their circle. Many of these kids thrive at school and are commonly the ones receiving the benefits of the halo effect described earlier. However, these traits can propel some toward a sense of entitlement and conceit. The cliques of popular kids that are stereotyped widely in teen movies can include individuals with the confident profile who believe that they are entitled to exclude others. Their extraverted demeanor and polite manners with teachers can disguise a more malicious streak that is reserved for peers who are perceived to cross them. Under more extreme conditions, such individuals who become filled with anger or hate can be the ringleaders of groups involved in more deliberate rule-breaking behavior.

Much of the work to harness the tremendous potential of children with the confident profile lies at home. Usually these kids are not receiving school accommodations or modifications because of their behavior through actions such as a 504 plan. Nevertheless, there can be many opportunities in the classroom to help these children apply their temperament endowments in a positive fashion and steer them away from traps. When children work in groups, deliberately pairing these kids with those in different social circles rather than allowing them to join up with other confident profile children can help them get to know others in a way that resists cliques and stereotypes. It is much easier to ignore the positive qualities in others and look down upon them if we have never bothered to get to know them at all.

Kids with the confident profile can also magnify their traits when given the proper opportunities. Encouragement to take school leadership positions or to turn school assignments into civil projects can bolster their developing temperament and propel them toward constructive applications of their abilities. A child who expresses concern for a particular societal problem learned about in a social studies class, for example, could be invigorated to translate these feelings into a community project or event. Such efforts, of course, can be very beneficial for all temperament types but may find particularly fertile ground in those with the confident profile.

Ironically, actions that help the school fit better with a confident profile child may include not giving them special treatment. Their behavioral indiscretions should be handled the same way as everyone else's, in part so that these children do not begin to believe that the standard rules do not apply to them. It is natural for teachers to be quite vigilant with more problematic students and to move swiftly and decisively when there are transgressions. Students of all types will be watching carefully to see that such a policy is applied equitably. Letting the rules slide for a subset of the students can breed contempt among those who see these laws being enforced only for them and impunity among those for whom the laws are ignored.

For children with the confident profile who are also intellectually bright, the level of challenge in the curriculum can sometimes be the issue. While the limits for behavior need to be consistent, the academic standards and expectations need to vary enough that all students are pushed to perform at their highest level. Supplemental or enrichment material can reduce boredom and keep school engaging for all students. At the same time, some children with the confident profile may not be as academically advanced as they might appear based on their temperament. It is important not to set these students up for frustration and failure by setting their workload and expectations beyond their true abilities.

The Anxious Profile
Some anxious children come across as defiant. If clinicians or parents can encourage the school to see the child as scared and uncomfortable rather than deliberately naughty, it can often be a crucial first step to paving

the way for a variety of positive changes. When problems do occur, such changes in perspective can usher in a much more sympathetic and forgiving stance on the part of school staff. Some insights into the potential triggers for these reactions and ways to manage them often spare the child many embarrassing outbursts that otherwise might push him or her to resist school further. Accommodations that may be helpful include providing the family and child with advance notice of what is coming at school so that the child can be fully prepared. Some anxious children do better when they are permitted to engage in new tasks more slowly and gradually so that they can build comfort and experience.

Advance notice of upcoming activities can be an opportunity to do some preliminary work that can result in the child being less worried when the time comes to begin that task at school. For example, if a parent knows that a new sport is about to be introduced in gym class, a personal introduction and practice beforehand at home can make the difference between an anxious child willing to give it a try in front of peers and a screaming meltdown that ends up in the assistant principal's office. For kids whose anxiety is high enough for them to be working with a counselor using cognitive-behavioral therapy, school-related challenges should definitely be a specific target that is addressed both in session and in therapy homework.

Other children with the anxious profile can be the least problematic children in the classroom, but sometimes at the expense of their learning. When confused, these kids are not the ones to raise their hands and ask for clarification or additional help. For these kids, teachers may do well to check in from time to time and have them demonstrate that they actually understand the concepts being taught.

The Moderate Profile

Last, what about those kids whose temperament fits the moderate profile best, and whose traits tend not to be particularly positive or negative? Is it worth a section on troubleshooting when there often isn't much trouble? The answer is yes. Without levels of traits that especially stand out, these kids may get neither the additional monitoring and intervention that more temperamentally challenging kids receive nor the extra praise or encouragement often bestowed on kids with the other profiles. In other words, they are apt to be left alone, especially if their intellectual aptitude is also somewhere near the middle.

If it appears that a child with the moderate profile is starting to fall through the cracks and not receive the academic attention that is needed and deserved, the child can be encouraged to take some steps to stay on the radar screen. If seating is not assigned, the child can move closer to the front. Parents can also encourage children with the moderate profile to engage more with their teacher by raising their hands when they know the answer and asking questions when they don't.

A parent of a moderate profile child can also help by being involved with the classroom and the teacher. While most teachers are not fond of overly intrusive parents, the occasional e-mail or phone call is often quite welcome and can help maximize positive engagement between the child and the school. Since these children can be less apt to express their thoughts, both negative and positive, parents may have to do this on their behalf. In addition, parents may want to try to build the child's enthusiasm for a learning topic through supplemental materials. If a child tends not to get too excited about things, this response can be interpreted as disinterest, which often breeds more disinterest from others. During a series on astronomy, for example, a night or two outside identifying the constellations with the child might make the lessons come to life. This little boost can stimulate additional learning opportunities in the classroom.

In summary, temperament is a huge factor in schools and other educational settings with the potential both to enhance and to inhibit a child's academic potential. Helping a child's temperament fit educational demands optimally involves actions designed to help the child adapt better to the school and modifications designed to help the school adapt best to the child. Such changes and accommodations, customized for each child's temperament, can be the result of intuitive adjustments performed informally by teachers or of more specific plans that are explicitly designed and implemented. Good communication between parents and teachers that encourages an open discussion about the child's (and teacher's) temperament is often a key initial step in creating an optimal fit that maximally stimulates further learning.

Chapter 11

Medications

Temperament and personality can change. Genetic and environmental forces have different levels of influence during various stages of development to accentuate or diminish traits over time, and for the most part we accept those changes as part of life. When particular traits result in a poor fit with a child's surroundings, a parent, teacher, or counselor can apply many of the suggestions outlined earlier to coach up or coach around these behaviors so that the child becomes more adaptive, which helps build positive developmental momentum. These interventions are accepted and encouraged without much fanfare or controversy about "personality engineering" or "brainwashing." But what about medications or even over-the-counter supplements as agents of temperament alteration, either as a by-product of treating mental illness or, even more provocative, as the intended result of taking a pill?

Since the mid-1990s, there has been an explosion in the number of children receiving psychiatric medications in the United States (Olfson et al., 2006). These drugs include stimulants for ADHD as well as mood stabilizers and antipsychotics that carry a host of potentially serious side effects. This surge has continued despite a continued lack of knowledge concerning the long-term effects of these medications on the developing brain. The study by Olfson documents that the number of medical visits that included an antipsychotic medication among children under 14 years of age rose by nearly a factor of eight from 1993 to 2009. One explanation for this rise in medication usage is that the floor that separates traits from illness has dropped sufficiently far to include millions of children who are now being treated for their temperament rather than their psychopathology. The debate and discussion that such possibilities stir up say much about our values as a society and some of their inconsistencies. Furthermore, the science of understanding potential personality changes due to medications lags well behind the political discourse. Here, we explore what is known about the ability of medications and other substances to modify temperament and personality and explore the implications of this potentially brave new world.

Temperament Change Associated With Psychiatric Treatment

When parents are deciding whether to use medications to treat emotional behavioral problems in a child, they very frequently state their wish that the medications change symptoms without changing who the child is, meaning the temperament or personality. This common request is eminently reasonable. Parents generally like their children and are naturally quite leery of any substance that might fundamentally alter the basic characteristics that define a child's core being. To prescribe a medication that transforms a child essentially into someone else would be counterproductive, misguided, and even creepy.

For example, a mother might bring a young boy struggling with ADHD for assessment and treatment with the hope that a medication such as methylphenidate (Ritalin) will help him attend better at school and not drift off so frequently into daydreams. She might also want to reduce his difficulty finishing homework assignments or his inability to sit quietly when the occasion calls for it, such as at church or during circle time at school. At the same time, this mother might adore this child's exuberance, his spontaneous displays of joy and affection, and his craving for new sensations and experiences. In discussions with the child's pediatrician or child psychiatrist, the goal of any medication would be to target the negative aspects of ADHD while preserving the positive aspects of the boy's temperament.

The physician, actually, wants exactly the same thing. Despite the mythology perpetuated by old books and movies such as *One Flew Over the Cuckoo's Nest*, there are no psychiatrists whose goal is to turn their patients into cookie cutter children who blandly follow rules without question. No physician I have ever met is trying to turn children into little "zombies," using my favorite word that comes up all the time when discussing medications with parents. How such an idea ever took hold is beyond my knowledge, but it is there nonetheless. Over the years, I have learned to state quite explicitly to parents who are carefully weighing the pros and cons of medication that to me, zombification is not an acceptable clinical outcome. If a child is sedated and lifeless, I say, then something will be done about it immediately. To my continual surprise, parents usually seem extremely relieved to hear this news.

Yet all appropriate reassurances aside, the weight of evidence described up to this point suggests that squelching psychiatric symptoms while leaving other elements of personality wholly intact may be a difficult thing to accomplish, whether through treatment with medication or anything else. As outlined in detail in Chapters 5 and 6, it looks quite convincing at this point that most of the problems treated by mental health professionals exist, at least on the surface, as extremes of a continuum of trait combinations that at less extreme levels would be described as temperament or personality traits. Emerging evidence further demonstrates that some of these continuums share common underlying physiology with regard to brain regions, genes, and environmental events. We are also reminded that all temperament dimensions traditionally have both positive and negative elements (Chapter 3). A child endowed with high levels of a particular dimension might then be expected to possess generous quantities of both its positive and negative components, the latter of which sound suspiciously like symptoms listed in books such as the DSM.

With the two domains being so closely intertwined, then, it may indeed be a challenge to effect symptom change without any personality change. Changing disorders without changing traits may be as complicated as targeting, for example, tumor cells with chemotherapy without affecting other rapidly growing and dividing tissues. The task is not impossible, but because the mechanisms governing the growth of both normal and cancerous cells have much in common, selecting only one type of cell for treatment is far from a straightforward task.

Listening to Prozac was published in 1993 by psychiatrist Peter Kramer. Released within a decade of the approval of fluoxetine (Prozac) by the FDA, the book chronicled the experiences of several patients who experienced personality change and even "transformation" after taking the antidepressant, and the implications of those changes. In addition to relieving symptoms of depression and anxiety, Kramer asserted that in his experience, a "substantial minority" of patients who took Prozac also reported being more confident, less shy, and calmer under stress. While one could easily argue that the book was written to raise rather than answer important questions, it became a wake-up call to the segment of society that was becoming increasingly suspicious of psychiatric medications. It challenged the prevailing assertion that the effect of medications was to reveal personality rather than alter it. Such claims continue to be made, and, as a practicing clinician, I must admit that few statements of gratitude are more rewarding to hear than parents thanking me after a child's successful treatment, saying that they now have their son or daughter back. Yet while *Listening to Prozac* did not dispute that treatment could work in such a way, it also suggested that for some people, what resulted from antidepressant use was not a return to a nondisease state but the creation of something altogether new.

Kramer's hypothesis of how such transformation could occur directly invoked the concept of temperament as a potential target of pharmacological treatment. Indeed, he noted the emerging research of that time demonstrating the involvement of core neurotransmitters such as dopamine, norepinephrine, and serotonin for both temperament traits and psychiatric disorders and concluded that we should have expected this conundrum to be present all along. "One conclusion we might draw from this understanding," he wrote, "is that medications that alter levels of, or transmission by, these substances *ought* to affect temperament" (Kramer, 1993, p. 175). His patient Sally, for example, was ostensibly being treated for her depressive symptoms, but it was her temperamental change of becoming less shy and more assertive that was more responsible for the difference in her life.

Embedded in Kramer's case examples are also speculations on the boundary between mental illness and character traits. While some of the patients quite easily met criteria for diagnoses such as major depression or an anxiety disorder, for other individuals the diagnosis was unclear. The case of Julia, who was somewhat controlling and excessively clean but did not quite meet criteria for either OCD or obsessive-compulsive personality disorder, illustrated how clinicians can question whether the focus of treatment is an illness, a temperament trait, or some sort of spectrum or "penumbra," as Kramer described it.

In my own practice with children and adolescents, I have certainly witnessed many changes after prescribing medications that would likely count as temperament or personality change if we had measured before and after treatment as such. When we treat ADHD with stimulant medications such as methylphenidate, many if not most of the kids become less impulsive and restless, and have an improved ability to regulate their attention. After prescribing selective serotonin reuptake inhibitors (SSRIs) such as fluoxetine, I certainly have observed less irritability and an overall feeling that irritating things simply bother a patient less. An adult patient once noted that she "didn't have anything to say" in psychotherapy because the usual conflicts and issues were no longer that compelling. In the majority of cases, parents perceive changes the way physicians hope; namely, they feel that treatment has brought their real child back or at least has allowed the child's true personality to emerge after the static noise of hyperactivity or irritability has settled down. Rarely have I witnessed personality transformations or what the child or parent describes as the emergence of a wholly new characteristic. More commonly, adolescents who were terribly anxious in social situations now find themselves somewhat less so, but none become complete extraverts who experience a complete absence of discomfort. On occasion, I do get a phone call from parents saying that the stimulant that was started for their child's ADHD has caused him or her to be listless and dull (i.e., a zombie) or, more commonly, increasingly intense and irritable. As mentioned previously, such reports bring swift action and the patient's return to a previous level of functioning.

It should be noted that similar, albeit less dramatic, changes have also occurred in the course of psychotherapy. A study examining the effect of a cognitive-behavioral intervention for temperamentally anxious children, for example, showed that levels of anxiety diminished as did the number of anxiety disorders in comparison to a monitor-only group (Rapee et al., 2010). In the course of psychotherapy, levels of shyness can diminish, assertiveness can grow, and overall mood can improve. These changes tend to be fairly gradual and usually in the desired direction, so parents and children seldom complain of them as unwanted or as the equivalent of medication side effects. Nevertheless, they would once again likely be detected during a formal temperament or personality assessment.

As described in Chapter 6, the degree of shared language between descriptions of temperament or personality traits and psychiatric symptoms might cause many to conclude that at least some degree of personality change is inevitable with any kind of successful treatment. Thus, what triggers the response of a grateful thank-you for relieving symptoms versus the odd discomfort that a child's personality has been fundamentally altered by treatment isn't obvious. For some, the distinction between a personality dimension and mental illness is "state versus trait." The family of a normally cheerful adolescent boy who becomes sullen and irritable during the course of a clinical depression will likely welcome the return of their bubbly and enthusiastic son in the course of antidepressant treatment, yet that same outcome for a boy who has always been somewhat reserved and serious could trigger the concern that something is now present that was not there previously. Another difference may lie in the magnitude of the change. It is one thing, for example, for a young girl to go from being painfully shy to slightly shy and quite another for her to become not shy at all, even if both instances involve progression along a quantitative continuum of behavior. Finally, the perception of true personality change may also be a function of whether or not that change was in the treatment plan from the beginning or a more unexpected by-product. When treating a child with attention problems, for example, a parent might well expect that peripheral functions such as organization or fidgetiness might also be affected, but when a child also becomes more compulsive and suddenly needs to have things lined up a particular way, then people begin to wonder if the treatment has overshot its mark.

Listening to Prozac certainly received its share of both praise and criticism. For some, the work was a decisive indictment of all that is wrong with the field of psychiatry in American culture, written by someone on the inside. Others, however, received the book as pure speculation from a person who should know better. Such criticism was easy to generate in the scientific community as the book was based on a small number of case examples rather than more systematic and controlled experiments. In his defense, Kramer acknowledged this limitation and never argued for decisive action based upon his few clinical reports, yet some believed that these speculations, even if labeled as such, should still be the product of more firmly grounded scientific evidence.

One might have expected that due to the amount of attention that the book and the medications received, a series of well-designed and tightly controlled studies were soon to follow. Surprisingly, however, these investigations continue to be published at a trickle. One of the most extensive studies on the subject to date was conducted at Northwestern University (Tang et al., 2009): 240 moderately depressed adults received treatment with the antidepressant paroxetine, a placebo, or cognitive therapy. Depression symptoms were assessed at multiple time points, as was personality using the self-report NEO-Five Factor Inventory (NEO-FFI). The primary personality variables that were measured were the higher-order dimensions of neuroticism and extraversion. Overall, both cognitive therapy and medication treatment resulted in changes in depression scores (decreased), neuroticism (decreased), and extraversion (increased). The changes in personality, however, remained significant even after statistically controlling for the changes in depression. Placebo resulted in moderate decreases in depression symptoms, a common finding in treatment studies of depression, but, interestingly, very little change in neuroticism or extraversion. Even more intriguing was the finding that the personality dimensions did eventually change, but only after the placebo patients (many of whom saw moderate improvement in depression) were offered and accepted medication treatment with paroxetine.

These results are a blow to the state effects hypothesis in depression-personality relations, which posits that what look like trait personality differences among depressed individuals are really a function of being in the state of depression. This perspective would predict that depressive symptoms and personality would move in lockstep together so that as depressive symptoms remit, neuroticism would decrease and extraversion would increase. This trend was indeed found for paroxetine, but the personality change remained robust even after taking into account the depression change. Even more compelling are the surprising results of placebo administration, for which depression scores changed while personality scores did not. Instead, the authors discussed a cause-correction model, by which medication treatment is thought to be effective by altering one of the main causes of depression, namely the underlying personality traits of high neuroticism and low extraversion.

With the inclusion of both a placebo and a psychotherapy group, this study represents a clear advance in the systematic examination of personality effects of medication. The use of the reliable and well-researched NEO-FFI also lends credence to their findings. At the same time, however, much more research is needed in this line of inquiry. There remains much to learn about personality changes with pharmacological treatment of other conditions such as various anxiety disorders, ADHD, eating disorders, and even psychotic disorders. There are almost no data in pediatric samples, or from instruments that purport to measure temperament rather than personality. In addition, personality or temperament assessment could be improved in future studies, perhaps by adding observer ratings to self-report questionnaires. Another important potential advance might be to reposition analyses to the facet level rather than higher-order dimensions. The vast majority of studies examine temperament at the highest level possible, namely broad dimensions such as extraversion and negative emotionality, yet to explore fully the potential effects of medications on temperament, it may be necessary to drill down to the components that make up those more general traits. Extraversion or surgency, for example, include several facets such as a tendency to enjoy more stimulating activities (high-intensity pleasure) as well as impulsivity. It is possible that medications preferentially affect some facets quite a bit and others hardly at all, with the end result being a rather moderate and bland change on the broad dimension. Such an analysis would also equip us more fully to answer the concerns of parents wondering whether or not to begin Ritalin treatment for their child. They want the level of impulsivity to decrease but not that enthusiasm and zest for life. Can a medication make such a fine distinction? We won't know until we specifically look.

Toward that end, our research group, with others, is hoping to undertake just such a study in children, using questionnaire and observer-based temperament assessments that can approach the question on both the broader dimensional and more detailed facet level. If successful, this study will undoubtedly not be the last word on the subject either. Likely, patients, their families, and their doctors will continue to worry about the unintended consequences on temperament and personality that result from a wide array of pharmacological agents designed to improve psychiatric symptoms. Because of the close alignment of temperament traits and symptoms, it seems unavoidable that both domains will be affected by any type of intervention, pharmacological or otherwise. Nevertheless, we may find cases in which medications cause some symptoms to change substantially while certain temperament traits, perhaps at finer levels, can change in different ways or remain unchanged.

Intentional Treatment of Temperament and Personality

While most of the discussion surrounding medications and temperament relates to changes induced in the course of treating specific psychiatric conditions, an equally important question arises regarding the appropriateness of using medications deliberately to change personality or temperament dimensions in the absence of definable illness. This possible new frontier is what Kramer (1993) referred to as "cosmetic psychopharmacology" and may be akin to the practice of using performance-enhancing substances to improve target characteristics in which a person already excels.

The use of medical procedures and pharmacological agents to enhance aspects of oneself that are not diseased is already well established in many other disciplines. According to the American Society for Aesthetic Plastic Surgery, over 9 million procedures were done in the United States in 2011 and the majority of Americans, even those making under $25,000 per year, approve of the practice (http://www.surgery.org). In sports medicine, the use of various compounds by elite athletes and weekend warriors alike to increase strength, endurance, and recovery times after an injury has left governing agencies for professional sports struggling to keep up with the science and technology of performance-enhancing agents that have invaded one sport after another. Other pharmacological indications that creep a little closer to disease treatment include things like the use of prescription acne medications.

Could psychiatry, or perhaps more appropriately mental health, be left behind in this movement? Traditional training in psychiatry teaches that antidepressants are not "happy pills," and their administration to nondepressed individuals thus will not elevate their mood. Case examples in *Listening to Prozac* (Kramer, 1993) challenge this belief somewhat, but more controlled evidence is certainly required. Thus far, however, there have been few studies. A study of healthy adults without depression who took the antidepressant paroxetine for a month did find increases in social affiliation and decreases in negative mood (Knutson et al., 1998). A few years later, Tse and Bond (2001) gave the SSRI citalopram to a small sample of adults and found increases in the trait of self-directedness compared to those who took placebo. A more recent study involved a sample of Danish adults who were not depressed themselves but had a first-degree relative with a history of clinical depression (Knorr et al., 2012). Personality was assessed at baseline and after 4 weeks of either escitalopram (10 mg per day) or placebo using the well-known Revised NEO Personality Inventory (Costa & McCrae, 1992) and the Eysenck Personality Inventory (Eysenck & Eysenck, 1975). While the authors hypothesized that there would be decreases in the trait of neuroticism, no statistically significant differences were found compared to placebo, although an effect was found for the trait of agreeableness (to the tune of about half of a standard deviation). While it would have been interesting to see if a few subjects experienced more dramatic changes, such data were presented only on a group level.

The case with other types of agents, however, is a bit more clear-cut. Stimulants like Ritalin and Adderall that are used to treat ADHD, for example, have been widely shown to improve memory and attention skills in healthy individuals, although the precise areas of improvement remain under study (Smith & Farah, 2011). This effect is likely driving the increasing popularity of stimulant use among high school and college youth as a study aid. According to the National Survey on Drug Use and Health, 12.3% of Americans between the ages of 21 and 25 have used a stimulant for "nonmedical" purposes (U.S. Department of Health and Human Services, 2009). Benzodiazepines, similarly, can help even those who don't have full-fledged anxiety disorders feel calmer and more relaxed.

The case for resisting, allowing, or even encouraging the use of psychiatric medications to improve behavioral traits and cognitive abilities has been reviewed in the literature (Cerullo, 2006; Farah et al., 2004; Franke, Lieb, & Hildt, 2012; Sahakian & Morein-Zamir, 2007). Arguments in favor of their use often relate to principles of individual freedom and even to societal gains resulting from a population that is smarter and less encumbered by maladaptive traits overall. Arguments urging restraint can rest on principles of fairness and access to these medications, especially given their lack of coverage by insurance policies. Even the individual freedom angle extolled by proponents can be challenged under the notion that if enough people begin to take medications to improve their personality and cognitive function, there will be pressure on everyone to do the same to keep up in the workforce or in society in general. From a more philosophical angle, a particularly troubling aspect of using medications like antidepressants to induce happiness is that one then bypasses the normal trials and tribulations that give that improved mental state substance and authenticity. In addition to the contention that the result of using medications to improve mental function would be more hollow and fragile in comparison to improvement gains through experience and hard work, the argument also evokes complaints of unfairness. Americans in particular cherish the ideal that to reap the benefits of something, a person should, to paraphrase an advertisement by investment company SmithBarney, obtain it the old-fashioned way, namely by earning it.

The President's Council on Bioethics (2003) specifically described an inhibited temperament alone as an inappropriate use of an SSRI and grouped this class of medications with drugs such as Ecstasy. The council also suggested that available medications used to adjust child temperament could result in a lack of tolerance for the full range of temperament variation. The council wrote, "The enhanced ability to make children conform to conventional standards could also diminish our openness to the diversity of human temperaments" (p. 88).

However, worries about using substances to change temperament seem to be reserved mainly for prescription medications. Herbal supplements like ginkgo biloba or vitamin B12 cause little public concern, while compounds such as caffeine to help us stay alert and alcohol to help us interact with others are firmly woven into the fabric of our society. Books such as *Smart Drugs and Nutrients* get published without firestorms of controversy (Dean & Morgenthaler, 1990). Illicit drugs such as methamphetamine or cannabis may result in a stronger change in personality traits, but their illegal status comes not from their ability to alter traits (albeit temporarily) but other qualities including addictive liability and high risk of adverse side effects.

Yet with the possible exception of stimulants used for cognitive enhancement, clinicians have not seen a tidal wave of individuals coming to the office who don't meet criteria for a psychiatric disorder asking for medications to augment or promote particular traits. Thus, many psychiatrists have been spared the moral dilemma of being asked to perform cosmetic psychopharmacology—for now. However, this situation may last only until a new agent comes on the scene that can actually deliver on the promise of reliable, robust, and safe changes in temperament or cognitive ability. Such a reprieve may be a relatively unusual case in which the science of how to do something does not outpace the ethical discourse regarding whether we should do something. I, for one, am glad for a little more time to think this one through.

For clinicians leery of prescribing medications for well individuals but who also don't want to overly restrict the use of treatments that could potentially benefit a large number of people, one convenient solution is simply to drop the threshold of a psychiatric diagnosis so that more people qualify as being ill. There are good indications that this has occurred over the past several decades, although the ability to prescribe more medications as a result is likely not the motivating factor. The CDC, for example, reported that the rate of ADHD rose about 3% per year over a decade (Pastor & Reuben, 2008). What is responsible for such an increase in diagnoses? People have blamed everything from pesticides on our food to the advanced age of new parents to reduced stigma of mental health conditions. Another factor that needs to be considered, however, is the increased awareness of these fuzzy boundaries between traits and psychopathology. With such an appreciation, the distinction between legitimate and cosmetic treatment becomes quite difficult. Indeed, the President's Council on Bioethics acknowledged that "the continuity of ADHD symptoms with ordinary behaviors" (2003, p. 81) makes it difficult to distinguish when a medication is being used to treat illness or to augment traits, thus opening the door for increased prescriptions for the latter.

For those expecting some kind of easy answer to these questions and concerns regarding the modification of temperament by medications either as a by-product of treatment for more "legitimate" illness or through intentional design, I'm afraid you will need to look elsewhere. It is clear to me that suffering due to a person's thoughts, behaviors, and actions does not suddenly appear at the threshold for a DSM disorder, and that medications can help to relieve some of that suffering. The bioethical principle of autonomy also teaches that the decision of whether or not to undertake a particular course of action rests with the individual. The physician, meanwhile, is to act more like a guide than a king. In the absence of a global decree on the subject, perhaps the complexity and contradictions that this issue stirs up compel clinicians and patients to have a frank and thoughtful discussion regarding a specific agent being considered for a specific person for a specific reason. That, in the end, may not be such a bad thing.

Credits

Figure 2.1: Reprinted from *Journal of the American Academy of Child & Adolescent Psychiatry*, Vol. 47, Issue 3, David C. Rettew, Robert R. Althoff, Levent Dumenci, Lynsay Ayer, James J. Hudziak, "Latent Profiles of Temperament and Their Relations to Psychopathology and Wellness," pp. 273–281, March 2008, with permission from Elsevier.

Figures 4.1 and **4.2:** Reprinted by permission from Macmillan Publishers Ltd: *Nature Reviews Neuroscience*, Vol. 9, Luiz Pessoa, "On the Relationship Between Emotion and Cognition," February 2008; permission from Nature Publishing Group.

Figure 5.1: Reprinted from *Journal of Child Psychology and Psychiatry*, Tina J. C. Polderman, Eske M. Derks, Jim J. Hudziak, Frank C. Verhulst, Daniëlle Posthuma, Dorret I. Boomsma, "Across the Continuum of Attention Skills: A Twin Study of the SWAN ADHD Rating Scale," pp. 1080–1087, August 2007, with permission from John Wiley and Sons.

Figure 6.1: Reprinted from *Journal of Anxiety Disorders*, Vol. 20, David C. Rettew, Alicia C. Doyle, Monica Kwan, Catherine Stanger, James J. Hudziak, "Exploring the Boundary Between Temperament and Generalized Anxiety Disorder: A Receiver Operating Characteristic Analysis," pp. 931–945, 2006, with permission from Elsevier.

Figure 6.3: Reprinted from *Comprehensive Psychiatry*, Vol. 47, David C. Rettew, Catherine Stanger, Laura McKee, Alicia Doyle, James J. Hudziak, "Interactions Between Child and Parent Temperament and Child Behavior Problems," pp. 412–20, September–October 2006, with permission from Elsevier.

References

Abikoff, H., Courtney, M., Pelham, W. E., Jr., & Koplewicz, H. S. (1993). Teachers' ratings of disruptive behaviors: The influence of halo effects. *Journal of Abnormal Child Psychology, 21*(5), 519–533.

Achenbach, T. M. (1991a). *Manual for the Child Behavior Checklist/4-18*. Burlington, VT: Department of Psychiatry, University of Vermont.

Achenbach, T. M. (1991b). *Manual of the Teacher Report Form and 1991 profile*. Burlington, VT: University of Vermont.

Achenbach, T. M., & Rescorla, L. A. (2000). *Manual for ASEBA preschool forms and profiles*. Burlington, VT: University of Vermont, Research Center for Children, Youth, and Families.

Achenbach, T. M., & Rescorla, L. A. (2001). *Manual for the ASEBA school-age forms and profiles*. Burlington, VT: University of Vermont, Research Center for Children, Youth and Families.

Akiskal, H. S., Kilzieh, N., Maser, J. D., Clayton, P. J., Schettler, P. J., Traci, Shea, M. . . . Keller, M. B. (2006). The distinct temperament profiles of bipolar I, bipolar II and unipolar patients. *Journal of Affective Disorders, 92*(1), 19–33. doi: 10.1016/j.jad.2005.12.033

Akiskal, H. S., Maser, J. D., Zeller, P. J., Endicott, J., Coryell, W., Keller, M., . . . Goodwin, F. (1995). Switching from "unipolar" to bipolar II: An 11-year prospective study of clinical and temperamental predictors in 559 patients. *Archives of General Psychiatry, 52*(2), 114–123.

Aksan, N., Goldsmith, H. H., Smider, N. A., Essex, M. J., Clark, R., Hyde, J. S., et al. (1999). Derivation and prediction of temperamental types among preschoolers. *Developmental Psychology, 35*(4), 958–871.

Allport, G. W. (1961). *Pattern and growth in personality*. New York: Holt, Rinehart and Winston.

Althoff, R. R., Rettew, D. C., Boomsma, D. I., & Hudziak, J. J. (2009). Latent class analysis of the Child Behavior Checklist Obsessive-Compulsive Scale. *Comprehensive Psychiatry, 50*(6), 584–592. doi: 10.1016/j.comppsych.2009.01.005

Althoff, R. R., Verhulst, F. C., Rettew, D. C., Hudziak, J. J., & van der Ende, J. (2010). Adult outcomes of childhood dysregulation: A 14-year follow-up study. *Journal of the American Academy of Child and Adolescent Psychiatry, 49*(11), 1105–1116. doi: 10.1016/j.jaac.2010.08.006

American Academy of Child and Adolescent Psychiatry. (2012). The child and adolescent psychiatrist. Retrieved from http://www.aacap.org/cs/root/facts_for_families/the_child_and_adolescent_psychiatrist

American Psychiatric Association. (1987). *Diagnostic and statistical manual of mental disorders* (3rd ed., rev.). Washington, DC: American Psychiatric Association.

Apter, A., Fallon, T. J., Jr., King, R. A., Ratzoni, G., Zohar, A. H., Binder, M. . . . Cohen, D. J. (1996). Obsessive-compulsive characteristics: From symptoms to syndrome. *Journal of the American Academy of Child and Adolescent Psychiatry, 35*(7), 907–912.

Asberg, M., Traskman, L., & Thoren, P. (1976). 5-HIAA in the cerebrospinal fluid: A biochemical suicide predictor? *Archives of General Psychiatry, 33*(10), 1193–1197.

Ayer, L., Rettew, D., Althoff, R. R., Willemsen, G., Ligthart, L., Hudziak, J. J., & Boomsma, D. I. (2011). Adolescent personality profiles, neighborhood income, and young adult alcohol use: A longitudinal study. *Addictive Behaviors, 36*(12), 1301–1304. doi: 10.1016/j.addbeh.2011.07.004

Barkley, R. A., & Benton, C. M. (1998). *Your defiant child: Eight steps to better behavior.* New York: Guilford.

Baron-Cohen, S., Knickmeyer, R. C., & Belmonte, M. K. (2005). Sex differences in the brain: Implications for explaining autism. *Science, 310*(5749), 819–823.

Barrett, P. M., Rapee, R. M., Dadds, M. M., & Ryan, S. M. (1996). Family enhancement of cognitive style in anxious and aggressive children. *Journal of Abnormal Child Psychology, 24*(2), 187–203.

Baumrind, D. (1991). The influence of parenting style on adolescent competence and substance use. *Journal of Early Adolescence, 11*, 56–95.

Bayley, N., & Shaefer, E. S. (1963). Maternal behavior, child behavior, and their intercorrelations from infancy through adolescence. *Monographs of the Society for Research in Child Development, 28*(3), 1–127.

Beardslee, W. R., Versage, E. M., & Gladstone, T. R. (1998). Children of affectively ill parents: A review of the past 10 years. *Journal of the American Academy of Child Adolescent Psychiatry, 37*(11), 1134–1141.

Biederman, J., Rosenbaum, J. F., Bolduc-Murphy, E. A., Faraone, S. V., Chaloff, J., Hirshfeld, D. R., & Kagan, J. (1993). A 3-year follow-up of children with and without behavioral inhibition. *Journal of the American Academy of Child Adolescent Psychiatry, 32*(4), 814–821.

Briggs-Myers, I., McCaulley, M. H., Quenk, N. L., Hammer, A. L., & Mitchell, W. D. (2009). *MBTI Step III manual: Exploring personality development using the Myers-Briggs Type Indicator Instrument.* Palo Alto, CA: Consulting Psychologists Press.

Buss, A. H., & Plomin, R. (1984). *Temperament: Early developing personality traits.* Hillsdale, NJ: Erlbaum.

Campbell, D. W., & Eaton, W. O. (1999). Sex differences in the activity level of infants. *Infant and Child Development, 8,* 1–17.

Capaldi, D. M., & Rothbart, M. K. (1992). Development and validation of an early adolescent temperament measure. *Journal of Early Adolescence, 12*(2), 153–173.

Caplan, P. J., & Hall-McCorquodale, I. (1985). Mother-blaming in major clinical journals. *American Journal of Orthopsychiatry, 55*(3), 345–353.

Carlson, G. A. (2009). Treating the childhood bipolar controversy: A tale of two children. *American Journal of Psychiatry, 166*(1), 18–24.

Caspi, A., Harrington, H., Milne, B., Amell, J. W., Theodore, R. F., & Moffitt, T. E. (2003). Children's behavioral styles at age 3 are linked to their adult personality traits at age 26. *Journal of Personality, 71*(4), 495–513.

Caspi, A., Henry, B., McGee, R. O., Moffitt, T. E., & Silva, P. A. (1995). Temperamental origins of child and adolescent behavior problems: From age three to age fifteen. *Child Development, 66*(1), 55–68.

Caspi, A., McClay, J., Moffitt, T. E., Mill, J., Martin, J., Craig, I. W., . . . Poulton, R. (2002). Role of genotype in the cycle of violence in maltreated children. *Science, 297*(5582), 851–854.

Caspi, A., Moffitt, T. E., Cannon, M., McClay, J., Murray, R., Harrington, H., . . . Craig, I. W. (2005). Moderation of the effect of adolescent-onset cannabis use on adult psychosis by a functional polymorphism in the catechol-O-methyltransferase gene: Longitudinal evidence of a gene X environment interaction. *Biological Psychiatry, 57*(10), 1117–1127. doi: S0006-3223(05)00103-4

Caspi, A., Moffitt, T. E., Newman, D. L., & Silva, P. A. (1996). Behavioral observations at age 3 predict adult psychiatric disorders: Longitudinal evidence from a birth cohort. *Archives of General Psychiatry, 53,* 1033–1039.

Caspi, A., Sugden, K., Moffitt, T. E., Taylor, A., Craig, I. W., Harrington, H., et al. (2003). Influence of life stress on depression: Moderation by a polymorphism in the 5-HTT gene. *Science, 301*(5631), 386–389.

Cerullo, M. A. (2006). Cosmetic psychopharmacology and the President's Council on Bioethics. *Perspectives in Biology and Medicine, 49*(4), 515–523.

Charney, D. S., Woods, S. W., Krystal, J. H., & Heninger, G. R. (1990). Serotonin function and human anxiety disorders. *Annals of the New York Academy of Sciences, 600,* 558–572; [discussion] 572–553.

Chess, S., Hertzig, M., G., Birch H., & Thomas, A. (1962). Methodology of a study of adaptive functions of the preschool child. *Journal of the American Academy of Child and Adolescent Psychiatry, 1,* 236–245.

Chess, S., & Thomas, A. (1996). *Temperament: Theory and practice.* New York: Brunner/Mazel.

Chutuape, M. A., & de Wit, H. (1995). Preferences for ethanol and diazepam in anxious individuals: An evaluation of the self-medication hypothesis. *Psychopharmacology (Berl), 121*(1), 91–103.

Clark, L. A., & Watson, D. (1991). Tripartite model of anxiety and depression: Psychometric evidence and taxonomic implications. *Journal of Abnormal Psychology, 100,* 316–336.

Clark, L. A., Watson, D., & Mineka, S. (1994). Temperament, personality and the mood and anxiety disorders. *Journal of Abnormal Child Psychology, 103,* 103–116.

Cloninger, C. R. (1999). *Personality and psychopathology.* Washington, DC: American Psychiatric Press.

Cloninger, C. R., Przybeck, T. R., & Svrakic, D. M. (1991). The Tridimensional Personality Questionnaire: U.S. normative data. *Psychological Reports, 69*(3), 1047–1057.

Cloninger, C. R., Przybeck, T. R., Svrakic, D. M., & Wetzel, R. D. (1994). *The Temperament and Character Inventory (TCI): A guide to its development and use.* St. Louis, MO: Center for Psychobiology of Personality, Washington University.

Cloninger, C. R., Sigvardsson, S., & Bohman, M. (1988). Childhood personality predicts alcohol abuse in young adults. *Alcohol Clinical and Experimental Research, 12*(4), 494–505.

Cohen, D. (1992). A power primer. *Psychological Bulletin, 112,* 155–159.

Collins, W. A., Maccoby, E. E., Steinberg, L., Hetherington, E. M., & Bornstein, M. H. (2000). Contemporary research on parenting. The case for nature and nurture. *American Psychologist, 55*(2), 218–232.

Compas, B. E., Forehand, R., Keller, G., Champion, J. E., Rakow, A., Reeslund, K. L., . . . Cole, D. A. (2009). Randomized controlled trial of a family cognitive-behavioral preventive intervention for children of depressed parents. *Journal of Consulting and Clinical Psychology, 77*(6), 1007–1020. doi: 10.1037/a0016930

Connolly, S. D., & Bernstein, G. A. (2007). Practice parameter for the assessment and treatment of children and adolescents with anxiety disorders. *Journal of the American Academy of Child and Adolescent Psychiatry, 46*(2), 267–283. doi: 10.1097/01.chi.0000246070.23695.06

Constantino, J. N., Cloninger, C. R., Clarke, A. R., Hashemi, B., & Przybeck, T. (2002). Application of the seven-factor model of personality to early childhood. *Psychiatry Research, 109*(3), 229–243. doi: 10.1016/S0165-1781(02)00008-2

Constantino, J. N., Davis, S. A., Todd, R. D., Schindler, M. K., Gross, M. M., Brophy, S. L., . . . Reich, W. (2003). Validation of a brief quantitative measure of autistic traits: Comparison of the Social Responsiveness Scale with the Autism Diagnostic Interview–Revised. *Journal of Autism and Developmental Disorders, 33*(4), 427–433.

Constantino, J. N., & Todd, R. D. (2003). Autistic traits in the general population: A twin study. *Archives of General Psychiatry, 60*(5), 524–530. doi: 10.1001/archpsyc.60.5.524

Cooper, M. L., Frone, M. R., Russell, M., & Mudar, P. (1995). Drinking to regulate positive and negative emotions: A motivational model of alcohol use. *Journal of Personal and Social Psychology, 69*(5), 990–1005.

Copeland, M. P., Daly, E., Hines, V., Mastromauro, C., Zaitchik, D., Gunther, J., & Albert, M. (2003). Psychiatric symptomatology and prodromal Alzheimer's disease. *Alzheimer Disease and Associated Disorders, 17*(1), 1–8.

Cornblatt, B. A., Lencz, T., Smith, C. W., Correll, C. U., Auther, A. M., & Nakayama, E. (2003). The schizophrenia prodrome revisited: A neurodevelopmental perspective. *Schizophrenia Bulletin, 29*(4), 633–651.

Costa, P. T., & McCrae, R. R. (1985). *The NEO Personality Inventory manual.* Odessa, FL: Psychological Assessment Resources.

Costa, P. T., & McCrae, R. R. (1992). *Revised NEO Personality Inventory and NEO Five-Factor Inventory: Professional manual.* Odessa, FL: Psychological Assessment Resources.

Culbert, K. M., Breedlove, S. M., Burt, S. A., & Klump, K. L. (2008). Prenatal hormone exposure and risk for eating disorders: A comparison of opposite-sex and same-sex twins. *Archives of General Psychiatry, 65*(3), 329–336. doi: 10.1001/archgenpsychiatry.2007.47

Dadds, M. R., Barrett, P. M., Rapee, R. M., & Ryan, S. (1996). Family process and child anxiety and aggression: An observational analysis. *Journal of Abnormal Child Psychology, 24*(6), 715–734.

Dean, W., & Morgenthaler, T. (1990). *Smart drugs and nutrients: How to improve your memory and increase your intelligence using the latest discoveries in neuroscience.* Petaluma, CA: Smart Publications.

De Clercq, B., De Fruyt, F., Van Leeuwen, K., & Mervielde, I. (2006). The structure of maladaptive personality traits in childhood: A step toward an integrative developmental perspective for DSM-V. *Journal of Abnormal Psychology, 115*(4), 639–657. doi: 10.1037/0021-843X.115.4.639

De Clercq, B., Rettew, D., Althoff, R. R., & De Bolle, M. (2011). Childhood personality types: Vulnerability and adaptation over time. *Journal of Child Psychology and Psychiatry*. doi: 10.1111/j.1469-7610.2011.02512.x

De Fruyt, F., Bartels, M., Van Leeuwen, K. G., De Clercq, B., Decuyper, M., & Mervielde, I. (2006). Five types of personality continuity in childhood and adolescence. *Journal of Personality and Social Psychology, 91*(3), 538–552.

De Pauw, S. S., & Mervielde, I. (2011). The role of temperament and personality in problem behaviors of children with ADHD. *Journal of Abnormal Child Psychology, 39*(2), 277–291. doi: 10.1007/s10802-010-9459-1

De Pauw, S. S., Mervielde, I., Van Leeuwen, K. G., & De Clercq, B. J. (2011). How temperament and personality contribute to the maladjustment of children with autism. *Journal of Autism and Developmental Disorders, 41*(2), 196–212. doi: 10.1007/s10803-010-1043-6

Dietrich, A., Riese, H., van Roon, A. M., Minderaa, R. B., Oldehinkel, A. J., Neeleman, J., & Rosmalen, J. G. (2009). Temperamental activation and inhibition associated with autonomic function in preadolescents: The TRAILS study. *Biological Psychology, 81*(1), 67–73.

Digman, J. M. (1990). Personality structure: Emergence of the five-factor model. *Annual Review of Psychology, 41*, 417–440.

DiLalla, L. F., & Jones, S. (2000). Genetic and environmental influences on temperament in preschoolers. In V. J. Molfese & D. L. Molfese (Eds.), *Temperament and personality development across the life span* (pp. 33–55). Mahwah, NJ: Erlbaum.

DiMaio, S., Grizenko, N., & Joober, R. (2003). Dopamine genes and attention-deficit hyperactivity disorder: A review. *Journal of Psychiatry and Neuroscience, 28*(1), 27–38.

Drechsler, R., Straub, M., Doehnert, M., Heinrich, H., Steinhausen, H. C., & Brandeis, D. (2007). Controlled evaluation of a neurofeedback training of slow cortical potentials in children with attention deficit/hyperactivity disorder (ADHD). *Behavioral and Brain Functions, 3*, 35. doi: 10.1186/1744-9081-3-35

Dugatkin, L. A., & Alfieri, M. S. (2003). Boldness, behavioral inhibition and learning. *Ethology Ecology and Evolution, 15*(1), 43–49.

Eaton, W. O., & Enns, L. R. (1986). Sex differences in human motor activity level. *Psychological Bulletin, 100*(1), 19–28.

Eddy, K. T., Keel, P. K., Dorer, D. J., Delinsky, S. S., Franko, D. L., & Herzog, D. B. (2002). Longitudinal comparison of anorexia nervosa subtypes. *International Journal of Eating Disorders, 31*(2), 191–201. doi: 10.1002/eat.10016

Else-Quest, N. M., Hyde, J. S., Goldsmith, H. H., & Van Hulle, C. A. (2006). Gender differences in temperament: A meta-analysis. *Psychological Bulletin, 132*(1), 33–72.

Erikson, E. (1950). *Childhood and society.* New York: Norton.

Ettelt, S., Grabe, H. J., Ruhrmann, S., Buhtz, F., Hochrein, A., Kraft, S., . . . Wagner, M. (2008). Harm avoidance in subjects with obsessive-compulsive disorder and their families. *Journal of Affective Disorders, 107*(1–3), 265-269. doi: 10.1016/j.jad.2007.08.017

Evans, D. E., & Rothbart, M. K. (2007). Developing a model for adult temperament. *Journal of Research in Personality, 41*, 868–888.

Eysenck, H. J. (1967). *The biological basis of personality.* Springfield, IL: Thomas.

Eysenck, H. J., & Eysenck, S. B. G. (1975). *Manual for the Eysenck Personality Inventory (adult and junior).* San Diego, CA: Digits.

Farah, M. J., Illes, J., Cook-Deegan, R., Gardner, H., Kandel, E., King, P., . . . Wolpe, P. R. (2004). Neurocognitive enhancement: What can we do and what should we do? *Nature Reviews Neuroscience, 5*(5), 421–425. doi: 10.1038/nrn1390

Forehand, R. L., Jones, D. J., & Parent, J. (2013). Behavioral parenting interventions for child disruptive behavior disorders and anxiety: What's different and what's the same? *Clinical Psychology Review, 33*, 133–145.

Forehand, R. L., & Long, N. (2010). *Parenting the strong-willed child.* New York: McGraw-Hill.

Fox, D. J., Tharp, D. F., & Fox, L. C. (2005). Neurofeedback: An alternative and efficacious treatment for attention deficit hyperactivity disorder. *Applied Psychophysiology and Biofeedback, 30*, 365–373.

Fox, N. A., Henderson, H. A., Rubin, K. H., Calkins, S. D., & Schmidt, L. A. (2001). Continuity and discontinuity of behavioral inhibition and exuberance: Psychophysiological and behavioral influences across the first four years of life. *Child Development, 72*(1), 1–21.

Franke, A. G., Lieb, K., & Hildt, E. (2012). What users think about the differences between caffeine and illicit/prescription stimulants for cognitive enhancement. *PLoS One, 7*(6), e40047. doi: 10.1371/journal.pone.0040047

Freud, A. (1965). *Normality and pathology in childhood: Assessments of development.* Madison, WI: International Universities Press.

Frick, P. J., & Morris, A. S. (2004). Temperament and developmental pathways to conduct problems. *Journal of Clinical Child and Adolescent Psychology, 33*(1), 54–68.

Fristad, M. A., Goldberg Arnold, J. S., & Leffler, J. (2011). *Psychotherapy for children with bipolar and depressive disorders*. New York: Guilford.

Ganiban, J. M., Ulbricht, J., Saudino, K. J., Reiss, D., & Neiderhiser, J. M. (2011). Understanding child-based effects on parenting: Temperament as a moderator of genetic and environmental contributions to parenting. *Developmental Psychology, 47*(3), 676–692.

Gapin, J. I., Labban, J. D., & Etnier, J. L. (2011). The effects of physical activity on attention deficit hyperactivity disorder symptoms: The evidence. *Preventive Medicine, 52*, S70–74. doi: 10.1016/j.ypmed.2011.01.022

Garon, N., Bryson, S. E., Zwaigenbaum, L., Smith, I. M., Brian, J., Roberts, W., & Szatmari, P. (2009). Temperament and its relationship to autistic symptoms in a high-risk infant sib cohort. *Journal of Abnormal Child Psychology, 37*(1), 59–78. doi: 10.1007/s10802-008-9258-0

Gartstein, M. A., & Rothbart, M. K. (2003). Studying infant temperament via the Revised Infant Behavior Questionnaire. *Infant Behavior and Development, 26*, 64–86.

Gest, S. D. (1997). Behavioral inhibition: Stability and associations with adaptation from childhood to early adulthood. *Journal of Personality and Social Psychology, 72*(2), 467–475.

Gillespie, N. A., Evans, D. E., Wright, M. M., & Martin, N. G. (2004). Genetic simplex modeling of Eysenck's dimensions of personality in a sample of young Australian twins. *Twin Research, 7*(6), 637–648. doi: 10.1375/1369052042663814

Glenn, A. L., Raine, A., Venables, P. H., & Mednick, S. A. (2007). Early temperamental and psychophysiological precursors of adult psychopathic personality. *Journal of Abnormal Psychology, 116*(3), 508–518. doi: 10.1037/0021-843X.116.3.508

Goldsmith, H. H., Buss, A. H., Plomin, R., Rothbart, M. K., Thomas, A. R., Chess, S., . . . McCall, R. B. (1987). Roundtable: What is temperament? Four approaches. *Child Development, 58*, 505–529.

Goldsmith, H. H., Buss, K. A., & Lemery, K. S. (1997). Toddler and childhood temperament: Expanded content, stronger genetic evidence, new evidence for the importance of environment. *Developmental Psychology, 33*(6), 891–905.

Goldsmith, H. H., Lemery, K. S., & Essex, M. J. (2004). Roles for temperament in the liability to psychopathology in childhood. In L. DiLalla (Ed.), *Behavior genetic principles: Development, personality, and psychopathology* (pp. 9–19). Washington, DC: APA Press.

References 245

Goldsmith, H. H., Reilly, J., Lemery, K. S., Longley, S., & Prescott, A. (1993). *Preliminary manual for the Preschool Laboratory Temperament Assessment Battery (Technical report version 1.0)*. Madison: Department of Psychology, University of Wisconsin-Madison.

Gordon, E. M., & Thomas, A. (1967). Children's behavioral style and the teacher's appraisal of their intelligence. *Journal of School Psychology, 5*, 292–300.

Gray, J. (1980). *Ivan Pavlov*. New York: Viking.

Gray, J. A. (1982). *The neuropsychology of anxiety: An enquiry into the functions of the septo-hippocampal system*. New York: Oxford University Press.

Gray, J. A. (1987). *The psychology of fear and stress*. New York: Cambridge University Press.

Gray, J. (1992). *Men are from Mars, women are from Venus*. New York: HarperCollins.

Greene, R. W. (1998). *The explosive child: A new approach for understanding and parenting easily frustrated, "chronically inflexible" children*. New York: HarperCollins.

Greene, R. W., Ablon, J. S. (2005). *Treating explosive kids: The collaborative problem-solving approach*. New York: Guilford.

Greene, R. W., Ablon, J. S., Goring, J. C., Raezer-Blakely, L., Markey, J., Monteaux, M. C., . . . Rabbitt, S. (2004). Effectiveness of collaborative problem solving in affectively dysregulated children with oppositional-defiant disorder: Initial findings. *Journal of Consulting and Clinical Psychology, 72*(6), 1157–1164. doi: 10.1037/0022-006X.72.6.1157

Guerin, D. W., Gottfried, A. W., Oliver, P. H., & Thomas, C. W. (2003). *Temperament infancy through adolescence*. New York: Kluwer Academic/Plenum.

Harkey, N., & Jourgensen, T. (2009). *Parenting by temperament: The new revised raising cuddlebugs and bravehearts*. Booksurge.

Hartshorne, J. K. (2010). Ruled by birth order? *Scientific American Mind, 20*, 18–19.

Hartshorne, J. K., Salem-Hartshorne, N., & Hartshorne, T. S. (2009). Birth order effects in the formation of long-term relationships. *Journal of Individual Psychology, 65*(2), 156–176.

Hellwig, B. (1896). *The four temperaments in children: Their appearance and treatment in rearing and in the school*. Paderbron: J. Esser.

Hettema, J. M., Neale, M. C., Myers, J. M., Prescott, C. A., & Kendler, K. S. (2006). A population-based twin study of the relationship between neuroticism and internalizing disorders. *American Journal of Psychiatry, 163*(5), 857–864.

Hettema, J. M., Prescott, C. A., & Kendler, K. S. (2004). Genetic and environmental sources of covariation between generalized anxiety disorder and neuroticism. *American Journal of Psychiatry, 161*(9), 1581–1587.

Hirshfeld-Becker, D. R., Masek, B., Henin, A., Blakely, L. R., Rettew, D. C., Dufton, L., . . . Biederman, J. (2008). Cognitive-behavioral intervention with young anxious children. *Harvard Review of Psychiatry, 16*(2), 113–125.

Hudziak, J. J. (2008). Genetic and environmental influences on wellness, resilience, and psychopathology: A family-based approach for promotion, prevention, and intervention. In J. J. Hudziak (Ed.), *Developmental psychopathology and wellness: Genetic and environmental influences* (pp. 267–286). Washington, DC: American Psychiatric Press.

Hudziak, J. J., Achenbach, T. M., Althoff, R. R., & Pine, D. S. (2007). A dimensional approach to developmental psychopathology. *International Journal of Methods in Psychiatric Research, 16*(S1), S16–S23.

Hudziak, J. J., Copeland, W., Rudiger, L. P., Achenbach, T. M., Heath, A. C., & Todd, R. D. (2003). Genetic influences on childhood competencies: A twin study. *Journal of the American Academy of Child and Adolescent Psychiatry, 42*(3), 357–363.

Hudziak, J. J., Copeland, W., Stanger, C., & Wadsworth, M. (2003). Screening for DSM-IV externalizing disorders with the Child Behavior Checklist: A receiver-operating characteristic analysis. *Journal of Abnormal Psychology, 42*(3), 357–363.

Hyman, S. E. (2009). How adversity gets under the skin. *Nature Neuroscience, 12*(3), 241–243. doi: 10.1038/nn0309-241

Inhelder, B., & Piaget, J. (1958). *The growth of logical thinking from childhood to adolescence.* New York: Basic Books.

Insel, T. R. (2010). The challenge of translation in social neuroscience: A review of oxytocin, vasopressin, and affiliative behavior. *Neuron, 65*(6), 768–779. doi: 10.1016/j.neuron.2010.03.005

Ivarsson, T., & Winge-Westholm, C. (2004). Temperamental factors in children and adolescents with obsessive-compulsive disorder (OCD) and in normal controls. *European Child and Adolescent Psychiatry, 13*(6), 365–372. doi: 10.1007/s00787-004-0411-1

Ivorra, J. L., Sanjuan, J., Jover, M., Carot, J. M., Frutos, R., & Molto, M. D. (2010). Gene-environment interaction of child temperament. *Journal of Developmental and Behavioral Pediatrics, 31*(7), 545–554.

Jackson, K. M., & Sher, K. J. (2003). Alcohol use disorders and psychological distress: A prospective state-trait analysis. *Journal of Abnormal Psychology, 112*(4), 599–613. doi: 10.1037/0021-843X.112.4.599

Janson, H., & Mathiesen, K. S. (2008). Temperament profiles from infancy to middle childhood: Development and associations with behavior problems. *Developmental Psychology, 44*(5), 1314–1328. doi: 10.1037/a0012713

Judd, L. L., Schettler, P. J., & Akiskal, H. S. (2002). The prevalence, clinical relevance, and public health significance of subthreshold depressions. *Psychiatric Clinics of North America, 25*(4), 685–698.

Jung, C. G. (1923). *Psychological types.* New York: Harcourt Brace.

Kagan, J. (1994). *Galen's prophecy.* Boulder, CO: Westview.

Kagan, J. (1997). In the beginning: The contribution of temperament to personality development. *Modern Psychoanalysis, 22*(2), 145–155.

Kagan, J., Reznick, J. S., & Snidman, N. (1988). Biological bases of childhood shyness. *Science, 240*(4849), 167–171.

Kagan, J., & Snidman, N. (2004). *The long shadow of temperament.* Cambridge, MA: Belknap.

Keller, M. C., Coventry, W. L., Heath, A. C., & Martin, N. G. (2005). Widespread evidence for non-additive genetic variation in Cloninger's and Eysenck's personality dimensions using a twin plus sibling design. *Behavior Genetics, 35*(6), 707–721.

Keltikangas-Jarvinen, L., Raikkonen, K., Ekelund, J., & Peltonen, L. (2004). Nature and nurture in novelty seeking. *Molecular Psychiatry, 9,* 308–311.

Kendler, K. S., McGuire, M., Gruenberg, A. M., O'Hare, A., Spellman, M., & Walsh, D. (1993). The Roscommon Family Study. III. Schizophrenia-related personality disorders in relatives. *Archives of General Psychiatry, 50*(10), 781–788.

Keogh, B. K. (2003). *Temperament in the classroom: Understanding individual differences.* Baltimore, MD: Paul H. Brookes.

Kim, S. J., Kang, J. I., & Kim, C. H. (2009). Temperament and character in subjects with obsessive-compulsive disorder. *Comprehensive Psychiatry, 50*(6), 567–572. doi: 10.1016/j.comppsych.2008.11.009

King, R. A. (1997). Practice parameters for the psychiatric assessment of children and adolescents. American Academy of Child and Adolescent Psychiatry. *Journal of the American Academy of Child Adolescent Psychiatry, 36*(10), 4S–20S.

Klein, R. G. (2011). Temperament: Half a century in the journal. *Journal of the American Academy of Child Adolescent Psychiatry, 50*(11), 1090–1092. doi: 10.1016/j.jaac.2010.07.013

Knorr, U., Vinberg, M., Mortensen, E. L., Winkel, P., Gluud, C., Wetterslev, J., . . . Kessing, L. V. (2012). Effect of chronic escitalopram versus placebo on personality traits in healthy first-degree relatives of patients with depression: A randomized trial. *PLoS One, 7*(2), e31980. doi: 10.1371/journal.pone.0031980

Knutson, B., Wolkowitz, O. M., Cole, S. W., Chan, T., Moore, E. A., Johnson, R. C., . . . Reus, V. I. (1998). Selective alteration of personality and social behavior by serotonergic intervention. *American Journal of Psychiatry, 155*(3), 373–379.

Kochanska, G., Philibert, R. A., & Barry, R. A. (2009). Interplay of genes and early mother-child relationship in the development of self-regulation from toddler to preschool age. *Journal of Child Psychology and Psychiatry, 50*(11), 1331–1338.

Kramer, P. D. (1993). *Listening to Prozac: A psychiatrist explores antidepressant drugs and the remaking of the self.* New York: Viking.

Kristal, J. (2005). *The temperament perspective: Working with children's behavioral styles.* New York: Paul H. Brookes.

Kristensen, P., & Bjerkedal, T. (2007). Explaining the relation between birth order and intelligence. *Science, 316*(5832), 1717. doi: 10.1126/science.1141493

Krueger, R. F., South, S., Johnson, W., & Iacono, W. (2008). The heritability of personality is not always 50%: Gene-environment interactions and correlations between personality and parenting. *Journal of Personality, 76*(6), 1485–1522. doi: 10.1037/a0030133

Krueger, R. F., & Tackett, J. L. (2003). Personality and psychopathology: Working toward a bigger picture. *Journal of Personality Disorders, 17*(2), 109–128.

Krueger, R. F., & Tackett, J. L. (Eds.). (2006). *Personality and psychopathology.* New York: Guilford.

Krueger, R. F., Watson, D., & Barlow D. H. (2005). Introduction to the special section: Toward a dimensionally based taxonomy of psychopathology. *Journal of Abnormal Psychology, 114*(4), 491–493. doi 10.1037/0021-843X.114.4.491

Kuntsche, E., Knibbe, R., Gmel, G., & Engels, R. (2006). Who drinks and why? A review of socio-demographic, personality, and contextual issues behind the drinking motives in young people. *Addictive Behaviors, 31*(10), 1844–1857. doi: 10.1016/j.addbeh.2005.12.028

Kuo, P. H., Chih, Y. C., Soong, W. T., Yang, H. J., & Chen, W. J. (2004). Assessing personality features and their relations with behavioral problems in adolescents: Tridimensional personality questionnaire and junior Eysenck personality questionnaire. *Comprehensive Psychiatry, 45*(1), 20–28.

Lakatos, K., Nemoda, Z., Birkas, E., Ronai, Z., Kovacs, E., Ney, K., . . . Gervai, J. (2003). Association of D4 dopamine receptor gene and serotonin transporter promoter polymorphisms with infants' response to novelty. *Molecular Psychiatry, 8*(1), 90–97.

LeDoux, J. E. (2000). Emotion circuits in the brain. *Annual Review of Neuroscience, 23*, 155–184. doi: 10.1146/annurev.neuro.23.1.155

Lemery, K. S., Essex, M. J., & Smider, N. A. (2002). Revealing the relation between temperament and behavior problem symptoms by eliminating measurement confounding: Expert ratings and factor analyses. *Child Development, 73*(3), 867–882.

Lengua, L. J., West, S. G., & Sandler, I. N. (1998). Temperament as a predictor of symptomatology in children: Addressing contamination of measures. *Child Development, 69*(1), 164–181.

Lerner, J. V., Lerner, R. M., & Zabski, S. (1985). Temperament and elementary school children's actual and rated academic performance: A test of a "goodness-of-fit" model. *Journal of Child Psychology and Psychiatry, 26*(1), 125–136.

Lieb, R., Wittchen, H. U., Hofler, M., Fuetsch, M., Stein, M. B., & Merikangas, K. R. (2000). Parental psychopathology, parenting styles, and the risk of social phobia in offspring: A prospective-longitudinal community study. *Archives of General Psychiatry, 57*(9), 859–866.

Liu, J., Portnoy, J., & Raine, A. (2012). Association between a marker for prenatal testosterone exposure and externalizing behavior problems in children. *Development and Psychopathology, 24*(3), 771–782. doi: 10.1017/S0954579412000363

Lonigan, C. J., Vasey, M. W., Phillips, B. M., & Hazen, R. A. (2004). Temperament, anxiety, and the processing of threat-relevant stimuli. *Journal of Clinical Child and Adolescent Psychology, 33*(1), 8–20.

Lord, C., Risi, S., Lambrecht, L., Cook, E. H., Jr., Leventhal, B. L., DiLavore, P. C., . . . Rutter, M. (2000). The Autism Diagnostic Observation Schedule–Generic: A standard measure of social and communication deficits associated with the spectrum of autism. *Journal of Autism and Developmental Disorders, 30*(3), 205–223.

Lubke, G. H., Hudziak, J. J., Derks, E. M., van Bijsterveldt, T. C., & Boomsma, D. I. (2009). Maternal ratings of attention problems in ADHD: Evidence for the existence of a continuum. *Journal of the American Academy of Child and Adolescent Psychiatry, 48*(11), 1085–1093. doi: 10.1097/CHI.0b013e3181ba3dbb

Luby, J. L., Svrakic, D. M., McCallum, K., Przybeck, T. R., & Cloninger, C. R. (1999). The Junior Temperament and Character Inventory: Preliminary validation of a child self-report measure. *Psychological Reports, 84*(3 Pt 2), 1127–1138.

Maccoby, E. E., & Martin, J. A. (1983). Socialization in the context of the family: Parent-child interaction. In P. H. Mussen (Ed.), *Handbook of child psychology* (4th ed., Vol. 4). New York: John Wiley.

Malmberg, A., Lewis, G., David, A., & Allebeck, P. (1998). Premorbid adjustment and personality in people with schizophrenia. *British Journal of Psychiatry, 172*, 308–313; [discussion] 314–305.

Markon, K. E., & Krueger, R. F. (2005). Categorical and continuous models of liability to externalizing disorders: A direct comparison in NESARC. *Archives of General Psychiatry, 62*(12), 1352-1359. doi: 10.1001/archpsyc.62.12.1352

Martel, M. M., & Nigg, J. T. (2006). Child ADHD and personality/temperament traits of reactive and effortful control, resiliency, and emotionality. *Journal of Child Psychology and Psychiatry, 47*(11), 1175-1183. doi: 10.1111/j.1469-7610.2006.01629.x

Martel, M. M., Nigg, J. T., & von Eye, A. (2009). How do trait dimensions map onto ADHD symptom domains? *Journal of Abnormal Child Psychology, 37*(3), 337–348. doi: 10.1007/s10802-008-9255-3

Martel, M. M., Nikolas, M., Jernigan, K., Friderici, K., & Nigg, J. T. (2010). Personality mediation of genetic effects on attention-deficit/hyperactivity disorder. *Journal of Abnormal Child Psychology, 38*(5), 633–643. doi: 10.1007/s10802-010-9392-3

Martin, R. P., Wisenbaker, J., Huttunen, M., Halverson, C. F., Kohnstamm, G. A., & Martin, R. P. (1994). Review of factor analytic studies of temperament measures based on the Thomas-Chess structural modal: Implications for the big five. In C. F. Halverson, G. A. Kohnstamm, & R. P. Martin (Eds.), *The developing structure of temperament and personality from infancy to adulthood* (pp. 157–172). Hillsdale, NJ: Erlbaum.

Maziade, M., Cote, R., Boutin, P., Boudreault, M., & Thivierge, J. (1986). The effect of temperament on longitudinal academic achievement in primary school. *Journal of the American Academy of Child Psychiatry, 25*(5), 692–696.

McClowry, S. G., Snow, D. L., & Tamis-LeMonda, C. S. (2005). An evaluation of the effects of INSIGHTS on the behavior of inner city primary school children. *Journal of Primary Prevention, 26*(6), 567–584. doi: 10.1007/s10935-005-0015-7

McCrae, R. R., & Costa, P. T. (2003). *Personality in adulthood: A five factor theory perspective* (2nd ed.). New York: Guilford.

McCrae, R. R., Costa, P. T., Jr., Ostendorf, F., Angleitner, A., Hrebickova, M., Avia, M. D., . . . Smith, P. B. (2000). Nature over nurture: Temperament, personality, and life span development. *Journal of Personality and Social Psychology, 78*(1), 173–186.

McGowan, P. O., Sasaki, A., D'Alessio, A. C., Dymov, S., Labonte, B., Szyf, M., . . . Meaney, M. J. (2009). Epigenetic regulation of the glucocorticoid receptor in human brain associates with childhood abuse. *Nature Neuroscience, 12*(3), 342–348. doi: 10.1038/nn.2270

Mebust, K., Rettew, D. C., & Hudziak, J. J. (2010). *Effect of ADHD on parenting: Evidence for an evocative gene-environment correlation.* Paper presented at the 57th Annual Meeting of the American Academy of Child and Adolescent Psychiatry, New York.

Mekertichian, L. K., & Bowes, J. M. (1996). Does parenting matter? The challenge of the behavioural geneticists. *Journal of Family Studies, 2*(2), 131–145.

Merikangas, K. R., He, J. P., Burstein, M., Swanson, S. A., Avenevoli, S., Cui, L., . . . Swendsen, J. (2010). Lifetime prevalence of mental disorders in U.S. adolescents: Results from the National Comorbidity Survey Replication—Adolescent Supplement (NCS-A). *Journal of the American Academy of Child and Adolescent Psychiatry, 49*(10), 980–989. doi: 10.1016/j.jaac.2010.05.017

Mervielde, I., & De Fruyt, F. (1999). Construction of the Hierarchical Personality Inventory for Children (HiPIC). In I. Mervielde, I. Deary, F. De Fruyt, & F. Ostendorf (Eds.), *Personality psychology in Europe*. Tiburg: Tiburg University Press.

Miettunen, J., Veijola, J., Lauronen, E., Kantojarvi, L., & Joukamaa, M. (2007). Sex differences in Cloninger's temperament dimensions—a meta-analysis. *Comprehensive Psychiatry, 48*(2), 161–169.

Miller, A. (1981). *Prisoners of childhood: The drama of the gifted child and the search for the true self*. New York: Basic Books.

MTA Cooperative Group. (1999). A 14-month randomized clinical trial of treatment strategies for attention-deficit/hyperactivity disorder. *Archives of General Psychiatry, 56*(12), 1073–1086.

Munafo, M. R., Yalcin, B., Willis-Owen, S. A., & Flint, J. (2008). Association of the dopamine D4 receptor (DRD4) gene and approach-related personality traits: Meta-analysis and new data. *Biological Psychiatry, 63*(2), 197–206. doi: 10.1016/j.biopsych.2007.04.006

Nigg, J. T. (2006). Temperament and developmental psychopathology. *Journal of Child Psychology and Psychiatry, 47*(3-4), 395–422.

Oldehinkel, A. J., Hartman, C. A., De Winter, A. F., Veenstra, R., & Ormel, J. (2004). Temperament profiles associated with internalizing and externalizing problems in preadolescence. *Development and Psychopathology, 16*(2), 421–440.

Olfson, M., Blanco, C., Liu, L., Moreno C., & Laje, G. (2006). National trends in the outpatient treatment of children and adolescents with antipsychotic drugs. *Archives of General Psychiatry, 63,* 679–685.

Pastor, P. N., & Reuben, C. A. (2008). Diagnosed attention deficit hyperactivity disorder and learning disability: United States, 2004–2006. *Vital Health Statistics*, Series 10 (237), 1–14.

Patterson, G. R., & Forgatch, M. (1987). *Parents and adolescents living together, part 1: The basics*. Champaign, IL: Research Press.

Pavlov, I. P. (1927). *Conditioned reflexes*. London: Oxford University Press.

Perlick, D. A., Rosenheck, R. A., Clarkin, J. F., Maciejewski, P. K., Sirey, J., Struening, E., & Link, B. G. (2004). Impact of family burden and affective response on clinical outcome among patients with bipolar disorder. *Psychiatric Services, 55*(9), 1029–1035. doi: 10.1176/appi.ps.55.9.1029

Pessoa, L. (2008). On the relationship between emotion and cognition. *Nature Reviews Neuroscience, 9*(2), 148–158.

Pezawas, L., Meyer-Lindenberg, A., Drabant, E. M., Verchinski, B. A., Munoz, K. E., Kolachana, B. S., . . . Weinberger, D. R. (2005). 5-HTTLPR polymorphism impacts human cingulate-amygdala interactions: A genetic susceptibility mechanism for depression. *Nature Neuroscience, 8*(6), 828–834.

Pfeifer, M., Goldsmith, H. H., Davidson, R. J., & Rickman, M. (2002). Continuity and change in inhibited and uninhibited children. *Child Development, 73*(5), 1474–1485.

Picchioni, M. M., Walshe, M., Toulopoulou, T., McDonald, C., Taylor, M., Waters-Metenier, S., . . . Rijsdijk, F. (2010). Genetic modelling of childhood social development and personality in twins and siblings with schizophrenia. *Psychological Medicine, 40*(8), 1305–1316. doi: 10.1017/S0033291709991425

Plaud, J. J. (2003). Pavlov and the foundation of behavior therapy. *Spanish Journal of Psychology, 6*(2), 147–154.

Pliszka, S. R., Carlson, C. L., & Swanson, J. M. (1999). *ADHD with comorbid disorders: Clinical assessment and management.* New York: Guilford.

Plomin, R. (2011). Commentary: Why are children in the same family so different? Non-shared environment three decades later. *International Journal of Epidemiology, 40*, 582–592.

Plomin, R., DeFries, J. C., & Loehlin, J. C. (1977). Genotype-environment interaction and correlation in the analysis of human behavior. *Psychological Bulletin, 84*(2), 309–322.

Polderman, T. J., Derks, E. M., Hudziak, J. J., Verhulst, F. C., Posthuma, D., & Boomsma, D. I. (2007). Across the continuum of attention skills: A twin study of the SWAN ADHD rating scale. *Journal of Child Psychology and Psychiatry, 48*(11), 1080–1087. doi: 10.1111/j.1469-7610.2007.01783.x

President's Council on Bioethics. (2003). *Beyond therapy: Biotechnology and the pursuit of human improvement.* Washington, DC: Dana Press.

Rapee, R. M., Kennedy, S. J., Ingram, M., Edwards, S. L., & Sweeney, L. (2010). Altering the trajectory of anxiety in at-risk young children. *American Journal of Psychiatry, 167*(12), 1518–1525. doi: 10.1176/appi.ajp.2010.09111619

Réale, D., & Festa-Bianchet, M. (2003). Predator-induced natural selection on temperament in bighorn ewes. *Animal Behavior, 65*, 463–470.

Réale, D., Gallant, B. Y., Mylene, L., & Festa-Bianchet, M. (2000). Consistency of temperament in bighorn ewes and correlates with behavior and life history. *Animal Behavior, 60*, 589–597.

Reiss, D. (2011). Parents and children: Linked by psychopathology but not by clinical care. *Journal of the American Academy of Child and Adolescent Psychiatry, 50*(5), 431–434. doi: 10.1016/j.jaac.2011.02.005

Reiss, D., Neiderhiser, J. M., Hetheringon, E. M., & Plomin, R. (2000). *The relationship code: Deciphering genetic and social influences on adolescent development*. Cambridge, MA: Harvard University Press.

Rescorla, L., Achenbach, T., Ivanova, M. Y., Dumenci, L., Almqvist, F., Bilenberg, N., . . . Verhulst, F. (2007). Behavioral and emotional problems reported by parents of children ages 6 to 16 in 31 societies. *Journal of Emotional and Behavioral Disorders, 15*(3), 130–142.

Rettew, D. C. (2007). Obsessive-compulsive disorder in the primary care setting. In E. A. Storch, G. R. Geffken, & T. K. Murphy (Eds.), *Handbook of child and adolescent obsessive-compulsive disorder* (pp. 351–377). Mahwah, NJ: Erlbaum.

Rettew, D. C. (2008). In this issue/abstract thinking: Child wellness and happiness. *Journal of the American Academy of Child and Adolescent Psychiatry, 48*(8), 775–776.

Rettew, D. C. (2009). Temperament: Risk and protective factors for child psychiatric disorders. In B. J. Sadock & V. A. Sadock (Eds.), *Kaplan and Sadock's comprehensive textbook of psychiatry* (9th ed., pp. 3432–3443). Philadelphia: Lippincott Williams and Wilkins.

Rettew, D. C. (2010). Refining our diagnostic system—cake or comorbid bread and fudge? *Journal of the American Academy Child and Adolescent Psychiatry, 49*(5), 441–443.

Rettew, D. C. (2012). Apples to committee consensus: The challenge of gender identity classification. *Journal of Homosexuality, 59*(3), 450–459. doi: 10.1080/00918369.2012.653313

Rettew, D. C. (2013). Child mental health blog. Retrieved from http://blog.uvm.edu/drettew/

Rettew, D. C., Althoff, R. R., Ayer, L. A., Rubin, D., & Hudziak, J. (2011). *Do trait versus disorder levels of behavior associate with the same genes?* Paper presented at the 58th Annual Meeting of the American Academy of Child and Adolescent Psychiatry, Toronto, ON.

Rettew, D. C., Althoff, R. R., Dumenci, L., Ayer, L., & Hudziak, J. J. (2008). Latent profiles of temperament and their relations to psychopathology and wellness. *Journal of the American Academy of Child and Adolescent Psychiatry, 47*(3), 273–281.

Rettew, D. C., Copeland, W., Stanger, C., & Hudziak, J. J. (2004). Associations between temperament and DSM-IV externalizing disorders in children and adolescents. *Journal of Developmental and Behavioral Pediatrics, 25*(6), 383–391.

Rettew, D. C., DiRuocco, L., Ivanova, M. Y., & Hudziak, J. J. (2011). *The Vermont family based approach: A new teaching model for child psychiatry assessments*. Paper presented at the annual meeting of the American Association of Directors of Psychiatric Residency Training, Austin, TX.

Rettew, D. C., Doyle, A., Althoff, R. R., Stanger, C., McKee, L., Copeland, W., & Hudziak, J. J. (2004). *Does fear of novelty in social and nonsocial domains exist together or apart? A latent class approach.* Paper presented at the 51st Annual Conference of the American Academy of Child and Adolescent Psychiatry, Washington, DC.

Rettew, D. C., Doyle, A. C., Kwan, M., Stanger, C., & Hudziak, J. J. (2006). Exploring the boundary between temperament and generalized anxiety disorder: A receiver operating characteristic analysis. *Journal of Anxiety Disorders, 20*(7), 931–945.

Rettew, D. C., Lynch, A. D., Achenbach, T. M., Dumenci, L., & Ivanova, M. Y. (2009). Meta-analyses of agreement between diagnoses made from clinical evaluations and standardized diagnostic interviews. *International Journal of Methods in Psychiatric Research, 18*(3), 169–184. doi: 10.1002/mpr.289

Rettew, D. C., van Oort, F., Verhulst, F. C., Buitelaar, J. K., Ormel, J., Hartman, C. A., . . . Hudziak, J. J. (2011). When parent and teacher ratings don't agree: The Tracking Adolescents' Individual Lives Survey (TRAILS). *Journal of Child and Adolescent Psychopharmacology, 21*(5), 389–397. doi: 10.1089/cap.2010.0153

Rettew, D. C., Rebollo-Mesa, I., Hudziak, J. J., Willemsen, G., & Boomsma, D. I. (2008). Non-additive and additive genetic effects on extraversion in 3314 Dutch adolescent twins and their parents. *Behavior Genetics, 38*(3), 223–233. doi: 10.1007/s10519-008-9192-5

Rettew, D. C., Stanger, C., McKee, L., Doyle, A., & Hudziak, J. J. (2006). Interactions between child and parent temperament and child behavior problems. *Comprehensive Psychiatry, 47*(5), 412–420.

Rettew, D. C., Vink, J. M., Willemsen, G., Doyle, A., Hudziak, J. J., & Boomsma, D. I. (2006). The genetic architecture of neuroticism in 3301 Dutch adolescent twins as a function of age and sex. *Twin Research and Human Genetics, 9*(1), 24–29.

Roberts, B. W., & DelVecchio, W. F. (2000). The rank-order consistency of personality traits from childhood to old age: A quantitative review of longitudinal studies. *Journal of Personality and Social Psychology, 126*(1), 3–25.

Roberts, B. W., Walton, K., & Viechtbauer, W. (2006). Patterns of mean-level change in personality traits across the life course: A meta-analysis of longitudinal studies. *Psychological Bulletin, 132*, 1–25.

Rothbart, M. K. (2004). Commentary: Differential measures of temperament and multiple pathways to childhood disorders. *Journal of Clinical Child and Adolescent Psychology, 33*(1), 82–87.

Rothbart, M. K., & Ahadi, S. A. (1994). Temperament and the development of personality. *Journal of Abnormal Psychology, 103*, 55–66.

Rothbart, M. K., Ahadi, S. A., & Evans, D. E. (2000). Temperament and personality: Origins and outcomes. *Journal of Personality and Social Psychology,* *78*(1), 122–135.

Rothbart, M. K., Ahadi, S. A., Hershey, K., & Fisher, P. (2001). Investigations of temperament at three to seven years: The Children's Behavior Questionnaire. *Child Development, 72,* 1394–1408.

Rothbart, M. K., & Derryberry, D. (1981). Development of individual differences in temperament. In M. E. Lamb & A. L. Brown (Eds.), *Advances in developmental psychology* (Vol. 1, pp. 37–86). Hillsdale, NJ: Erlbaum.

Rothbart, M. K. (1986). Longitudinal observation of infant temperament. *Developmental Psychology, 22,* 356–365.

Rothbart, M. K. (2011). *Becoming who we are: Temperament and personality in development.* New York: Guilford.

Rueda, M. R., Checa, P., & Santonja, M. (2008). *Training executive attention: Lasting effects and transfer to affective self-regulation.* Paper presented at the annual meeting of the Cognitive Neuroscience Society, San Francisco, CA.

Rueda, M. R., Rothbart, M. K., McCandliss, B. D., Saccomanno, L., & Posner, M. I. (2005). Training, maturation, and genetic influences on the development of executive attention. *Proceedings of the National Academy of Sciences (USA), 102*(41), 14931–14936. doi: 10.1073/pnas.0506897102

Sahakian, B., & Morein-Zamir, S. (2007). Professor's little helper. *Nature, 450*(7173), 1157–1159. doi: 10.1038/4501157a

Sallquist, J. V., Eisenberg, N., Spinrad, T. L., Reiser, M., Hofer, C., Zhou, Q., . . . Eggum, N. (2009). Positive and negative emotionality: Trajectories across six years and relations with social competence. *Emotion, 9*(1), 15–28. doi: 10.1037/a0013970

Saudino, K. J. (2005). Behavioral genetics and child temperament. *Journal of Developmental and Behavioral Pediatrics, 26*(3), 214–223.

Saudino, K. J., & Cherny, S. S. (2001). Sources of continuity and change in observed temperament. In R. N. Emde & J. K. Hewitt (Eds.), *Infancy to early childhood: Genetic and environmental influences on developmental change* (pp. 89–110). New York: Oxford University Press.

Saudino, K. J., Cherny, S. S., Emde, R. N., & Hewitt, J. K. (2001). Parental ratings of temperament in twins. In R. N. Emde & J. K. Hewitt (Eds.), *Infancy to early childhood: Genetic and environmental influences on developmental change* (pp. 73–88). New York: Oxford University Press.

Schiffman, J., Walker, E., Ekstrom, M., Schulsinger, F., Sorensen, H., & Mednick, S. (2004). Childhood videotaped social and neuromotor precursors of schizophrenia: A prospective investigation. *American Journal of Psychiatry, 161*(11), 2021–2027. doi: 10.1176/appi.ajp.161.11.2021

Schinka, J. A., Busch, R. M., & Robichaux-Keene, N. (2004). A meta-analysis of the association between the serotonin transporter gene polymorphism (5-HTTLPR) and trait anxiety. *Molecular Psychiatry, 9*(2), 197–202.

Schinka, J. A., Letsch, E. A., & Crawford, F. C. (2002). DRD4 and novelty seeking: Results of meta-analyses. *American Journal of Medical Genetics, 114*(6), 643–648. doi: 10.1002/ajmg.10649

Schneider, M. L., Moore, C. F., Suomi, S. J., & Champoux, M. (1991). Laboratory assessment of temperament and environment enrichment in rhesus monkey infants (Macaca mulatta). *American Journal of Primatology, 25,* 137–155.

Schwartz, C. E., Kunwar, P. S., Greve, D. N., Moran, L. R., Viner, J. C., Covino, J. M., . . . Wallace, S. R. (2010). Structural differences in adult orbital and ventromedial prefrontal cortex predicted by infant temperament at 4 months of age. *Archives of General Psychiatry, 67*(1), 78–84. doi: 10.1001/archgenpsychiatry.2009.171

Schwartz, C. E., Snidman, N., & Kagan, J. (1999). Adolescent social anxiety as an outcome of inhibited temperament in childhood. *Journal of the American Academy of Child and Adolescent Psychiatry, 38*(8), 1008–1015.

Schwartz, C. E., Wright, C. I., Shin, L. M., Kagan, J., & Rauch, S. L. (2003). Inhibited and uninhibited infants "grown up": Adult amygdalar response to novelty. *Science, 300*(5627), 1952–1953.

Sheese, B. E., Voelker, P. M., Rothbart, M. K., & Posner, M. I. (2007). Parenting quality interacts with genetic variation in dopamine receptor D4 to influence temperament in early childhood. *Development and Psychopathology, 19*(4), 1039–1046.

Shiner, R. L. (2000). Linking childhood personality with adaptation: Evidence for continuity and change across time into late adolescence. *Journal of Personality and Social Psychology, 78*(2), 310–325.

Shiner, R. L., Masten, A. S., & Tellegen, A. (2002). A developmental perspective on personality in emerging adulthood: Childhood antecedents and concurrent adaptation. *Journal of Personality and Social Psychology, 83*(5), 1165–1177.

Shirley, M. (1933). *The first two years. Vol. III: Personality manifestations.* Minneapolis: University of Minnesota Press.

Smith, M. E., & Farah, M. J. (2011). Are prescription stimulants "smart pills"? The epidemiology and cognitive neuroscience of prescription stimulant use by normal healthy individuals. *Psychological Bulletin, 137*(5), 717–741. doi: 10.1037/a0023825

South, S. C., Krueger, R. F., Johnson, W., & Iacono, W. (2008). Adolescent personality moderates genetic and environmental influences on relationships with parents. *Journal of Personality and Social Psychology, 94*(5), 899–912. doi:10.1037/0022-3514.94.5.899

Stefanacci, L., & Aramal, D. G. (2002). Some observations on cortical inputs to the macaque monkey amygdala: An anterograde tracing study. *Journal of Comparative Neurology, 451*, 301–323. doi: 10.1002/cne.10339

Stringaris, A., Maughan, B., & Goodman, R. (2010). What's in a disruptive disorder? Temperamental antecedents of oppositional defiant disorder: Findings from the Avon longitudinal study. *Journal of the American Academy of Child and Adolescent Psychiatry, 49*(5), 474–483.

Sulloway, F. J. (1996). *Born to rebel.* New York: Vintage.

Sussman, A., & Ha, J. (2011). Developmental and cross-situational stability in infant pigtailed macaque temperament. *Developmental Psychology, 47*(3), 781–791.

Swanson, J. M., Schuck, S., Mann, M., Carlson, C., Hartman, K., Seargeant, J. A., . . . McCleary, R. (2006). *Categorical and dimensional definitions and evaluations of symptoms of ADHD: The SNAP and SWAN Rating Scales.* Irvine: University of California Press.

Swedo, S. E. (1994). Sydenham's chorea: A model for childhood autoimmune neuropsychiatric disorders. *JAMA, 272*(22), 1788–1791.

Swedo, S. E., Leckman, J. F., & Rose, N. R. (2012). From research subgroup to clinical syndrome: Modifying the PANDAS criteria to describe PANS (pediatric acute-onset neuropsychiatric sydrome). *Pediatrics and Therapeutics, 2*(2), 1–8.

Swing, E. L., Gentile, D. A., Anderson, C. A., & Walsh, D. A. (2010). Television and video game exposure and the development of attention problems. *Pediatrics, 126*(2), 214–221. doi: 10.1542/peds.2009-1508

Tang, T. Z., DeRubeis, R. J., Hollon, S. D., Amsterdam, J., Shelton, R., & Schalet, B. (2009). Personality change during depression treatment: A placebo-controlled trial. *Archives of General Psychiatry, 66*(12), 1322–1330. doi: 10.1001/archgenpsychiatry.2009.166

Thomas, A., & Chess, S. (1977). *Temperament and development.* New York: Brunner/Mazel.

Thomas, A., Chess, S., Birch, H. G., Hertzig, M. E., & Korn, S. (1963). *Behavioral individuality in early childhood.* New York: New York University Press.

Thorndike, E. L. (1920). A constant error in psychological ratings. *Journal of Applied Psychology, 4*(1), 25–29.

Tillman, R., Geller, B., Craney, J. L., Bolhofner, K., Williams, M., Zimerman, B., . . . Beringer, L. (2003). Temperament and character factors in a prepubertal and early adolescent bipolar disorder phenotype compared to attention deficit hyperactive and normal controls. *Journal of Child and Adolescent Psychopharmacology, 13*(4), 531–543.

Tse, W. S., & Bond, A. J. (2001). Serotonergic involvement in the psychosocial dimension of personality. *Journal of Psychopharmacology, 15*(3), 195–198.

U.S. Department of Health and Human Services. (2009). *Results from the 2008 National Survey on Drug Use and Health: National findings.* Substance Abuse and Mental Health Services Administration. Retrieved from http://www.oas.samhsa.gov/nsduh/2k8nsduh/2k8Results.pdf

Van Gestel, S., & Van Broeckhoven, C. (2003). Genetics of personality: Are we making progress? *Molecular Psychiatry, 8,* 840–852.

van Oers, K., Drent, P. J., Dingemanse, N. J., & Kempenaers, B. (2008). Personality is associated with extrapair mating in great tits, Parus major. *Animal Behavior, 76,* 555–563.

Verweij, K. J., Zietsch, B. P., Medland, S. E., Gordon, S. D., Benyamin, B., Nyholt, D. R., . . . Wray, N. R. (2010). A genome-wide association study of Cloninger's temperament scales: Implications for the evolutionary genetics of personality. *Biological Psychology, 85*(2), 306–317. doi: 10.1016/j.biopsycho.2010.07.018

Viken, R. J., Rose, R. J., Kaprio, J., & Kosenvuo, M. (1994). A developmental genetic analysis of adult personality: Extraversion and neuroticism from 18 to 59 years of age. *Journal of Personality and Social Psychology, 66*(4), 722–730.

Walker, E., & Lewine, R. J. (1990). Prediction of adult-onset schizophrenia from childhood home movies of the patients. *American Journal of Psychiatry, 147*(8), 1052–1056.

Watson, D., Gamez, W., & Simms, L. J. (2005). Basic dimensions of temperament and their relation to anxiety and depression: A symptom-based perspective. *Journal of Research in Personality, 39,* 46–66.

Weaver, I. C. (2007). Epigenetic programming by maternal behavior and pharmacological intervention: Nature versus nurture: Let's call the whole thing off. *Epigenetics, 2,* 22–28.

Webb, E. (1915). Character and intelligence. *British Journal of Psychology Monographs, 1*(3), 1–99.

Wechsler, D. (1991). *Wechsler Intelligence Scale for Children—Third Edition (WISC III).* San Antonio, TX: Psychological Corporation.

Wegiel, J., Kuchna, I., Nowicki, K., Imaki, H., Marchi, E., Ma, S. Y., . . . Wisniewski, T. (2010). The neuropathology of autism: Defects of neurogenesis and neuronal migration, and dysplastic changes. *Acta Neuropathologica, 119*(6), 755–770. doi: 10.1007/s00401-010-0655-4

Weissman, M. M., Pilowsky, D. J., Wickramaratne, P. J., Talati, A., Wisniewski, S. R., Fava, M., . . . Rush, A. J. (2006). Remissions in maternal depression and child psychopathology: A STAR*D-child report. *JAMA, 295*(12), 1389–1398.

Westen, D., & Harnden-Fischer, J. (2001). Personality profiles in eating disorders: Rethinking the distinction between axis I and axis II. *American Journal of Psychiatry, 158*(4), 547–562.

Whittle, S., Yucel, M., Fornito, A., Barrett, A., Wood, S. J., Lubman, D. I., . . . Allen, N. B. (2008). Neuroanatomical correlates of temperament in early adolescents. *Journal of the American Academy of Child and Adolescent Psychiatry, 47*(6), 682–693.

Wildes, J. E., Marcus, M. D., Crosby, R. D., Ringham, R. M., Dapelo, M. M., Gaskill, J. A., & Forbush, K. T. (2011). The clinical utility of personality subtypes in patients with anorexia nervosa. *Journal of Consulting and Clinical Psychology.* doi: 10.1037/a0024597

Winnicott, D. (1953). Transitional objects and transitional phenomena. *International Journal of Psychoanalysis, 34,* 89–97.

Wonderlich, S. A., Lilenfeld, L. R., Riso, L. P., Engel, S., & Mitchell, J. E. (2005). Personality and anorexia nervosa. *International Journal of Eating Disorders, 37*(Suppl.), S68–S71; [discussion] S87–S69. doi: 10.1002/eat.20120

Woodruff, T. J., Axelrad, D. A., Kyle, A. D., Nweke, O., Miller, G. G., & Hurley, B. J. (2004). Trends in environmentally related childhood illnesses. *Pediatrics, 113*(4 Suppl.), 1133–1140.

Wright, A. J., Krueger, R. F., Hobbs, M. J., Markon, K. E., Eaton N. R., & Slade, T. (2013). The structure of psychopathology: Toward an expanded quantitative empirical model. *Journal of Abnormal Psychology, 122*(1), 281–294. doi: 10.1037/a0030133

Zohar, A. H., & Felz, L. (2001). Ritualistic behavior in young children. *Journal of Abnormal Child Psychology, 29*(2), 121–128.

Zucker, K. J., & Bradley, S. J. (1995). *Gender identity disorder and psychosexual problems in children and adolescence.* New York: Guilford.

Zucker, K. J., Wood, H., Singh, D., & Bradley, S. J. (2012). A developmental, biopsychosocial model for the treatment of children with gender identity disorder. *Journal of Homosexuality, 59*(3), 369–397. doi: 10.1080/00918369.2012.653309

Index